Antonia Clare

JJ Wilson

speakout

Advanced

Students' Book

with ActiveBook

CONTENTS

CONTENTS

LISTENING/DVD	SPEAKING	WRITING
	talk about names	write a personal profile; learn to plan your writing
listen to a radio programme about a personality test	talk about ways to improve your language learning; discuss the results of a personality test	
listen to a discussion about portraits of famous people	speculate about people based on their portraits; learn to use vague language	
BBC **Francesco's Venice:** watch an extract from a programme about Venice	describe a treasured possession	write a description of an object
	talk about words of wisdom	
listen to people talking about their experiences of a living library	discuss controversial statements	write a discursive essay; learn to use linking devices
listen to people discussing whether we can trust the news we read; learn to express doubt	debate how to deal with untrustworthy employees	
BBC **The Making of Me: Vanessa-Mae:** watch an extract from a documentary about a famous violinist	plan and take part in a panel discussion	write a summary of an opinion
	talk about special holiday memories	write a description of a place for a guidebook; learn to add detail
listen to people describing the space where they work	discuss work spaces; describe your ideal space to work/study	
listen to a proposal for a scheme to improve a city	plan and present a proposal to improve your local area; learn to suggest modifications	
BBC **An African Journey:** watch an extract from a travel programme about Africa	talk about your country; develop a documentary proposal	write a proposal for a documentary about your country
listen to and read film synopses	talk about issues related to crime and punishment	
listen to people talking about someone they admire	discuss social issues and solutions	write a problem-solution essay; learn to use parallelism
listen to people discussing what they would do if they witnessed a crime; learn to add emphasis	talk about how to deal with different moral dilemmas	
BBC **Blackadder:** watch an extract from a comedy set during the First World War	present the arguments for the defence and the prosecution in a court case	write a summary of a court case
listen to a radio programme about when and how you should reveal a secret	talk about secrets	write a narrative; learn to use time phrases
	debunk a myth	
listen to a conversation about WikiLeaks	discuss questions related to freedom of information; learn to manage a conversation	
BBC **North and South:** watch an extract from a drama set in 19th century England	describe seven secrets about yourself	write personal facts people don't know about you

COMMUNICATION BANK PAGE 158   AUDIO SCRIPTS PAGE 164

CONTENTS

CONTENTS

PARTS OF SPEECH

1A Complete the text with the words/phrases in the box.

according	to forget
remembering	changed
Interestingly	It's being suggested
the	get hold of	might	on

Has Google made us stupid?

The rise of Google and other search engines has ¹_____ the way we remember information, ²_____ to research. Because we now have access to all ³_____ information we could possibly want at the touch of a button, we no longer need to store so much information in our heads. ⁴_____ that this is actually changing the way our brains store and recall information. We're quite likely ⁵_____ information which we believe we can find online and more likely to remember something which we ⁶_____ not be able to access on the internet. We are now better at remembering where we can ⁷_____ the information than we are at ⁸_____ the information itself. ⁹_____, the brain is a malleable organ, which changes according to our circumstances. So, it's not just Google that can change the way we remember things. We have always looked to 'experts' to remember things for us. And even in more informal ways, long-term couples also learn to rely ¹⁰_____ each other for remembering information. Now, where did I put my keys?

B Match the words in the box above with parts of speech 1–10.

1. present participle
2. past participle
3. infinitive with *to*
4. adverb
5. definite article
6. multi-word verb
7. modal verb
8. passive
9. gerund
10. dependent preposition

ERROR CORRECTION

2A Correct the mistakes. There is one mistake in each sentence.

1. One of the most interesting of things about my job is the people I meet.
2. I haven't seen my parents since five years.
3. I studied geography at university so I'm knowing a lot about different countries.
4. I haven't told nobody about my hobby.
5. Its difficult to find work these days.
6. I've been to Spain many times in last few years.
7. Do you think it's enough warm for me to go without a coat?
8. I adore to live by the sea.

B Find one example of each mistake in sentences 1–8 above.

a) incorrect tense
b) incorrect word order
c) incorrect pronoun
d) incorrect preposition
e) incorrect punctuation
f) incorrect verb pattern
g) missing word
h) extra word

C Rewrite three of the sentences to make them true for you. Compare your sentences in pairs.

PRONUNCIATION

3A Work in pairs. Which underlined sound is the odd one out?

1. f<u>ie</u>rce   s<u>ee</u>k   h<u>ea</u>r
2. b<u>ough</u>t   h<u>ou</u>se   c<u>ow</u>
3. s<u>ai</u>l   bl<u>a</u>me   aw<u>a</u>re
4. c<u>a</u>lm   b<u>ea</u>r   h<u>ea</u>rt

B ▶ L.1 Listen and check.

C ▶ L.2 Listen and tick the words you hear. Then read the pairs of words aloud.

1. badge   batch
2. thistle   this'll
3. of   off
4. vision   fission
5. rise   rice
6. pig   pick

MULTI-WORD VERBS

4A Read the definitions. Complete the multi-word verbs with the words in the box.

look	work	get	watch	hold
carry	make	come		

1. communicate your message clearly
2. meet/find by chance
1. _____  across
2. _____
3. search for information, e.g. in a dictionary
4. invent, e.g. a story
3. _____  up
4. _____
5. continue
6. wait
5. _____  on
6. _____
7. be careful
8. calculate something
7. _____ out
8. _____

B Work in pairs. What should you do when you hear a new multi-word verb? Write advice using some of the multi-word verbs above.

When you come across a new multi-word verb …

REGISTER

5 Read sentences a)–f). Answer questions 1–3 for each sentence.

a) All guests must be signed in by a member.
b) A bunch of people turned up at his place well after midnight.
c) The committee reached an affirmative decision with regard to termination of his contract.
d) Are you gonna be at the game on Saturday?
e) Great food, this.
f) Payment shall be subject to the fulfilment of clause 5.3.

1. Is the sentence formal or informal? How do you know?
2. Where might you see/hear it?
3. Can you rephrase the sentence to change the register?

UNIT I

origins

BBC
speakout DVD

> What's in a name? p8

> What are you like? p11

> This is me p14

> Francesco's Venice p16

SPEAKING

1A Read the questions and think about your answers.

1 What are the origins of your first name?

2 How much do you know about your family name?

3 Do you have any nicknames? How did you get them?

4 Do people ever confuse your name or make mistakes with it?

5 Why do you think some names become fashionable/unfashionable?

B Work in pairs. Ask and answer the questions in Exercise 1A.

VOCABULARY names

2A Read sentences 1–8 and answer questions a)–f) about the words/phrases in bold.

1 My **given name** is Stephen but I have a Greek **surname** – Theodorakopoulos – and a Spanish **middle name** – Gonzalo!

2 My **maiden name** is Popova but my **married name** is Edelstein.

3 I was **named after** my grandmother.

4 I'm from a famous family and it's not easy to **live up to my name**.

5 I worked hard for twenty years and **made a name for myself** in film.

6 He used to be **a household name** but young people don't know him.

7 I **put my name forward** for class president.

8 Even though she was innocent, it took her years to **clear her name**.

a) Which are on your passport/identity document?

b) Which might change in your lifetime?

c) Which are related to reputation?

d) Which is in honour of someone else?

e) Which means 'volunteered'?

f) Which means 'famous'?

B Work in pairs. Complete the sentences in any way you choose.

1 One given name that I really like is …

2 I have made/would like to make a name for myself as a …

3 … should be a household name because he/she …

4 One job I'd never put my name forward for is …

5 … is so famous that everyone knows him/her by his/her nickname: …

KŐRÖSI CSOMA SÁNDOR 1784 - 1842

READING

3A Work in pairs and discuss the questions.

1 What do you think are the world's most common first names?

2 What are the most common family names in your country?

3 Why do you think people change their names?

B Read the article and complete the sentence.

The main idea of the text is that …

C Answer the questions.

1 What do the results of Mehrabian's research show us?

2 Who is Pamela Satran?

3 What does Angela Baron think of employers who give people jobs on the basis of names?

4 According to Satran, what influences the way people name their children?

4A Work in pairs and discuss the questions.

1 Who do you agree with more: Mehrabian or Satran?

2 How has your name affected you in life?

3 Why do you think certain names are associated with success?

4 The research for this article was done in the US. Do you think the same is true of names in your country?

B What do you think words/phrases 1–8 mean? Use a dictionary to help you if necessary.

1 frumpy (paragraph 1)

2 get lumped with (paragraph 1)

3 reach the top of the tree (paragraph 4)

4 cut and dried (paragraph 5)

5 call-backs (paragraph 6)

6 take a … dim view of (paragraph 7)

7 celebrities are leading the field in the bizarre forename stakes (paragraph 8)

8 outlandish (paragraph 9)

THE NAME GAME

1 We've all got one – the friend with the impossibly glamorous name that leaves the Peters, Katherines and Margarets among us feeling somewhat, well, frumpy. Sometimes life (or in this case parents) isn't fair. But it's not as if the first name you get lumped with at birth actually has an impact on your success in later life. Is it?

2 Albert Mehrabian, professor emeritus of psychology at the University of California, certainly thinks so. 'Names generate impressions, just like a person's appearance can generate a positive or negative impression,' he says. 'But names also have an impact when you're not physically present, such as when you send in a CV.'

3 Mehrabian has researched people's instinctive reactions to hundreds of first names. It's striking how many positive associations some names carry, and how negative the connotations of others turn out to be – particularly when it comes to linking names with 'success', which Mehrabian takes to include ambition, intelligence, confidence and other such valuable workplace attributes.

4 So what kind of name does it take to reach the top of the tree career-wise? Based on research in the US, Mehrabian says that Alexander scores 100 percent for 'success'. William gets 99 percent and John 98 percent. For the girls, Jacqueline rates very highly, as do Diana, Danielle and Catherine. Although Katherine, Mehrabian points out, does slightly better than Catherine.

5 But can the impact of a first name really be that cut and dried? Pamela Satran, co-author of eight baby-naming books, is less convinced that the power of a name can be quantified.

6 'There isn't that much hard evidence that's absolutely conclusive,' says Satran. She recalls one American study where researchers submitted identical CVs to a number of employers. The forename on half of the CVs was Lashanda, 'seen as a stereotypical African-American name,' says Satran. The name on the other half was Lauren – seen as much more white and middle class. In one study, Lauren got five times more call-backs than Lashanda, says Satran, but in another study the rate was similar for both names. 'I've seen similarly conflicting studies,' Satran adds.

7 Angela Baron, an adviser at the Chartered Institute of Personnel and Development, takes an understandably dim view of employers who make decisions on the basis of first names. 'People do make emotive judgements,' she says, but 'we shouldn't be recruiting people on that basis. Good interviewers will be aware that what they need to look for are skills, experience and what [the interviewee] can do for the business.'

8 Celebrities are leading the field in the bizarre forename stakes, with Jordan (a British model) calling her daughter Princess Tiaamii and Jermaine Jackson (Michael Jackson's brother) lumbering his son with … wait for it … Jermajesty. But non-celebrity parents aren't far behind.

9 'My pupils have increasingly outlandish names,' says one secondary school teacher from north London. She cites 'poorly spelt names' such as Amba, Jordon, Charlee and Moniqua, and what she calls 'absurd names' like Shaliqua and Sharday. How will such names affect her students when they go out to get a job? 'I think it's a serious disadvantage,' she says.

10 Albert Mehrabian agrees that 'deliberately misspelt names are disastrous.' But Pamela Satran has a more relaxed take: 'How these names are perceived is something that's changing very rapidly,' she says. 'Celebrity culture and ethnic diversity have made people much more eager to look for a wide range of names of their own. The thinking is if you have a special name, that makes you a special person.'

GRAMMAR the continuous aspect

5A Check what you know. Why is the continuous form used in these sentences?

1 These days it's getting easier and easier to change your name.

2 She's always talking as if she's a household name, but she's only been on TV once!

3 I'm considering naming my dog after my hero: Che Guevara.

4 The author of the book has been trying to think of a good name for months.

5 My partner was reading a book about babies' names when I got home.

6 I was hoping to borrow your car, if that's OK.

B Check your answers. Match uses a)–f) with sentences 1–6 above.

a) to describe a background action that was in progress when another (shorter) action happened   5

b) to talk about something that's incomplete, temporary, or still in progress (often emphasising the length of time)

c) to talk about situations that are in the process of changing

d) to emphasise repeated actions (that may be annoying)

e) for plans that may not be definite

f) to sound tentative and less direct when we make proposals, inquiries, suggestions, etc.

page 128 **LANGUAGEBANK**

PRACTICE

6 Which underlined verbs would be better in the continuous form? Why? Change them as necessary.

1 John's not in the office. He might <u>have</u> lunch.
'Have' should be in the continuous form because the action is still in progress.

2 I'm fed up. We'<u>ve waited</u> for an hour!

3 She <u>owns</u> a small house by the river.

4 Can you be quiet? I <u>try</u> to work.

5 The letter arrived today. She <u>had expected</u> news since Monday.

6 That chicken dish <u>tasted</u> great.

7 Who <u>do</u> these keys <u>belong</u> to?

8 By next September, we <u>will have lived</u> here for twenty-five years.

9 I <u>work</u> on a project at the moment.

10 My partner <u>made</u> dinner when I got home so I helped.

7 Complete the sentences to make them true for you. Make the verbs negative if necessary.

1 I work … / I've been working …

2 I study … / At the moment I'm studying …

3 I usually write … / I've been writing …

WRITING a personal profile

8A Read the personal profile. Where do you think it will appear?

introduction

Author:
Danny Garcia
Date:
February 27, 2011

Hello, everyone. My name is Danny Garcia. I'm a lifelong resident of London, UK – born and bred here. I'm working to achieve my dream of getting a master's degree, and I'm delighted to be in BLED 514, Multicultural Education.

The area of multicultural education has been a long-term interest of mine. It began when I got my job as an English teacher at a school in London, where I have worked for ten years. I hope to deepen my understanding of the subject during this term.

This is not my first foray into higher education. I have a bachelor's degree in English which I finished in 2000. It's quite a shock to go back to university and jump right into master's level courses!

My passion is basketball. I used to play every day but I don't have time now. I have two great kids who are my world and keep me going. Lily, who's five, is the oldest and Justin, who's three, is the baby of the family. My wife is a paediatrician and she's also from London. We met ten years ago when we were hiking separately and I got lost and she rescued me!

I'm looking forward to participating in this class. Good luck, everyone!

reply

forward

send message

B Read the guidelines for writing a personal profile. To what extent does Danny Garcia's profile follow them?

1 Share positive things.
2 Keep it short: condense rather than using very long sentences.
3 Choose specific details and examples, not generalisations.
4 Don't lie, boast or exaggerate.
5 Keep it informal and friendly.

9 Which information in the box would you include in a profile for: a blog, a social networking site, a job application?

where you're from   family information
likes/dislikes   hobbies   talents and skills
education/grades/qualifications   goals and plans
favourite music/food   religious or spiritual beliefs
address   pet peeves   groups you belong to
job   trips and unusual experiences

speakout TIP

When you write, always remember your audience. Who will read your work? What do they expect (think about content, length, tone and formality)? What do they know about the topic? Think of writing as a conversation that takes place through space and time.

LEARN TO plan your writing

10A Discuss. Which of the following things do you do when you write? What does it depend on?

1 Brainstorm ideas.
2 Write notes.
3 Write an outline.
4 Discuss your ideas with someone before writing.
5 Visualise your readers and imagine how they will react to your piece.
6 Write the first draft quickly and roughly.

B Look at the outline of a personal profile for a job application. What job might it be?

Introduction: name and where I'm from
Interests: love children, music, dance
Skills: play guitar & piano, drawing, costume-making
Experience: worked as a summer volunteer in Bournemouth Children's Centre, 2010
Goals for the future: run a nursery for 2–4 year-olds

11 Write a personal profile as part of a class profile. Follow stages 1–4 below.

1 Think about your audience and what you need to include. Make notes.
2 Write an outline for your profile.
3 Write your profile (200 words). Check it and make any corrections.
4 Share your profile with other students. What common features are there in your class, e.g. professions, goals and plans, where you're from, etc.?

▶ **GRAMMAR** | describing habits   ▶ **VOCABULARY** | personality   ▶ **HOW TO** | talk about routines/habits

SPEAKING

1A Look at the questionnaire. Do statements 1–12 apply to you? Mark each statement:

✓✓ strongly agree ✓ agree ✗ disagree ✗✗ strongly disagree

B Work in pairs and compare your answers. Are you a good language learner? What could you do to improve?

GRAMMAR describing habits

2A Look at the questionnaire again and underline verbs/expressions used to describe present or past habits. Add examples to complete the table.

present habit	past habit
1 *will* + infinitive without *to* *I'll look* for clues that will help me.	8 *would* + infinitive without *to* _____
2 *is always* + *-ing* _____	9 *was always* + *-ing* *I was always looking* for new ways to …
3 *keep (on)* + *-ing* She *keeps on calling* me.	10 *kept* (on) + *-ing* _____
other phrases to describe a present habit	other phrases to describe a past habit
4 *I have an inclination to/I'm _____ to*	11 *I was forever making mistakes.*
5 *I'm prone to/I tend to/I have _____ to*	12 *I was prone to*
6 *As a _____*	13 _____
7 *Nine times _____*	

B ▶1.1 Listen and write sentences 1–3. Check your answers in the audio script on page 164.

C ▶1.2 Listen to the sentences being said in two different ways. What effect does the change in pronunciation have on the meaning?

⟶ page 128 **LANGUAGEBANK**

PRACTICE

3A Add the words in the box to sentences 1–8.

> to   as   would   is   looking   of   a̶   keeps

1 I have /ᵃ tendency to sleep in late.
2 My mother prone to worrying about everything.
3 He failing his driving test.
4 I'm not inclined be very laid-back.
5 I'm always for new things to learn.
6 A rule, I try not to work at the weekend.
7 Nine times out ten I'll be right about my first impressions.
8 As a child I spend hours reading.

B Make two or three of the sentences in Exercise 3A true for you. Compare your ideas in pairs.

Are you a good language learner?

Good language learners find a style of learning that suits them.

1 I'm always watching videos or reading articles in English and that helps me a lot.

2 I'm quite analytical, so I have a tendency to focus on the grammar and on being accurate.

3 I'm an extrovert and I enjoy talking to people. I learn a lot just by speaking and listening.

Good language learners are actively involved in the language learning process.

4 I'm always looking for opportunities to use and learn the language outside class.

5 As a rule, I'm happy to take risks with language and experiment with new ways of learning.

6 I can usually identify where I have problems, so generally I focus on improving those areas.

Good language learners try to figure out how the language works.

7 I'm inclined to be very analytical. Like a detective, I'll look for clues that will help me understand how language works.

8 I have a good ear for language, so nine times out of ten I'll just know if something is wrong. I use my instinct and when I don't know, I guess.

9 I'm prone to making mistakes with grammar, so I'll often compare what I say with what others say. This helps me to check that I'm using correct grammar and vocabulary.

Good language learners try to overcome their feelings of frustration or lack of confidence.

10 When I started, I tended to get frustrated because I kept making mistakes. Now, I've learnt not to be embarrassed.

11 At first, I would spend hours studying grammar rules, but I didn't have the confidence to speak. So I set myself goals to improve my pronunciation and speak as much as possible.

12 I realise that learning a language takes time and dedication, and I just need to keep practising.

VOCABULARY personality

4A Work in pairs. Brainstorm adjectives for describing people's personalities.

B Look at the words in the box. Give examples of how people with these qualities might behave.

Someone who is open-minded likes to consider different points of view.

> thoughtful   perceptive   obsessive   inspirational   over-ambitious
> conscientious   obstinate   neurotic   open-minded   prejudiced
> apathetic   insensitive   solitary   rebellious   mature   inquisitive

C Find a word in the box above to describe someone who:

1 notices things quickly and understands situations and people's feelings well.

2 has an unreasonable dislike of a thing or a group of people.

3 is not interested or willing to make the effort to do anything.

4 is determined not to change their ideas, behaviour or opinions.

5 deliberately disobeys people in authority or rules of behaviour.

6 spends a lot of time alone because they like being alone.

7 is unreasonably anxious or afraid.

8 is willing to consider or accept other people's ideas or opinions.

D Work in pairs and write definitions for the other words in Exercise 4B. Choose three words your friends would/wouldn't use to describe you.

▶ page 148 **VOCABULARYBANK**

LISTENING

5A Read the radio programme listing below and answer the questions.

1 What does the Myers-Briggs Test Indicator do?

2 Who uses it?

3 Do you think this type of test can be useful? Why/Why not?

B ▶ 1.3 Listen to the programme and answer the questions.

1 According to the programme, what is one of the biggest stressors at work?

2 What kinds of people do the MBTI test?

3 What kinds of questions does the interviewer ask Mariella?

How Myers-Briggs Conquered the Office

It was created by a mother and daughter team, neither of whom were trained as psychologists, yet today it is the world's most widely used personality indicator, used by leading companies like Shell, Procter and Gamble, Vodafone and the BBC. In this BBC radio programme, Mariella Frostrup tells the story of The Myers-Briggs Type Indicator (MBTI), created by Katherine Briggs and her daughter Isabel Briggs Myers. Participants are asked a series of questions intended to reveal information about their thinking, problem-solving and communication styles. At the end of the process each participant is handed one of sixteen four-letter acronyms which describes their 'type'. ENTPs are extrovert inventors, ISTJs are meticulous nit-pickers. Mariella finds out what type she is – will it change the way she works?

6A What do the following expressions from the programme mean?

1 sweeping generalisers

2 detail-obsessed nit-pickers

3 obsessive planners

4 last-minute deadline junkies

5 recharge your batteries

6 flat-pack furniture

B Listen again. Choose the option, a), b) or c), which best describes Mariella's answer to the question.

1 How do you like to recharge your batteries at the end of the day?

 a) She goes out for a nice meal.

 b) She stays at home and reads a book.

 c) She watches TV and goes to bed.

2 If you have ever had the opportunity to put together any flat-pack furniture, how did you go about it?

 a) She always follows the instructions carefully.

 b) She finds the whole process infuriating, so she doesn't buy flat-pack furniture.

 c) She tends to lose the instructions and the parts.

3 If you imagine that a friend of yours gives you a call and says, 'I've just been burgled.' What would you do? What would your reaction be?

 a) First, she would ask her friend how she was feeling.

 b) First, she would be concerned about the practicalities, then she would ask about feelings.

 c) She would only ask about the practical details.

4 How do you go about doing the food shopping?

 a) She generally keeps a careful list of all the things she needs. Then she buys it all online.

 b) She hates internet shopping, so she goes to the supermarket once a week.

 c) She buys most of her food on the internet, but she doesn't use a list so she forgets things.

C Work in pairs. Answer the questions in Exercise 6B for you and compare your answers.

SPEAKING

7A Read about the different types of people in the Myers-Briggs test below. Mark your position on each scale to work out your profile, e.g. ENTJ.

B Turn to page 158 to read more about your profile. Do you agree with the description?

C Compare your profiles with other students. Are they similar or different?

I Introvert •••••••••••••••|•••••••••••••••• Extrovert **E**

Enjoys spending time alone. Tends to think first, act later.

Finds being with others relaxing. Tends to act first, think later.

N Intuition •••••••••••••••|•••••••••••••••• Sensing **S**

Likes to change things and find their own solutions to problems. Looks to the future and tends towards idealism.

Uses the practical information around them to solve problems. Enjoys the present and tends towards realism.

T Thinker •••••••••••••••|•••••••••••••••• Feeler **F**

Makes decisions using objectivity and logic.

Decides by listening to their own and others' feelings.

J Judging •••••••••••••••|•••••••••••••••• Perceiving **P**

Approaches life in a structured way, making plans and organising things.

Finds structure limiting, likes to keep their options open and go with the flow.

VOCABULARY *PLUS* idioms for people

8A Look at the idioms in bold and try to work out the meanings.

1 He's a bit of a **yes-man**. He agrees with anything the boss says.

2 Apparently, the new engineer knows what he's doing. He's a real **whiz kid**.

3 She knows everything about everyone. She's the office **busybody**.

4 There is never a quiet moment with Kate. She's a real **chatterbox**.

5 It was very annoying of him. Sometimes Joe could be a real **pain in the neck**.

6 She is a **dark horse**. I didn't know she had written a novel.

7 He's had plenty of experience. He's an **old hand** at the job.

8 My grandmother has the same routine every day. She's very **set in her ways**.

9 Jack has always been a bit of a rebel. He's the **black sheep** of the family.

10 I'm glad we've invited Sinead. She's always the **life and soul** of the party.

B Work in pairs. Which of the idioms in Exercise 8A would you use in the following situations?

1 You have suggested a new way of working, but your colleague is reluctant to change the way he does things.

2 You feel sure that you can trust the person you have asked to do a job because he has a lot of experience.

3 Your friend loves talking.

4 You discover that your colleague is the lead singer in a successful band. She has never mentioned it.

5 You have to complete your tax return by tomorrow. You hate doing it.

6 Your young nephew shows you how to play a new computer game. He has already applied to work as a games developer with Nintendo.

7 Your postman is always asking questions about your private life.

8 You always invite your sister when you're having a party, because she makes people laugh.

speakout TIP

Understanding and using English idioms is particularly important for Advanced learners. Here are four ideas to help you try to remember idioms.

1 Translation – are any of the idioms in Exercise 8A the same in your language?

2 Group by topic – do you know any other idioms for describing personality?

3 Visualise – can you think of images to help you remember the idioms in Exercise 8A?

4 Personalise – can you use the idioms in 8A to talk about people you know?

C Use the expressions in Exercise 8A to talk about people in your own life, or people in the news/film/television/politics.

▶ page 148 **VOCABULARYBANK**

| ▶ **FUNCTION** | speculating | ▶ **VOCABULARY** | images | ▶ **LEARN TO** | use vague language |

VOCABULARY images

1A Look at the portraits from the National Portrait Gallery, London. Read what the sitters said about their portraits and match quotations 1–3 with portraits A–C. Were they happy with their portraits? Why/Why not?

1 I'd rather be thought of as it were through what I've written than my own **physical presence** because I think it's such a **dismal** physical presence most of the time. But he doesn't make me look so … you know … the usual take on me is that I'm this monkish recluse and he doesn't quite endorse that view of me.
– *Alan Bennett*

2 I think it's a wonderful picture. I know it doesn't make me look particularly good-looking, but I'm not good-looking so that's alright. I don't feel as though I have been **caricatured** or anything, but what I think it does look like, it looks like a portrait of intelligence. It's got this incredible **flicker** about it, of energy, which is her energy more than mine, but it's … my image is invested in her … her power and her concentration.
– *Germaine Greer*

3 It's very hard to see yourself in the picture or any image of yourself. But when I look at that now, you see that was done a few years ago and when I first **posed** for Peter I must have been thirty-eight or thirty-nine. It was unveiled when I was forty. And that this whole process of having a portrait done, paradoxically because you know a portrait is supposed to in some way preserve you, it suddenly made me very aware of my mortality and I mean I'm approaching forty; yes it's a great honour and very **flattering**. But they say they are going to do a portrait for the National Portrait Gallery. But of course I immediately think, oh but that's where all these dead people are hung up.
– *Kazuo Ishiguro*

B Work in pairs. Check you understand the meaning of the words in bold. Can you use other words to explain them?
dismal – dull, depressing

FUNCTION speculating

2A Look at each portrait more carefully. Work in pairs and discuss the questions.
1 What can you say about the person's character from the picture?
2 What job do you think they do?

B ▶1.4 Listen to people discussing the portraits and make notes. What do they say about each person's:
• character/appearance?
• possible job?

A

C In which portrait do they say the person:
1 has a kind of intensity to their face?
2 looks like he's in a world of his own?
3 is trying to make a statement: 'this is the sort of person I am'?
4 looks intellectual or thoughtful?
5 has something knowing in their eyes, as if they've got a secret?
6 is trying to make a point about how ridiculous or absurd his life is?

D Listen again to check your ideas.

3 Look at the language used for speculating. Read audio script 1.4 on page 164 and find some examples of this language.

I suppose/guess/reckon he's about …
I'd say he/she looks/doesn't look …
I wonder what he/she …
I'd hazard a guess (that) …
If I had to make a guess, I'd say (that) …
I'm pretty sure he/she …
There's something … about him/her.
He/she gives the impression of being …
He/she could be …
It seems like he/she … /It seems to me …
It looks to me as if he/she …
It makes me think (that) maybe he/she …
It might suggest (that) …

▐▐▐➡ page 128 **LANGUAGEBANK**

To sound fluent in English, avoid long pauses in your speech by using fillers like *er* and *erm*. Vague language (*sort of/ kind of/ you know*) and hedges (*I suppose/ probably/ I guess I'd*) are also used as fillers. Read audio script 1.4 on page 164 and find examples of fillers.

6A Correct the mistakes in the sentences.

1 I'll be there soon. I just have a couple things to do.
2 Why don't we meet at exactly 8-ish?
3 I left a lot of stuffs at the hotel, but I can pick it up later.
4 Don't worry. We've got a plenty of time.
5 We've sort finished the accounts.
6 There'll be about forty and so people attending.

B ▶1.5 Listen to the corrected sentences. Find examples of the following:

1 linking between words which end in a consonant sound and words which begin with a vowel sound.

I just have a couple of things to do.

2 elision (when a sound disappears) between two consonant sounds, e.g. must be /mʌsbiː/.

Why don't we meet at about eight-ish?

C Mark the links between words in the following examples. Try saying the phrases.

1 It looks as if he's got a lot of work to do.
2 She looks about fifty or so.
3 It's a bit dark, isn't it?
4 I've got a couple of things to ask.

D ▶1.6 Listen and check. Then listen and repeat.

SPEAKING

7A Work in pairs. Look at the portraits on page 158 and follow the instructions.

B If you had a portrait painted of you, where would you be? What kind of portrait would you like to have? Compare your ideas with other students.

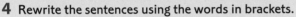

4 Rewrite the sentences using the words in brackets.

1 I guess she's a bit lonely. (It / seems / me)
2 It looks as though he's angry. (gives / impression)
3 I think she's probably an actress. (reckon)
4 If you asked me, I'd say she was happy with her life. (had / make / guess)
5 I'd definitely say that he's not telling us everything. (pretty)
6 I think she could be an only child. (hazard / guess)

LEARN TO use vague language

5 Look at the examples of vague language. Some are from the conversation in Exercise 2B. Why do the speakers use vague language? Does it sound formal or casual?

Vague nouns: *thing, stuff, bit*   *There's something knowing in his eyes.*
Quantifiers: *one or two, a few, a couple of, a lot of, plenty of, loads of, a bit (of)*   *She looks a bit puzzled to me.*
Vague numbers: *around, about fifty, more or less, fifty or so*   *Would you say he's in his sixties?*
Generalisers: *sort of, kind of, you know*   *This guy looks kind of … intellectual.*
List completers: *and stuff, and so on, or something (like that)*   *He could be a novelist or a playwright, or something like that.*

DVD PREVIEW

1 Work in groups. Look at the photo and discuss the questions.

1 What do you know about this city? Think about its geography and history.

2 Have you been there? Would you like to go?

3 What would it be like to live in Venice? How might it be different from where you live now?

2 Read the programme information. Why do you think Francesco is a good person to host the programme?

BBC Francesco's Venice

Francesco's Venice is a BBC documentary that tells the story of the great Italian city, Venice. Francesco da Mosto, a historian and writer, explains how this city – with no firm ground, no farmland and no army – acquired its power and fame. During the series, da Mosto describes the city's history and shows how his own family's fortunes have been closely related to the fortunes of Venice. In this episode, he goes to a house that his family built centuries ago and imagines his ancestors' lives as merchants.

3 Complete the sentences about Francesco's house with the words in the box.

> warehouse   storeys   bequeathed
> modest   showroom   rotting

1 The house is damp and in terrible condition, and the wood is _____.

2 Chiara da Mosto _____ the house to another family after falling out with her relatives.

3 This room was a _____. They used it to store goods before selling them.

4 It served as a _____. They used it to show goods to clients.

5 It used to be a more _____ building, not as big or beautifully decorated as now.

6 The house was two _____ high. The living room was on the first floor.

▶ DVD VIEW

4 Watch the DVD. Number the scenes in the order they appear.

a) Francesco stands on the balcony and looks across the canal.

b) He sails a small boat and looks at the house.

c) He walks through the house.

d) He imagines his ancestors and other people inside the house.

5A Answer the questions.

1 Why does the story of his ancestors' home break Francesco's heart?

2 When did his ancestors build the house?

3 What happened to the house in 1603?

4 Apart from living there, what did his ancestors use the house for?

B Watch the DVD again to check.

6 Work in pairs and discuss the questions.

1 What did you think of Francesco's house?

2 What did you find interesting about his story?

3 Does your personal family history involve any particular countries or cities? Which ones?

speakout a possession

7A ▶ 1.7 Listen to someone talking about a treasured family possession. What is the object? What does she say about the points below?

- **Background:** the history of the object.
- **Physical description:** what it looks/feels/sounds/smells like.
- **Value:** why it is so important.
- **Memories:** what feelings or stories are associated with it.

B Listen again and tick the key phrases you hear.

keyphrases

(It) has been in my family for four generations.

My grandmother inherited it.

It has sentimental value.

(It) was bequeathed to me.

I should repair it.

I will always treasure it.

8A Now think about a treasured possession of your own or a place that is special to your family. Make notes on the points in Exercise 7A.

B Work in groups and take turns. Tell each other about your possession/place.

writeback a description of an object

9A Read a description of an object. Why is the object special to the writer?

I own an antique gramophone player that belonged to my grandfather and then my father. It was made in Germany in the 1920s and has a heavy base made of pine wood and a large brass horn. In the days before cassette players, CDs and iPods, this is how people listened to music at home.

The gramophone reminds me of my childhood because when we went to my grandfather's house in Essex, near London, he used to play records on it. While his grandchildren were running and bellowing all over the house, he would be sitting there drinking tea and listening to a scratchy recording of a Bach sonata or Fauré's *Requiem*.

When he died, the gramophone was handed down to my father. It sat in the corner of the living room where a light skin of dust settled upon it. It was a piece of furniture, an heirloom that no one used or noticed but that just seemed to belong there, just as now it belongs in its own special corner of my living room. I don't know if many people nowadays would recognise a gramophone if they saw one, but I treasure the object because of the memories associated with it.

B Write about an object or place that is important to you. Use the key phrases to help.

NAMES

1 Underline the correct alternatives.

1 He was innocent but it took him years to *live/clear/make* his name.

2 I was named *before/after/of* my grandfather.

3 My married name is Kovacs but my *maiden/principle/single* name is Warsawski.

4 Zara made a name for *self/her/herself* as the best designer in the business.

5 He's a good actor but not a *house/household/family* name like Brad Pitt or Johnny Depp.

6 His real name is Keanu but his *nickname/friendly name/fun name* is Nunu.

THE CONTINUOUS ASPECT

2A Complete the pairs of sentences using the same verb. Use one simple form and one continuous form. Some verbs are in the negative.

1 a) My friend _____ to visit next week.

b) Harada is Japanese. He _____ from Osaka.

2 a) I _____ a cold for two weeks – I can't seem to get rid of it.

b) I _____ tennis lessons for two years.

3 a) My office _____ painted yesterday so I worked from home.

b) The garden _____ really beautiful when I was a child, but now it's a mess.

4 a) The children _____ homesick at all – they love travelling.

b) The economy _____ any better so our jobs are still at risk.

5 a) They knew me already because I _____ for that company before.

b) I was exhausted because I _____ for sixteen hours without a break.

B Work in pairs. Discuss why we use the simple or continuous forms in the sentences above.

In 1a) it's a future plan so this uses the present continuous.

DESCRIBING HABITS

3A Find and correct the mistakes in sentences 1–6. There is one mistake in each sentence.

1 I'm prone leaving things until the last minute, and then I always have to rush.

2 I don't tend needing as much sleep as I used to.

3 I keep forget people's birthdays.

4 My parents were always very strict and they wouldn't to let me out late at night.

5 I'm more inclination to phone people than to send them a text.

6 I'm always tidy my house. I can't stand it when it's in a mess.

B Work in pairs. Change information in the sentences above to write three or four sentences about your partner (guess if necessary). Then compare your sentences to check.

A: I guess you're prone to leaving things until the last minute.

B: Actually, I tend to be quite organised.

PERSONALITY

4A Complete the words in sentences 1–6.

1 We're m_____ enough to disagree but still respect each other.

2 You're right. I hadn't noticed. That's very pe_____ of you.

3 He was a very o_____ man. He refused to do what I asked.

4 She is a c_____ teacher. She prepares her lessons carefully.

5 It's important to remain o_____-m_____ and consider all options.

6 I'd have asked more questions, but I didn't want to seem too i_____.

B Work in pairs and take turns. Choose a word from Exercise 4A and describe an occasion when you can be like this. Can your partner guess the word?

A: In the office, I work hard and make 'to do' lists.

B: Conscientious?

SPECULATING

5A Match the sentence halves.

1 I reckon

2 If I had to make a guess,

3 I wonder if

4 She gives the impression

5 I'd hazard

6 There's something

7 It looks to me

8 I'm pretty

a) as if Nataly has an artistic streak.

b) a guess that Felix has a tendency to be a little absent-minded.

c) Guido's probably obsessive about keeping his house tidy.

d) of being a little apathetic about politics.

e) sure that Olga is a fitness fanatic.

f) I'd say that Monika is a conscientious student.

g) Alex has a solitary side to his nature?

h) mysterious about Martha.

B Write two or three sentences speculating about things that might happen in the next year. Compare your ideas with other students.

If I had to make a guess, I'd say that the government will change within the next twelve months. I'm pretty sure this government won't get through the next elections.

UNIT 2

opinion

BBC speakout DVD

▶ **Words of wisdom**   p20

▶ **Changing your mind**   p23

▶ **Who do you trust?**   p26

▶ **The Making of Me**   p28

READING

1 Work in pairs. Which pieces of advice a)–i) do you agree/disagree with? Why?

a) Don't worry about other people's opinions.

b) If you want anything said, ask a man. If you want anything done, ask a woman.

c) If it looks good on your CV, it's worth doing.

d) Don't mix business with family.

e) Don't explain. Just do what needs to be done.

f) Use every chance you get.

g) If you don't like something, change it. If you can't change it, change your attitude.

h) Show that you have confidence in your abilities.

i) Respect everyone.

2A Read the article. Match speakers 1–7 with advice a)–i) above. There are two extra pieces of advice.

B Work in groups and discuss which pieces of advice in the article surprised you. Have you ever been in a similar position to the people in the text? What did you do?

VOCABULARY learning

3A Find expressions in the article with the following meanings.

1 finding out how something is done in a particular place or situation (introduction)

2 was criticised by someone (paragraph 1)

3 believed that my feelings are correct (paragraph 2)

4 use the chances you get (paragraph 3)

5 don't stop trying to achieve something (paragraph 3)

6 changed a person deeply, e.g. the way they understand the world (paragraph 4)

7 feel deeply that you can succeed (paragraph 6)

8 in a position in which you quickly have to learn something difficult (paragraph 7)

Words from the wise

Everyone needs words of wisdom. When we're learning the ropes or things are going wrong, we all need help. Sometimes it's the wise words of our mentors that set us free. But we also need to watch out for advice that sounds good, but doesn't work. The trick is to know the difference between the two.

1 Rubem Alves, educator, writer

In the 1960s, I was in the United States doing post-graduate work. Although I never explicitly criticised the government, I came under attack for my political sentiments. My professor then gave me the following advice: 'Rubem,' he said, 'never explain yourself. For your friends, it's unnecessary. For your enemies, it's pointless.'

2 May Chen, web designer

When I was starting out in my twenties, I did some really boring jobs because people kept telling me, 'It'll look good on your CV.' Had I been more confident, I wouldn't have listened. I could have done more interesting things if I'd trusted my instincts. So I got a nice CV, but now I regret wasting my twenties. If only I'd known then what I know now.

3 Jane Goodall, primatologist and conservationist

When I was about ten years old and dreaming of going to Africa, living with animals and writing books about them, everyone laughed at me. Africa was far away and full of dangerous animals, and only boys could expect to do those kinds of things. But my mother said, 'If you really want something and you work hard and you take advantage of opportunities – and you never, ever give up – you will find a way.' The opportunity was a letter from a friend inviting me to Kenya. The hard work was waitressing at a hotel to earn money for the trip – and spending hours reading books about Africa and animals, so I was ready when Dr Louis Leakey offered me the opportunity to study chimpanzees.

B Look at questions 1–8 and choose at least four that you are happy to answer. Compare your answers with other students.

1 When were you last on a steep learning curve? What was the most difficult thing to learn?

2 In what situations do you always trust your instincts?

3 What opportunities have you taken advantage of?

4 Have you ever told yourself 'never give up'? What was the situation?

5 Can you think of a great event or person that had a profound effect on you?

6 Do you know anyone who has come under attack for things he/she said or believed?

7 Can you think of a situation or place in which you had to learn the ropes?

8 Has anyone ever told you to 'believe in yourself'? Who? When? Why?

4 Felipe Massa, Formula 1 driver

In 2006, I became team-mates with Michael Schumacher. I knew Schumacher as a legend, the man who had broken practically every record in Formula 1. But the most profound effect Schumacher had on me was when the great champion said, 'People will speak badly about you one day and well about you the next. Ignore them. The important thing is to do your work as well as you can.'

5 David Satcher MD, US Surgeon General

When I left home to attend Morehouse College, my father – who did not even have the privilege of completing elementary school – accompanied me to the bus stop and gave me the most important advice I ever received: 'Son, when you get there, you're going to meet a lot of people that have a whole lot more than you. You may even meet some that have less than you do. But no matter who you meet, treat everybody with respect.' Those are words I still live by.

6 Stefan Orogovitz, brain surgeon

A journalist once asked me, 'Why do brain surgeons have such large egos?' I told her, 'We need them. We lose ninety-five percent of our patients.' If I'd known that statistic when I was learning the ropes, I'd be selling insurance today. How can you keep working with figures like that? There's only one way: do all you can, never apologise, believe in yourself and always tell the truth.

7 Xhang Li, businesswoman

When my husband and I first began in the real estate business, we were on a steep learning curve and it caused some friction. Everyone told us, 'Marriage and business don't mix.' I wish we hadn't listened to their advice. They were so wrong! We're a great team because of our great marriage. But for our trust in each other, we would never have become so successful.

GRAMMAR conditionals and regrets

4A Look at paragraphs 2, 6 and 7 in the article above. Underline four conditional sentences and three phrases to describe regrets.

B Check what you know. Answer the questions.

1 Instead of *if* + past simple, two of the conditional sentences use alternative forms. What forms are they?

2 Are these forms more or less formal than an *if* clause?

3 Two of the phrases to describe regrets use the same verb tense. What tense is this?

C Look at the sentences you underlined again. Which one is a mixed conditional? Read the rules to check.

Rules:
1 Use *if* + past perfect and *would* + present continuous/present simple to form a mixed conditional.
2 Use a mixed conditional to say that if something in the past had been different, the present would be different.

▶ page 130 **LANGUAGE**BANK

PRACTICE

5A Complete the story with one word in each gap.

One day, a poor stonecutter worked chipping stone from the side of a mountain. Tired and hungry, he said, 'I wish I had ¹_____ born a rich man.' A magic spirit heard him and transformed him into a rich man. He enjoyed his new life, but one day the sun burnt him. He said, 'The sun is more powerful than me. I ²_____ I was the sun instead of a rich man.' So the magical spirit transformed him into the sun. Now he shone down on the earth. But one day a cloud passed in front of him. 'The cloud is more powerful than me! ³_____ I known this, I would have asked to become a cloud!' The magical spirit turned him into a cloud. Now he blocked the sun and caused cold weather, but one day the wind blew the cloud away. He said, 'If I had been stronger, I could ⁴_____ stopped the wind. I wish I was the wind.' The spirit granted his wish. He blew and blew, creating dust storms and hurricanes, but when he tried to blow a mountain over, he failed. '⁵_____ for my weakness, I would have blown that mountain down. If ⁶_____ I had been transformed into a mountain, I would be the strongest of all.' Again, the spirit helped him. Now, he stood huge and immovable. But one day he felt something chipping at him. It was a stonecutter. 'The stonecutter is the most powerful!' he said. 'If only I had known this, I ⁷_____ have remained a stonecutter. I ⁸_____ making all these wishes and I want to be a stonecutter again.' And so the magic spirit turned him back into a poor stonecutter.

B Complete the moral of the story in any way you choose. Compare your ideas with other students.

A wise person …

C ▶ 2.1 Which sentences 1–8 in the story can use contractions? Listen and check. Then listen and repeat.

In sentence 1, 'had' can be contracted: 'I wish I'd been born …'

SPEAKING

6A Complete the sentences and make them true for you.

1 If there's one thing I've learnt …
2 One thing I'd never …
3 One thing I wish I'd known when I was …
4 If I had a personal motto, it would be …
5 My mother/father/mentor/friend always told me …

B Work in groups and take turns. Read your sentences and give some background, explaining what you wrote. Try to use contractions.

VOCABULARY PLUS metaphors

7A Read the metaphor and choose the correct meaning.

I'm over the hill.

a) I can't do something well enough because I'm too old.

b) I have done the most difficult part of a task.

B Discuss the questions.

1 Can you think of other examples of metaphors?

2 Why are metaphors used?

3 How do they help to communicate an idea?

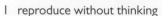

speakout TIP

Metaphors sometimes come in patterns: *your career is a journey*; *time is money*; *ideas are food*; *good is up* and *bad is down*. It is useful to write these metaphors together in your notebook. This helps you to remember them. Do this with the metaphors in exercises 8 and 9. Which ones are similar in your language?

8 Read the paragraph and underline four metaphors related to journeys. Match them with meanings 1–4.

When I graduated, everyone said, 'You'll go far.' I joined a law firm and quickly reached the peak of my profession. But then my career started to go downhill. I argued with colleagues and lost some cases. I found myself at a crossroads: either I could continue working there or I could take a risk and start my own firm.

1 go badly

2 having to choose one thing or another

3 have a great future *(You'll) go far.*

4 become number one

9A Work in pairs. Student A: read the paragraph below and underline four metaphors related to ideas. Match them with meanings 1–4. Student B: turn to page 159.

When I was a philosophy student at university, one day my professor said, 'OK, here's an idea. For some, this might be hard to swallow, but I have a proposal. Instead of making you take exams, in which you just regurgitate the book, at the end of term you all give a talk about something you found interesting in class.' He paused. Silence. 'It's just food for thought,' he said. 'You don't have to decide now.' None of us had done anything like this before. But, as if to prove it wasn't just a half-baked idea, at the end of term, he made us do it. It was the best thing I did in four years at university.

1 reproduce without thinking

2 difficult to believe/accept

3 badly thought-out

4 something to think about

B Read your paragraph to your partner twice. Which metaphors did he/she notice? Teach the four metaphors to your partner.

10 Replace the underlined phrases with metaphors and any necessary verbs.

1 My teachers said, 'You have a great future ahead of you.' *You'll go far.*

2 A friend told me she was related to Albert Einstein, but I find that difficult to believe.

3 You should keep some time free to visit the National Gallery when you're in Edinburgh.

4 He had a badly thought-out plan to start a website selling cars.

5 I began my career by winning two tennis tournaments, but then things started to go wrong.

6 Our dog had been sick for years and was expected to die at any moment.

7 He was at the height of his career when he decided to retire.

8 Someone once said 'all children are born geniuses'. That's something for us to think about.

11A Work in pairs and think of two:

• half-baked ideas that could change the world.
  Allow all schools to be run by the students.

• tips for reaching the peak of your profession.

• things you can't afford (either the money or time) to do.

• activities you would do if you put aside some time for yourself.

• reasons why famous people's careers go downhill.

• things you heard in the news that you find hard to swallow.

B Explain your ideas to other students.

➠ page 149 VOCABULARYBANK

▶ **GRAMMAR** | verb patterns ▶ **VOCABULARY** | opinions ▶ **HOW TO** | talk about opinions

LISTENING

1A Read about living libraries. Do you think they are a good idea?

Living books: changing people's opinions by talking to them

The idea of the 'living library' originated in Scandinavia. 'Readers' come to the library to borrow real people in the same way that they would normally borrow books. They can then take them away to a corner for a fifteen-minute chat, in the course of which they can ask any questions they like and hear real live answers. The idea is that by doing this, the 'reader' will start to uncover some of the preconceptions that they may have, and the 'book' is able to try and dispel a few of the typical stigmas, stereotypes and prejudices they encounter in their everyday lives.

B ▶ 2.2 Listen to two people talking about being in a living library. Which speaker, Alex (A) or Saba (S):

1 volunteered to talk about their life as a student?
2 is curious about other types of people?
3 met a woman who lost her sight due to an illness?
4 was nervous about being able to answer the questions?
5 thinks that student ideologies haven't changed much since the 1960s?
6 learnt about the people who have inspired a blind person?

2 Listen again and answer the questions.

1 What was written in the catalogue next to 'student'?
2 How did Alex feel about this?
3 What did Alex expect the man to do?
4 In fact, what happened?
5 What was the first thing Saba noticed about Karrie?
6 What opinion is Karrie hoping to change?
7 How does being blind affect Karrie's life?
8 Why does she feel that she is a good judge of character?

VOCABULARY opinions

3A Underline the correct alternatives.

1 Everyone has *preconceptions/stereotypes* about what a drug addict is.
2 They *raise the stereotypes/challenge the stereotypes* that people hold about immigrants.
3 I was beginning to *have second thoughts/have a second opinion* about the whole idea.
4 It's important to *be an open mind/keep an open mind*.
5 His attitude is very *narrow-minded/thin-minded*.
6 The experience was *eye-opening/eye-closing* as we talked so directly.
7 I saw the situation from a whole new *perspective/view*.
8 I didn't find his argument very *persuading/convincing*.

B Respond to situations 1–5 using the prompts and phrases from Exercise 3A.

1 You are supposed to get married next month, but you're feeling nervous about the decision.
   I'm having *second thoughts about getting married.*
2 You spend a week living in a small community with a very different lifestyle to your own. It gives you a new outlook on life.
   It was an … experience. It has …
3 You meet your new father-in-law and he is a policeman. You had ideas about the kind of person he is, which you discover are wrong.
   I had some …
4 Politicians are arguing that nuclear power is safe. You are not sure how true that is.
   I don't find …
5 You used to think it would be great not to work, but then you lost your job.
   Losing my job …

C Work in pairs and answer the questions.

1 Can you think of any situations which have made you change your mind about something?
2 Have you ever had second thoughts about a decision you have made?

▐▶ page 149 **VOCABULARYBANK**

GRAMMAR verb patterns

4A Check what you know. Underline the correct alternatives to complete what people said about living libraries.

1 It was great being able to say those things you're usually scared *to say/say/saying* and ask questions you're usually afraid to ask.

2 We were given the freedom *to ask/ask/asking* questions without having to worry about *to be/be/being* judged. I admit *to feel/feel/feeling* a little nervous about a few of the questions.

3 I wanted *to offer/offer/offering* some insights into my job and I was determined *to challenge/challenge/challenging* a few misconceptions.

4 I enjoyed *to talk/talk/talking* to different people. I learnt more about where my arguments for *to be/be/being* a vegan fall down. I had to apologise for not always being able to answer the question properly.

5 They advised me *to be/be/being* as honest as possible about my feelings.

6 *To sleep/Sleep/Sleeping* outside in the middle of winter isn't the problem. Coping with how people treat you is much harder *to deal/deal/dealing* with.

B Look at Exercise 4A again. Find an example of verb + *-ing* or infinitive with *to* for situations 1–9 below.

1 after a preposition (sentence 2)
   worry about being judged

2 after an adjective (sentence 1)

3 to express a purpose (sentence 3)

4 after certain verbs, e.g. *recall, admit, keep, mention* (sentence 2)

5 after a noun, often as a semi-fixed phrase (sentences 2 and 4)

6 after certain verbs, e.g. *hope, wish, expect, fail, need, want* (sentence 3)

7 after *like, love,* etc. (sentence 4)

8 when used as a noun (subject or object) (sentence 6)

9 after a verb + object, e.g. *advise someone, remind someone, prefer something* (sentence 5)

C Which structure (verb + *-ing* or infinitive with *to*) is used in each situation? Are there any situations in which both structures can be used?

1 worry about being judged = verb + -ing

D Match examples 1–3 with rules a)–c).

1 They seem to have forgotten why we came here.

2 Not understanding people's reasons for why they do the things they do is a big problem.

3 He is always being stopped by police just for the way he looks.

Rules:

a) Passive infinitive or *-ing* form _____
   Use the passive infinitive or *-ing* form to talk about actions which are done to the subject.

b) Perfect infinitive or *-ing* form _____
   Use the perfect infinitive or *-ing* form to emphasise when one action happens before another.

c) Negative infinitive or *-ing* form _____
   Negative infinitives and *-ing* forms can often be made the subject of a sentence, like gerunds.

PRACTICE

5A Complete the sentences with the correct form of the verb in brackets.

1 I didn't expect _____ (feel) so embarrassed, but the questions they asked were so personal.

2 _____ (Meet) Linda and _____ (have) the chance to talk to her about her experience was enlightening.

3 They had the opportunity _____ (ask) me about anything that they wanted.

4 It's hard _____ (imagine) what it's like to live with a disability.

5 I wouldn't even contemplate _____ (leave) the country.

6 She had refused _____ (marry) the man her parents had chosen for her.

7 Somehow he seemed _____ (lose) all the money already.

8 He is fed up with _____ (be) called rude names.

B Work alone and think of:

• one thing you would never consider doing.

• something you regret doing/not doing.

• three things you find hard to tolerate.

• something you have recently been persuaded to do.

C Compare your ideas in pairs.

SPEAKING

6A Mark the statements below with a number from 1–5 (1 = strongly agree, 5 = strongly disagree).

Medical advances will soon mean that people will live until they are 200 years old.

Individual countries do not have the right to interfere with the affairs of another country.

Books will always exist – people like the feel of paper.

Students, not the state, should pay university tuition fees.

Women should be promoted to top jobs in business and politics before men.

B Work in groups. Discuss two of the statements and modify them until everyone in the group agrees with what they say.

C Compare your new statements with the rest of the class.

page 130 **LANGUAGEBANK**

WRITING a discursive essay

7A Look at the photo. What do you think are the main reasons for homelessness? What is the best way to reduce the problem?

B Read the essay. Does the writer share your ideas?

Are we doing enough to help the homeless?

Homelessness is a major problem in any big city. There are regular attempts by authorities to clear the streets of the homeless, typically in cities hosting events like the Olympics. Homelessness doesn't look good and it makes politicians feel uncomfortable. Is enough being done to resolve the problem, **however**?

Many people assume that homeless people live on the streets as a result of drug or alcohol misuse. **Consequently**, they assume we can do little to help as drugs will continue to be a problem. **Additionally**, charitable organisations already help the homeless, **so** this may be sufficient. In my opinion, this approach ignores the bigger picture.

There is no doubt that drug abuse is a major contributing factor leading to homelessness. **On the other hand**, there are increasing numbers of people who are homeless because of the lack of affordable housing. **In addition to this**, as unemployment increases, more people struggle to keep up with payments on their homes.

A frightening number of the homeless are families with children. They are, **in fact**, the fastest growing part of the homeless population. **Furthermore**, it's not only the unemployed who cannot afford housing. According to a recent survey, more than a quarter of homeless people (25–40 percent) actually work. **Nevertheless**, they still cannot afford to pay for accommodation.

In today's society, it is unacceptable that working people cannot afford to pay for a house to live in. **For this reason**, it's essential that governments ensure people are paid sufficient wages. **Likewise**, since housing prices are so high, governments should focus on providing accommodation for low-income families. **In conclusion**, the responsibility for homelessness should not just be left to charities, but as a society we need to help people before they find themselves on the streets.

8 Look at the guidelines for writing a discursive essay. How far does the essay in Exercise 7B follow the guidelines?

1 Include an introductory paragraph.
2 Divide your essay into for and against sections.
3 Use linking words and phrases.
4 Write a concluding paragraph.

LEARN TO use linking devices

9A Complete the table with phrases in bold from the essay.

introduce additional information (meaning 'and')
what is more, another (problem/issue/point, etc.), _____, _____, _____, _____

indicate a contrast with what has come before (meaning 'but')
in contrast, on the contrary, conversely, _____, _____, _____

follow a logical argument (meaning 'therefore')
thus, hence, accordingly, as a result, _____, _____, _____

prove your point
evidently, obviously, indeed, to conclude/_____, _____

Most linking words come at the beginning of a sentence (followed by a comma), or in the middle of the sentence (usually with a comma before and after the linker). Some linkers can be used at the end of clauses. Underline an example in the essay of where the linker appears at the beginning, in the middle and at the end of a sentence.

B Delete the incorrect alternative in each sentence.

1 Most computer users have, *in conclusion/evidently/in fact*, never received any formal keyboard training. *As a result,/However,/So* their keyboard skills are inefficient.

2 He is old and unpopular. *On the contrary/Furthermore/In addition to this*, he has at best only two more years of political life left.

3 Some of the laws were contradictory. Measures were taken to clarify them, *accordingly/as a result/hence*.

4 What he said was true. It was, *nevertheless/thus/however*, unkind.

5 I don't mind at all. *Indeed/In fact/To conclude*, I was pleased.

6 Many employees enjoy music in the workplace. *However/Conversely/In addition to this*, some people find it distracting or, *indeed/in fact/obviously*, annoying.

10A Work in groups. Choose a statement from Exercise 6A and discuss the arguments for and against it.

B Plan an essay about your statement. Write a few key sentences using linking words.

C Write a discursive essay (250–300 words).

SPEAKING

1A Work in groups and discuss the questions.

1 Which professions are the most/least trusted by the public?

2 Do you think public trust in certain professions has changed over the years? Why/Why not?

B Read the article about the most and least trusted professions in the UK. Would the results be the same in your country?

In a recent UK poll to find the most trustworthy professions, doctors came first. Ninety-two percent of people trust them. Other highly trusted professions included teachers, judges and clergy. Near the bottom of the list were business leaders and journalists, but politicians came last. Only thirteen percent of people trust them.

Three of the most trusted professions gave us their comments.

Dr David Bailey, doctor

'I qualified when I was twenty-three years old. I've every intention of working until I'm sixty-five, so I've got a real vested interest in making sure that my patients think I am trustworthy. You do that by the way you behave towards people.'

Mary Davis, teacher

'We make every effort to get to know each individual pupil and we also try very hard to be part of the community. As well as knowing the pupils, we get to know their families.'

Professor Justin Lewis, university professor

'We don't have an axe to grind. Our business is doing research; teaching. In good faith, we try and produce things that are of value to society in general.'

VOCABULARY idioms of opinion

2A Work in pairs. Underline two idioms in the article and check you understand them.

B Work in pairs. Underline the idioms in sentences 1–4 and choose the best definitions.

1 I'm going to play devil's advocate. Let's imagine the company goes bankrupt. What happens to the employees?

a) give a very negative opinion about someone or something

b) say something unlikely or unpopular so people will think about the issue more carefully

2 I'm going to speak my mind. I think this situation is absolutely terrible and we have to find a solution.

a) change your opinion after reconsidering something

b) say what you really believe

3 If you have to make a decision, it's no use sitting on the fence. You must choose one or the other.

a) being unable to commit yourself to one opinion or one side

b) asking lots of people to help you make a difficult decision

4 Let's not beat about the bush. You have committed a serious crime, and now you must pay for it.

a) give an opinion based on false evidence

b) talk a lot, but avoid directly addressing the most important point

C Which idioms in Exercise 2B can be used to introduce opinions or knowledge?

FUNCTION introducing opinions

3A ▶ 2.3 **Listen to a debate. What issue are the speakers discussing and what conclusion do they reach?**

B Listen again and tick the ideas that are mentioned.

1 Journalists have an axe to grind.
2 Most journalists are truly impartial.
3 Some journalists are there to sell newspapers.
4 A journalist's job is to get proof and ask for evidence.
5 Journalists want the truth.
6 Good journalists make the case for both sides.
7 There are many libel trials because people don't like what is written about them.
8 Some journalists 'give others a bad name'.

4A What words do you think complete the expressions for introducing opinions? Which do you know? Which do you use?

If you want my honest ¹_____, …
Quite ²_____, …
The reality is … /In reality, …
According ³_____ (the statistics/the facts/her), …
From what I can ⁴_____, …
As far as I'm ⁵_____, …
To my knowledge, …
Look at it this way.
If you ⁶_____ me, …

B Read audio script 2.3 on page 166. Which of the expressions above can you find?

▸ page 130 LANGUAGEBANK

5A Underline the correct alternatives.

1 *In/Of/By* reality, all the recent political and business scandals have eroded people's trust in these professions.
2 From what I can *learn/gather/get*, nurses are extremely trustworthy. They were voted the most trusted professionals in the USA from 2004–2008.
3 As far as I'm *opinionated/concern/concerned*, postal workers are the most trustworthy profession.
4 To my *knowledge/view/opinion*, there are no professions that are 'squeaky clean'; all of them have 'bad apples'.
5 If you *tell/inquire/ask* me, librarians are the most trustworthy people; they have no reason to lie.
6 If you want my *truest/honest/perfect* opinion, I'd say trust nobody, ever.

B Do you agree with opinions 1–6 above? Why/Why not?

LEARN TO express doubt

6A ▶ 2.4 **Listen to three extracts from the debate in Exercise 3A. Tick the phrases you hear for expressing doubt.**

1 I find that highly unlikely.
2 I'm really not sure about that.
3 That's debatable.
4 I don't know about that.

B Which expression above shows the most doubt?

C ▶ 2.5 **Listen to four sentences using the expressions above. Notice the intonation on the modifiers *really* and *highly*. Listen again and repeat.**

SPEAKING

7A Read about three real cases of untrustworthy behaviour at work. If you were the boss in these cases, what would you do? What would it depend on? Think of some ideas and make notes.

CASE 1
Someone in your company has been stealing pens and other supplies from the office. You discover that it's one of your best workers.

CASE 2
One of the teachers at your school frequently calls in sick on Mondays. You notice holiday photos on his Facebook page which were taken on one of the days he was 'off sick'.

CASE 3
An employee at your advertising agency has used her company credit card to pay for expensive meals and tickets to events. You know that she wasn't with clients on those days.

B Compare your ideas with other students. If you were the boss, what options would you have? Debate the issue.

C What do you think the bosses really did? Turn to page 159 to find out. Do you think they did the right thing?

DVD PREVIEW

1A Work in groups. Check you understand the words/phrases in bold.

1 Do you think musicians like Beethoven or artists like Picasso are born with an **innate talent**, or would you **put their success down to** a **lifelong passion** or intensive training?

2 Do you agree that any parent can train their child to become world-class at something or does the child need to be born **academically/artistically gifted**?

3 If you can **inherit** eye and hair colour from a parent, do you think it is possible to also inherit personality **traits**?

4 How much do you think a parent is able to **shape** their child's future and success?

B Discuss the questions in Exercise 1A.

2 Read the programme information and answer the questions.

1 What is Vanessa's special talent?

2 Who was influential in helping Vanessa to become a professional musician?

3 What does Vanessa hope to learn from taking part in the programme?

BBC The Making of Me: Vanessa-Mae

Vanessa-Mae first hit the international music scene at the age of ten and was the youngest violinist ever to record Beethoven and Tchaikovsky violin concertos. Over eight million record sales have propelled her onto the Rich List and into celebrity status. But her success has been accompanied by a turbulent relationship with her mother, who was the prime force behind her career as a young musician. In the BBC documentary *The Making of Me*, Vanessa investigates how much of her ability was inherited, how much was shaped by her mother and how much was down to her own work. Was it nature or nurture that played the bigger part?

▶ DVD VIEW

3 Watch the DVD and answer the questions.

1 In what way was Vanessa's relationship with her mother unusual?

2 Does Vanessa feel that she was born with her musical gift, or that she developed her talent purely through the amount of practice she did? What does she say about this?

3 Is Vanessa happy about her childhood? Why/Why not?

4A Complete the extracts.

1 With a fortune in excess of _____, Vanessa-Mae is one of Britain's most successful young musicians.

2 This beautiful instrument has given me so much _____ and _____ and _____ in my life. It has basically _____ my life.

3 I was always made to appreciate that the love my mother had for me was _____.

4 To help Vanessa find the answer, science will test her body and her _____. She'll be observed by _____ … and be pushed to the limit.

5 Emotionally, I may have become the person I became because of the _____ in my life.

6 It was my blood, my sweat and my _____ that brought me here today.

B Watch the DVD again to check.

5 Work in pairs and discuss the questions.

1 Do you think Vanessa's mother made the right decisions about how to bring up her daughter? Why/Why not?

2 Are your own successes a result of your natural ability (inherited from your parents), your own hard work, or just pure luck?

3 Do you think your parents' interests and achievements have shaped your own? Have you inherited personality traits from members of your family?

speakout a panel discussion

6A ▶ 2.6 Listen to someone debating the role of nature versus nurture. Which side of the argument does she present? What examples does she give to justify her ideas?

B Listen again and tick the key phrases you hear.

> ### keyphrases
>
> I'd like to begin by stating that …
>
> As I see it … / What I think is …
>
> I would say it depends on …
>
> What you need to consider is …
>
> I think it's ridiculous to suggest …
>
> I absolutely reject the idea that …
>
> So, to conclude I would have to argue that …
>
> Does anyone have a question … ? / Are there any other questions?
>
> That's a good question because …

C Which key phrases are used to:
- introduce the argument?
- justify an opinion?
- conclude?
- invite questions?
- respond to questions?

7A Work in groups. Think of points 'for' and 'against' the following statement.

Children should start school younger than they do now.

B Prepare to argue either 'for' or 'against' the statement. Follow the instructions.
- Choose a speaker for your group.
- Help them to prepare their argument.
- Make notes on how to introduce the argument, justify the opinion and conclude. Use the key phrases.

C The speakers take turns to present their arguments. Listen and ask questions at the end. Which case was argued the most clearly?

writeback a summary

8A Read the summary. What are the key points? Do you agree with the writer's opinion?

> ### Should your child learn a musical instrument?
>
> **Anna:** Music in a child's life has many benefits. Some even claim that early exposure to classical music for very young children (even before they are born) helps them to become more intelligent, the so-called 'Mozart Effect'. The claims are unsubstantiated, but there is no question that classical music is soothing to the soul. They may not become musical prodigies, but exposing your children to songs and nursery rhymes from a young age will give them a feel for rhythm and language, and encourage them to appreciate the beauty of music as they grow.
>
> At school, children who learn musical instruments are generally more successful and perform better in tests. It may be that learning music also helps children to develop their reasoning skills, learn about problem-solving and decision-making. It can also be great for confidence-building and is a valuable experience which helps to broaden their understanding and appreciation of the world around them.
>
> Obviously, there are costs and commitments involved with teaching a child a musical instrument. But, if you ask me, it's one of the most precious gifts you can offer a child and one which he or she will appreciate for a lifetime.

B Write a summary (200–220 words) of your opinion about one of the issues in Exercises 6A or 7A .

LEARNING

1 Find and correct the mistakes in sentences 1–8. There are five mistakes.

1 I've only been working here for two weeks so I'm still learning the chains.

2 You are so talented, you should believe on yourself.

3 He came under attack for his political beliefs.

4 I decided to make advantage of the opportunity.

5 David didn't need to think because he trusted on his instincts.

6 That film had a profound effect on me at an early age.

7 If you really want to be the best, never give up.

8 It's a difficult course and Frank's on a steep learning curb.

CONDITIONALS AND REGRETS

2A Choose one of the scenarios below. Write as many sentences as you can, using past conditionals and regrets.

- Several years ago you had a great idea for a book, but you were too busy to write it. The story involved a schoolboy magician and his two friends who fight against evil by using magic. Then the Harry Potter books appeared.

- You have a safe, steady job, but you are totally bored. As a teenager you were a really good dancer and had the opportunity to go to the best dance school in the country. You gave it up because the profession seemed too risky.

- A few years ago you saw a wonderful house for sale. You thought about buying it, but hesitated because of the long commute to work. By the time you decided to make an offer, it was already sold. You frequently dream about living in that house.

B Compare your ideas with other students.

OPINIONS

3A Work alone. Prepare to talk about some of the following topics.

1 Describe the national stereotype for your country. Do you think it is an accurate description?

2 Name three kinds of prejudice or stereotype people are trying to challenge in your country.

3 Describe a person you had a preconception about, who turned out to be very different.

4 What do you think leads to people becoming narrow-minded/open-minded about an issue?

5 What is the best way to change someone's perspective about a topic?

6 Talk about something you decided to do, but then had second thoughts about.

7 Describe a film/book which you would consider eye-opening. Why?

8 Can you think of any convincing/unconvincing arguments in the media at the moment?

B Work in pairs. Talk about as many of the topics as you can in five minutes.

VERB PATTERNS

4A Complete the sentence stems so they are true for you.

1 I would never expect …

2 In my school, we were required …

3 I've always been interested in …

4 I'd love to have the chance …

5 Recently, I've been making plans …

6 It's impossible …

7 I don't mind …

8 I'd advise you …

B Compare your ideas in pairs.

INTRODUCING OPINIONS

5A Use a word from each box to complete the conversations.

according	can	if	my
~~honest~~	reality	quite	I'm

concerned	to	gather	
~~opinion~~	frankly	you	is
knowledge			

1 A: If you want my _honest_ _opinion_, she should apologise.

  B: _____ _____, I agree.

2 A: _____ _____ the statistics, we're the industry's most successful company.

  B: As far as _____ _____, statistics are worthless.

3 A: To _____ _____, the painting hasn't been sold yet.

  B: _____ _____ ask me, the price is too high.

4 A: From what I _____ _____, there's a lot of corruption in sport.

  B: The _____ _____, there's corruption everywhere, not only in sport.

B Play devil's advocate. Choose three of the topics below and write sentences using the expressions in Exercise 5A. Read your sentences to other students. Say what you think of their ideas.

- politics and politicians

As far as I'm concerned, taxpayers should never pay for politicians to have a second home in the capital.

- sport
- technology
- a film or TV programme
- classical music

BBC VIDEO PODCAST

Watch people talking about advice they have given and received on ActiveBook or on the website.

Authentic BBC interviews

www.pearsonELT.com/speakout

UNIT 3

SPEAKING
> Describe a holiday memory
> Talk about your work space
> Present a proposal

LISTENING
> Listen to people describing their work spaces
> Listen to a proposal for a city improvement scheme
> Watch a BBC travel programme about Africa

READING
> Read an article about memorable holiday moments
> Read a city guide
> Read a report about solutions to urban problems

WRITING
> Write a guidebook entry
> Write a documentary proposal

BBC CONTENT
▯ Video podcast: What is your favourite place?
◉ DVD: An African Journey

places

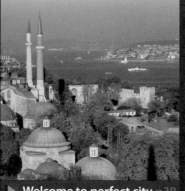

▶ **Lonely planet** p32　　▶ **Your space** p35　　▶ **Welcome to perfect city** p38　　▶ **An African Journey** p40

VOCABULARY landscapes

1A Work in pairs. Match the words in the box with synonyms 1–8. Use a dictionary to help you.

> picturesque   tranquil   bustling   magnificent
> ancient   deserted   ~~run-down~~   unspoilt

1 shabby, dilapidated, in a bad state *run-down*
2 calm, quiet, peaceful
3 stunning, breathtaking
4 old, historic
5 unchanged, not altered by tourism
6 busy, full of people and noise
7 beautiful, lovely, pretty, attractive, pleasant
8 empty, uninhabited

B Complete the sentences with adjectives from Exercise 1A.

1 The flower market was _____ with shoppers.
2 The view from the tower was _____.
3 We wandered around the _____ walled city. Life there hadn't changed for centuries.
4 Tourists haven't discovered the area yet, so the beaches are completely _____.

C Look at the photos. Use the vocabulary to describe the scenes.

READING

2A Read the introduction to the article. Who took the photos? Can you guess where they were taken?

B Read the article and match stories 1–3 with photos A–C.

C Read the article again and answer the questions.

1 How did Alistair arrive at the scene?
2 What example(s) of spontaneity does he mention?
3 What is the Malecón and what happens there?
4 Which things in the photo and the text capture the essence of Havana for Anthony?
5 What is special about the houses in Matera?
6 How did Greg feel when he left the town?

SPEAKING

3A Think of a 'snapshot' moment of a special holiday. Think about where you were, what kind of holiday it was, how you felt at the time and why the memory is important to you.

B Compare your 'snapshot moments' with other students. Who has the best description/story?

A

Every month the BBC *Lonely Planet Magazine* runs a photo competition. They ask readers to send in pictures they have taken on their travels and tell the story behind them.

1 Sangkhlaburi, Thailand: Taking the plunge
'We were in a long-tail boat crossing the Khao Laem reservoir in Sangkhlaburi, close to the Burmese border in Western Thailand, when our driver took us on a detour to Thailand's longest wooden bridge. As he cut the engine and we idled up to the bridge for a closer look, some local boys were enjoying a bombing (diving) competition. When they saw us, they seized the moment to showcase some of their diving and one after the other plunged into the water. We were only there for a few minutes but this impromptu performance remains one of the highlights of my time in Thailand. This shot embodies the spontaneity of the country, and its people's vibrancy.'
Alistair McDonald was on a two-week holiday in Thailand.

2 Havana, Cuba: Seeing the light
'The Malecón is a five-mile-long, six-lane sea road, laid out by US Marines from 1901 and fronted by nineteenth-century buildings in various states of disrepair. It is where Habaneros★ hang out and party at the weekends and is the unique fingerprint of Havana. When I got there, the sun was starting to set. There was a warm breeze blowing and a strong sea swell, with waves crashing against the sea wall. The sun was barely peeping through the clouds when I noticed a 1950s Pontiac approaching in the distance. I waited until it drew closer before pressing the shutter. For me this photo captures the essence of Havana: a uniquely photogenic city frozen in time for fifty years.'
Anthony McEvoy was in Cuba for work and a short holiday.
★*Habaneros* – people born in Havana, Cuba

3 Matera, southern Italy: Time stands still
'Nothing could have prepared me for my first sight of the Sassi di Matera. I wasn't sure what to expect from a cave town where the locals live in the same houses as their ancestors did 9,000 years ago. I felt like I'd wandered onto a film set. The jumble of stacked cave houses appeared to tumble down a ravine. Adding to the magic of the place was the fact that I was the only person there and it felt like a ghost town. I left feeling slightly humbled – maybe it was knowing that my hotel room was once a cave dwelling for a family of ten and their livestock!'
Greg Jackson spent his summer holiday last year in Italy.

GRAMMAR noun phrases

4 Look at the ways in which noun phrases can be modified. Add the underlined sections in the text to the appropriate category below.

Rules:

A noun phrase is a group of words which functions as a unit to describe the noun. Information can be added before or after the noun in different ways.

1 Compound nouns

A noun can be used to modify a noun. Sometimes these are written as two words, sometimes as one word, and sometimes they are hyphenated.

cave houses   *fingerprint*   *candy-floss*   ¹_____

2 Compound adjectives

Adjectives can be used to modify the noun, using hyphens.

long-tail boat (a boat with a long tail)

When the noun part is plural, it becomes singular in a compound.

nine-year-old girl (the girl is nine **years** old)   ²_____

3 Adverb + adjective combinations

refreshingly cool breeze   ³_____

4 Adjectives

When several adjectives come before the noun, they need to be in a specific order.

Value adjectives (which give your opinion) come first, followed by size, age, shape, colour, origin and material.

delicious slice of home-made apple pie   ⁴_____

5 Prepositional phrases and participle clauses

These occur after the noun.

Prepositional phrases:

a camera **for filming short video clips**   ⁵_____

Participle clauses:

waves **crashing against the sea wall**   ⁶_____

⮕ page 132 **LANGUAGEBANK**

5 Put the words/phrases in the correct order to make sentences.

1 home-made / a slice of / chocolate / delicious / on top / cherries / with / cake

2 a / mountain bike / bright red / with fifteen gears / heavy-duty / brand new

3 Greek / seafood / it's a / of the best / fresh / restaurant / some / small / in the area / which serves

4 cashmere / very expensive / black / with extra-long sleeves / a / jumper

5 with / a / soup / traditional / freshly-baked / bean / Tuscan / bread.

6 a / medieval / castle / ancient / steep / on top of a very / hill / fascinating

6A Look at the extra detail added to the noun phrases below. What parts of speech in Exercise 4 have been added each time?

The **shop** serves **tarts** and **coffee**.

1 The **shop** serves **custard tarts** and **good coffee**.

custard tarts = compound noun; good coffee = adjective + noun

2 The **shop** serves **delicious hand-made custard tarts** and **extraordinarily good strong black espresso coffee**.

3 The **shop** serves **delicious hand-made custard tarts with a sprinkle of cinnamon on top** and **tiny cups of extraordinarily good strong black espresso coffee**.

4 The **old pastry shop in central Lisbon** serves **delicious hand-made custard tarts with a sprinkle of cinnamon on top** and **tiny cups of extraordinarily good strong black espresso coffee**.

B Work in pairs. Add more detail to the following noun phrases.

1 The man lives in a house.

2 There was a piece of cheese on the table.

3 The shop sells furniture.

4 The boy enjoyed the cake.

5 The streets were empty.

6 The bus was crowded.

C Write three complex noun phrases describing:

1 a place you have visited.

2 something you have enjoyed eating/cooking.

3 something you bought recently.

D Compare your sentences with other students.

WRITING a description of a place

7A Read the *Lonely Planet* guidebook entry for Lisbon. Make notes about the city under the following headings.

- Location
- Nearby sights
- Things to see/do
- History
- Architecture
- Food and drink

Situated on the southwestern coast of Portugal and overlooking the Rio Tejo, Lisbon offers all the delights you'd expect of Portugal's star attraction. Gothic cathedrals, majestic monasteries and quaint museums are all part of the colourful cityscape, but the real delights of discovery lie in wandering the narrow lanes of Lisbon's lovely backstreets.

As bright yellow trams wind their way through curvy tree-lined streets, Lisboêtas stroll through the old quarters, much as they've done for centuries. Village-life gossip in old Alfama is exchanged at the public baths or over fresh bread and wine at tiny patio restaurants, as fadistas (proponents of fado, Portugal's traditional melancholic singing) perform in the background.

Meanwhile, in other parts of town, visitors and locals chase the ghosts of Pessoa (a Portuguese poet) in warmly lit 1930s-era cafés. Yet, while history is very much alive in ancient Lisbon, its spirit is undeniably youthful.

In the hilltop district of Bairro Alto, dozens of restaurants and bars line the narrow streets, with jazz, reggae, electronica and fado filling the air and revellers partying until dawn. Nightclubs scattered all over town make fine use of old spaces, whether on riverside docks or tucked away in eighteenth-century mansions.

The Lisbon experience encompasses so many things, from enjoying a fresh pastry and bica (espresso) on a petite leafy plaza to window-shopping in elegant Chiado or watching the sunset from the old Moorish* castle.

Just outside Lisbon, there's more to explore: the magical setting of Sintra, glorious beaches and traditional fishing villages.

* *Moorish* – relating to the Moors (Muslim people from Northern Africa)

B Work in pairs and discuss the questions.

1 What tense(s) does the writer use to describe Lisbon? Why?
2 Do you think the language in the article sounds formal or informal? Why?
3 Do you think the writer likes the place? Why/Why not?

LEARN TO add detail

8A What kinds of details did the writer add to improve the sentences below?

1 Trams travel along the streets of the old town, where many locals walk.
2 In Alfama, people gossip in the public baths, or in restaurants where they enjoy bread, wine and traditional Portuguese music.
3 In Bairro Alto, you can find many restaurants and bars which play live music.
4 Nightclubs around the town can be found in all kinds of interesting places, near the docks and in old mansions.
5 In Lisbon you can do many things, like enjoy a coffee at a pavement café, go window-shopping or visit the castle.
6 Outside Lisbon, it is worth visiting the town of Sintra, and also beaches and fishing villages along the coast.

> **speakout TIP**
>
> Add colour. Details help to make your writing more colourful and interesting for the reader. Try to use a rich range of vocabulary and add details (colours, shapes, sounds, smells, tastes, feelings) to help the reader experience your description. Underline the sections in the article which add colourful detail to the description.

B Read the description below. Underline phrases which refer to the senses and identify each sense.

Approaching the central square, you can hear the voices of the market sellers, advertising their wares. The sweet smell of fruit ripened in the hot sun lingers in the air, mixing with the aroma of strong, fresh coffee and petrol fumes from the small, three-wheeled motorised vans the local farmers, or 'contadini', use to bring their produce to market. Each stall has mountains of different coloured fruits and vegetables, firm red peppers, purple beans, tomatoes of all shapes and sizes. There's a liveliness in the air, as the old ladies haggle over the price of the cherries and wave their arms in rebuke at the younger workers.

9A Plan a guidebook entry. Choose a place you know well. Make some notes using the headings in Exercise 7A. Think about how you can add some interesting detail.

B Write your guidebook entry (200–250 words).

▶ **GRAMMAR** | relative clauses ▶ **VOCABULARY** | adjectives ▶ **HOW TO** | talk about a personal space

SPEAKING

1A Work with other students. Look at the photos and discuss the questions.

1 What can you guess about the profession/ age/gender of the people who work in these rooms?

2 Do you think these rooms look like good spaces in which to work? Why/Why not?

3 What type of space is good to work in? What qualities does it need (e.g. light, view, furniture)?

B Match quotations 1–3 with photos A–C. Check your answers on page 162.

1 'This room sold the place for me because it gets the morning sun and then that's it.'

2 'I have to have a lot of colour around me. It makes me feel happy.'

3 'When I'm in my chair I feel like Goldfinger or one of the other Bond villains.'

C Discuss. What is good or bad about the space where you work or study?

VOCABULARY adjectives

2A Read descriptions 1–6. Are they from an advertisement, a ratings website, or a piece of fiction? How do you know?

1 Beautiful, roomy Suffolk cottage. Spacious living area, generous bedrooms, sleeps eight, shady patio for outdoor dining; call 01865 558569

2 Danziger's gloomy, airless room suited his mood. He lay on the mattress, listening to the whirr of the water pipes, and wondered where his youth had gone.

3 We found the room comfortable, even though the décor – bright yellow and green stripes – was a bit gaudy. It also got quite chilly at night.

4 Airy flat. Huge windows. Sunny living room. Peaceful location. Sleeps four. €895 per month.

5 Entering through a grey door, she saw grey walls enclosing a grey space and said, 'What a dreary room. This looks like a good place to die.'

6 The room was a bit poky. There wasn't much space, but for £60 a night in London, we couldn't complain.

B Underline all the adjectives in Exercise 2A. Which are positive and which are negative? Think of more examples to describe a place or room.

🎙 speakout TIP

Many descriptive adjectives end in -y. Some come from the root word, e.g. *dirty, noisy, smelly*. Others do not have a root word, e.g. *happy, pretty, silly*. So, if we don't know the meaning, we need to guess from the context. Do the adjectives in exercise 2A have a root word?

3A Are the bold vowel sounds long or short? Underline the odd one out in each set.

1 dreary/city/really

2 gaudy/body/naughty

3 gloomy/footie/roomy

4 hockey/jokey/poky

5 shady/ready/daily

6 bury/airy/ferry

B ▶ 3.1 Listen and check. Then listen again and repeat.

▐▶ page 150 **VOCABULARYBANK**

LISTENING

4A ▶ 3.2 Listen to two people describing the space where they work. What types of space do they describe? What is good and bad about them?

B Listen again. Who uses the following phrases: speaker 1 or speaker 2?

> open plan   one drawback   all crammed up
> a stone's throw away   somewhere nice to hang out
> it gets quite chaotic   a little haven of tranquillity

C Work in pairs. Use some of the phrases in the box to describe where you work or live.

GRAMMAR relative clauses

5 Read six blog comments from people describing where they work. Do you sympathise with their views?

1	Most people who do creative work need a quiet place, but I need noise and movement and chaos to create anything.
2	I've shared offices with lots of great talkers, none of whom were bad people, but I need silence to work.
3	My work space can be anywhere I feel physically comfortable, warm and relaxed.
4	I shared an artist's studio for two years. One day I arrived to find six people asleep on the floor, at which point I decided to work from home. Home is the best work space for me.
5	I love antiques, so everything in my house is old. Even the leather chair, on which I sit every day, is an antique.
6	The best work spaces for me are those whose major characteristic is brightness. I just need big windows.

6A Check what you know. Look at comments 1 and 2 in Exercise 5 and underline the relative clauses. Which is a defining relative clause? Which is a non-defining relative clause? What is the difference?

B Underline the relative clauses in comments 3–6.

C Match descriptions a)–f) with the relative clauses in Exercise 5.

a) a formal sentence in which a preposition comes before the relative pronoun (*which/who/when*, etc.) 5

b) a fixed prepositional phrase with *which* or *when* in a non-defining relative clause

c) the possessive *whose* (used only before nouns)

d) a relative pronoun after *some of, all of, none of*, etc.

e) a defining relative clause with no relative pronoun

f) a defining relative clause in which the relative pronoun (*who, which*, etc.) can be replaced by *that*

D Work in pairs and answer the questions.

1 In what kinds of clauses can you sometimes use *that* instead of *who, where, when*, etc.?

2 Why is a comma used in sentences 2, 4 and 5 before the relative clause?

3 Which relative pronoun has been omitted from sentence 3? Why is this possible?

⫸ page 132 **LANGUAGEBANK**

PRACTICE

7 Cross out the incorrect option in each sentence.

1 My aunt and uncle, _____ cook well, spend most of their time in the kitchen.

 a) both   b) both of whom   c) who both

2 That's the run-down little bar _____ we first met.

 a) in which   b) where   c) which

3 The hill _____ overlooks a secluded hotel off the beaten track.

 a) on where the castle was built   b) on which the castle was built   c) which the castle was built on

4 The group of friends, _____ I've known for ages, went on a yearly holiday together.

 a) who   b) of which   c) a few of whom

5 We decided to go home in 1997, _____ we had travelled to thirty-five countries.

 a) at which point   b) since when
 c) by which time

6 The food _____ they served was wonderful.

 a) –   b) that   c) what

7 We watched the election, _____ was never in doubt.

 a) the result of which   b) that result
 c) whose result

8 She was the person _____ for our information.

 a) on whom we relied   b) whom we relied
 c) who we relied on

SPEAKING

8A Design your ideal space for work/study. Think about the following topics and make notes.

- type of room
- decoration
- size
- special features
- objects/furniture
- view

B Work in groups. Take turns to describe your ideal space.

VOCABULARY *PLUS* prefixes

9 Read about a hotel. Why is it famous?

Hotel Chelsea

TRAVEL

To say that the Hotel Chelsea has an interesting history would be an understatement. Since the early twentieth century, the hotel has been home to dozens of celebrities. The fame of the building itself pre-dates its fame as a hotel; when it was constructed in 1883 as a block of flats, it was New York's tallest building. It became a hotel in 1905. Although prosperous at first, during a period of maladministration the hotel began to <u>degenerate</u>. It went bankrupt and changed hands in 1939. Its proactive new managers soon got it up and running again and, in the post-war era, its fame grew.

As a part of the New York artistic scene, the hotel is irreplaceable. Its famous residents have included actors, artists, singers, writers and numerous anti-establishment figures. Frida Kahlo, Jean-Paul Sartre, Jackson Pollock, Marilyn Monroe, Bob Dylan, Jimi Hendrix, Madonna and Uma Thurman all lived there for a while, and the hotel has been immortalised (and some would say overexposed) in dozens of songs, books and films (*9½ Weeks, The Interpreter*). Always a place of non-conformity, the hotel's management sometimes allowed penniless residents to pay for their rooms with artworks, some of which still hang in its lobby today. Its famous residents have found the hotel conducive to creativity. Arthur C Clarke and Jack Kerouac wrote, respectively, *2001: A Space Odyssey* and *On the Road* while living in the hotel, and Madonna used it for a photo shoot for one of her books. Unfortunately, the hotel is also associated with artistic misbehaviour and tragedy. One of numerous examples of wild adventures behind its closed doors, the poet Dylan Thomas collapsed in room 205 of the hotel after partying too hard. He died four days later.

10A Read the text again. Find and underline an example of each prefix in the first column of the table.

prefix	meaning	example
de ir im non un	*negatives/ opposites/reverse*	*degenerate*
under over		
mal mis		
pre post		
pro anti		

B Complete the second column of the table with the meanings in the box.

> ~~negatives/opposites/reverse~~   size or degree
> time (before or after)   wrong or bad
> attitude or opinion (for or against)

C What types of words do we use the prefixes with (e.g. nouns, verbs, adjectives)?

*We use un- with adjectives like **un**interesting and **un**happy, and adverbs like **un**fortunately.*

D Work in groups. Add your own examples to the third column of the table.

11 One statement about prefixes is true. Correct the false statements.

1 When we add a prefix to the root word, the spelling of the root word usually changes.

2 We cannot add more than one prefix at a time to root words.

3 Learning to recognise prefixes helps us to build our vocabulary and guess unknown words.

4 There are rules that tell us which prefixes we can add to each root word.

12A Complete the words by adding prefixes.

1 a place that is ____known to most tourists because it's ____exposed in the media

2 a hotel, restaurant, bar or café that looks ____descript but is ____rated

3 a hotel, restaurant, bar or café that you think is ____attractive and a bit ____rated

4 a building that is ____inhabitable because it was ____managed in the past

5 a threatened habitat that is ____replaceable, but ____possible to save

B Work in pairs. How many examples of places in Exercise 12A can you think of? Compare your ideas with other students.

A place that is unknown to most tourists is Regent's Canal in London. You can walk nine miles along it from Camden Market to Little Venice, and it's great!

⫸ page 150 **VOCABULARYBANK**

São Paulo

VOCABULARY city life

1A Work in groups and discuss the questions.

1 Have you been to any of the cities in the photos?

2 What do you think might be good about living in them? What problems might there be?

3 What is good and bad about the city or town where you live?

4 What other problems connected with urban living can you think of?

It can be quite stressful because everyone's always in a rush.

B Read the article. Does it mention any of the issues you discussed in Exercise 1A?

Welcome to Perfect City

Environmental psychology is a field of science that looks at the ways in which we are affected by our surroundings. Almost every aspect of the built environment, from the colour of hospital walls to the type of grass used in parks, can have a dramatic impact on crime, health, education, commerce and happiness. *BBC Focus Magazine* reports on how psychologists are teaming up with designers to build spaces that are safer and healthier.

Classic trick

In the mid-nineties in Montreal, it was discovered that playing classical music through the public address system would drive away crowds of loitering teenagers and cut crime. The idea soon caught on. Now, classical music is played in over sixty underground stations in London.

Stop signs

Sometimes less is more – towns such as Bohmte in Germany have found that the best way to slow traffic is to remove all road signs and markings. Without these guides, drivers have to slow down and negotiate rights of way with other drivers, cyclists and pedestrians.

Dipping distractions

Researchers in Manchester found that pickpockets took advantage of pedestrians distracted by confusing environments. By removing visual clutter and making spaces easier to navigate, pedestrians are more aware of their surroundings and less likely to become victims of crime.

Delays stress

Commuting long distances isn't necessarily stressful, but delays are. A study of rail commuters found the highest levels of stress hormone cortisol among those who perceived their journey as unpredictable. Real-time transport updates, such as a text message sent to your phone letting you know exactly when the next bus will arrive, have been found to reduce stress.

2A Complete the sentences with the words in the box.

| amenities   infrastructure   congestion |
| abandonment   tolls   regeneration |

1 The best thing to do with loitering teenagers is to give them _____ such as sports facilities.

2 The city can't host a major international event because it doesn't have the _____. The transport links are poor and the power supply often fails.

3 The _____ of run-down old buildings used to be a real problem where I live, but the area has undergone urban _____, so now it's full of nice shops and houses.

4 There's always traffic _____ in the city centre. They should introduce more _____, so people have to pay to bring cars into the centre.

B Which three words in the box contain suffixes that turn them into nouns? What are the root words of these nouns?

FUNCTION making a proposal

3A ▶ 3.3 Listen to someone proposing an idea to improve an area of their city. What is the idea? What is the speaker proposing to do now?

B Complete the notes. Then listen again to check.

– Harrogate Council to set up cycle hubs in the next
¹_____ years.

– Idea: to increase ²_____ use.

– Hubs to go in the city ³_____ , where many cyclists go.

– Will make the environment ⁴_____ for cyclists.

– Benefits of cycling: fast, good for environment,
⁵_____ and good for fitness.

Beijing

Istanbul

5 Some of the sentences below contain extra words. Cross out the extra words and tick the correct sentences.

1 Hello, everyone. To start up with, I'm going to talk briefly about Manor Studios.

2 Just to give a bit of background information, Manor Studios was where some great films were made in the 1930s, but it's now very run down.

3 The main goals objective of our proposal is to start a project to renovate the building.

4 The aim of the project is to use the building as a film museum.

5 What we plan to do is but renovate the main studio and paint the whole building.

6 We're going to build a new entrance and knock down some walls.

7 This idea is too feasible because the buildings and the location still have great potential.

8 This solution will help us to put Manor Studios to use in the community.

9 In the first of instance, our plan would mean an investment of about one million euros.

10 The long-term benefits include bringing jobs and tourism to the area.

11 So, basically, what is we're proposing is to re-establish the building in the community as a film museum.

12 So that's our plan. Is there anything that needs the clarification?

4A Put phrases a)–g) under the correct headings below.

a) The main goal/objective of our proposal is to

b) The short-term/long-term benefits include …

c) To sum up, we're proposing …

d) Is there anything that needs clarification?

e) This idea is feasible because …

f) To start with, I'm going to talk briefly about …

g) We're going to build/develop/come up with …

Introducing your proposal

Just to give a bit of background information, …

1 _____

Stating the purpose

The aim of the project is to …

2 _____

Describing your idea

What we plan to do is …

3 _____

Justifying your idea

This solution will help us to …

4 _____

Listing the benefits

In the first instance, this would mean …

5 _____

Summarising your proposal

So, basically, what we're proposing is to …

6 _____

Soliciting questions

Does anyone have any questions?

7 _____

B Which expressions were used by the speaker in Exercise 3A? Read audio script 3.3 on page 167 to check.

▶ page 132 **LANGUAGEBANK**

LEARN TO suggest modifications

6 Look at phrases a)–f) which are used to suggest modifications or changes to a proposal. Answer questions 1–4.

a) I'd like to propose a compromise.

b) Let's try to come up with a solution.

c) Let's look at it another way.

d) How about if we combine our ideas?

e) Is there any way we can reduce the costs?

f) Is there any leeway regarding the schedule?

1 Which two expressions mean we should put separate ideas together?

2 Which two expressions ask if there is flexibility to change a plan?

3 Which expression means we should think of an answer to a problem?

4 Which expression asks to rethink a problem?

SPEAKING

7A Work in groups. Think of an area you know, for example part of your city, and make notes on the questions below.

1 What problems does the area have? Think about:

- buildings
- user-friendliness
- facilities
- safety
- appearance
- noise levels

2 How could the area be improved?

3 What would be the benefits for the community?

B Your group is applying for a €1,000,000 grant to improve the area. Plan a proposal using the structure in Exercise 4A. Decide who will say which part and practise the proposal.

C Present your proposal to the class.

DVD PREVIEW

1 Work in pairs and discuss the questions.

1 Do you enjoy travelling? What are the best and worst things about it?

2 What is your favourite way to travel? Why?

3 Have you ever visited (or heard about) a country that you prefer to your own? Would you like to live there? How would your lifestyle change?

2 Read the programme information. What do you think Serpent's family business might be?

BBC An African Journey

After four decades of reporting from the continent, Jonathan Dimbleby returns to Africa on a 7,000-mile journey to discover how it is changing. He starts his African journey in the capital of Mali, Bamako, the fastest-growing African city. Here, he meets some of the individuals who are changing the face of the continent. As new and cheaper technologies arrive in Mali, they are rapidly changing the lives of many of Mali's inhabitants. Jonathan finds the city in the grip of moped mania and meets Serpent and his brother, who are running a successful family business.

▶ DVD VIEW

3 Watch the DVD and answer the questions.

1 How is Bamako changing?

2 What is Serpent's family business?

3 Why is it successful?

4 How is cheaper technology transforming the lives of people in Bamako?

4A Complete the extracts.

1 This series is not about failure or despair, but _____ and hope.

2 West Africa's largest nation is the Republic of _____.

3 I'm using the fastest-growing means of transport here, the _____.

4 There are now more than _____ mopeds in a city of two million people.

5 The economy has grown on average by _____ percent a year for over a decade.

6 It takes _____ minutes to put [a moped] together.

B Watch the DVD again to check.

5 Work in pairs. How do you think other cheaper technologies could transform the lives of people in developing countries? Think of specific examples.

speakout your country

6A ▶ 3.4 Listen to two people from Canada and Argentina. Make notes on what they say about their countries.

B Compare your notes in pairs. What do they say in answer to the questions below? Which questions <u>don't</u> they answer?

1 What is special about your country?

2 What are the highs and lows of living in your country?

3 How would you describe your country geographically? What features would you focus on in a documentary about your country?

4 Is your country experiencing any particular changes at the moment? Do you feel strongly about any of them?

5 Does your country have any interesting customs or events? What are they?

6 What are the similarities and differences between your country and your neighbouring countries?

C Listen again. How do the speakers complete the key phrases? Check your answers in audio script 3.4 on page 167.

keyphrases

(Canada) has one of the highest … in the world.

On the downside, I suppose, you have to deal with …

I would describe (Canada) as geographically …

We're very lucky in (Canada) to have …

Undoubtedly one of the best things about (Argentina) is the …

People are very warm … and we've got a great sense of …

(Argentinians), we've got a sense of longing for …

7A Work in pairs. Ask and answer the questions in Exercise 6B. Do you have similar answers?

B Work in groups. Read the instructions for developing a documentary proposal. Decide what you would include in a programme about your country and make notes.

Lights, camera, action!

You need to pitch a plan for a short documentary about your country. Think about your audience – who is the documentary for? Think about your purpose – what issue would you like to focus on? What do you want people to learn from your video? What attitude do you want them to leave with? Think about your plan – how will you make your information engaging and appealing? Who/Where will you film? Will you include interviews? What will you call the documentary?

C Present your ideas to the class.

writeback a proposal

8A Read the sample proposal. Do you think this pitch would receive funding? Why/Why not?

The music of our heritage

This documentary would examine the importance of the National Folkloric Festival (Festival Nacional de la Mejorana) in Panama. The mejorana is a small guitar, and the music and dance associated with it form an important part of Panama's cultural heritage. Nowadays though, fewer people know how to make the instrument or how to play it.

The aim of the documentary would be to film the four-day festival in order to raise awareness of the mejorana and the consequences of losing this tradition in favour of more modern music.

During the festival, groups from all around the country gather to enjoy Panamanian folklore. There are musical performances, dances, singing, bull fights, traditional competitions and an ox-cart parade. It is a colourful and spectacular occasion. The documentary would highlight the atmosphere at the festival, filming music and dance performances, and interview young and old visitors to gather opinion about the importance of the mejorana and of protecting the traditional customs that are an integral part of Panamanian life.

B Write a short proposal (200–250 words) for your documentary idea. Use the instructions in Exercise 7B.

LANDSCAPES

1A Match the sentence halves.

1 It was a shabby little restaurant,
2 In the summer the normally calm,
3 Hong Kong is a
4 Loreto is an ancient
5 With its largely unspoilt
6 The beach was completely

a) hillside town with cobbled streets.
b) deserted and not safe for swimming.
c) tranquil streets fill with tourists.
d) but the food was exquisite.
e) natural beauty, Vietnam is a top tourist destination.
f) bustling, fascinating city.

B Choose three adjectives from Exercise 1A. Use them to describe places you know to your partner.

shabby —The tapas bar near where I live has been run by the same couple for thirty years. It's a bit shabby now and needs to be redecorated.

NOUN PHRASES

2A Add detail to sentences 1–4 using words/phrases in the box.

cups of	old	brand-new
steaming hot	top-of-the-range	
five-mile-long	farm	
laptop	on top of the hill	
cross-country	Japanese green	
to keep me awake	in the rain	
with all the latest graphic technology		

1 I drink tea.
2 They bought the house.
3 I bought a computer.
4 She went for a run.

B Work in pairs and take turns. Extend the descriptions of the nouns in the box by adding one extra piece of information each time.

a book	coffee	a cake
cigars	the house	a day

A: an old book
B: an old book with torn-out pages

ADJECTIVES

3A Read about three places. Complete the descriptive adjectives.

1 The Pear Tree is a g_____, dark bar which has live bands playing every night. It's quite p_____ with uncomfortable wooden chairs and there isn't much space, but it's a great place for musicians and artists to gather.

2 Jackie Brown's Café is a large café with a r_____ interior. Set in a picturesque part of the city, it is very a_____, with huge windows that look out onto a big park. People come to chat, drink the excellent coffee and look at the stunning views.

3 Bangles II is a bright, loud hangout for the city's trendsetters. It has a g_____, multicoloured decor and a DJ who plays hip hop and acid jazz while the clientele sips cocktails. A real summer hangout with large windows, it gets c_____ in winter.

B Work in pairs and discuss which places in exercise 3A you would most like to visit regularly/work in.

RELATIVE CLAUSES

4A Underline the correct alternatives to complete the riddles.

1 I am taken from a mine and shut in a wooden case *of which/from which/which* I am never released, but almost everyone uses me. What am I?

2 I have a little house *which I live alone/that I live alone/in which I live alone*. It has no doors or windows and if I want to go out, I have to break through the wall. What am I?

3 What is one question *to which you can never answer 'yes'/which you can never answer 'yes'/that you can never answer 'yes' for*?

4 A barrel of water weighed ten pounds. Someone added something to it, *to which point/by when/at which point* it weighed four pounds. What did they add?

B Try to solve the riddles without looking at the answers.

C Match the answers in the box with riddles 1–4.

Are you asleep?	lead in a pencil
a hole	a chick in an egg

MAKING A PROPOSAL

5 Work in pairs and complete the proposal. You may need to add more than one word in each gap.

1 Just _____ give _____ background information, I have ten years' experience in marine research.

2 _____ main objective _____ proposal _____ get funds for marine research in Australia.

3 _____ aim _____ project _____ document the gradual destruction of Australia's Barrier Reef.

4 _____ plan _____ is measure the coral every week for a year.

5 Then _____ come up _____ a plan to minimise the damage.

6 _____ idea _____ feasible _____ it follows previous research on the reef.

7 I hope _____ solution _____ help _____ slow down the destruction of the reef.

8 _____ first instance, _____ mean talking to Australian authorities about the problem.

9 _____ long-term benefits _____ preserving the reef with all its diversity of marine life.

10 _____ basically, _____ proposing is _____ carry out the study in a year and find solutions after that.

11 _____ anyone _____ questions?

BBC VIDEO PODCAST

Watch people talking about travel plans and experiences on ActiveBook or on the website.

Authentic BBC interviews

SPEAKING
> ❱ Talk about criminal justice
> ❱ Discuss social issues
> ❱ Discuss moral dilemmas
> ❱ Argue a court case

LISTENING
> ❱ Listen to people describe someone they admire
> ❱ Listen to a discussion about witnessing a crime
> ❱ Watch a BBC comedy

READING
> ❱ Read an article about a miscarriage of justice
> ❱ Read an essay about gun control

WRITING
> ❱ Write a problem-solution essay
> ❱ Summarise a court case

BBC CONTENT
> 🔲 Video podcast: What legal or social issues concern you?
> ◉ DVD: Blackadder

UNIT 4

justice

> ▶ Conviction   p44

> ▶ Social justice   p47

> ▶ Do the right thing   p50

> ▶ Blackadder   p52

READING

1A Work in pairs. Look at the film poster and the headline of the article. Use the phrases in the box to predict what you think happens in the story.

> free innocent brother   shocking story
> elderly neighbour   arrested for murder
> life sentence   had an alibi   trained as a lawyer
> fraudulent evidence   appeal   courtroom

B Read the article to check your ideas.

2 Work in pairs and answer the questions.

1 Why did Betty believe that her brother would not be charged with the murder?

2 Did she ever believe that Kenny had committed the crime?

3 What prompted Betty to go to law school?

4 What was the effect of her brother's case on her personal life?

5 What evidence did Betty use in order to prove her brother's innocence?

6 How did she obtain the evidence?

3 Discuss. Would you do the same as Betty Anne Waters? Why/Why not?

VOCABULARY crime collocations

4 Make collocations by matching words in A with words in B. Then complete sentences 1–8.

A

> under   brought (to)   previous   make
> perfect   protest   fresh   early

B

> alibi   convictions   (an) appeal   evidence
> release   justice   innocence   arrest

1 The prisoners continued to _____ their _____.

2 The police have found _____ _____ which proves that Tilly was at the scene of the crime.

3 A man is _____ _____ following the suspicious death of his wife.

4 Simon has obtained an _____ _____ from prison.

5 He had a _____ _____ and the police let him go.

6 The crime went unsolved and the perpetrators were never _____ to _____.

7 My client is planning to _____ an _____ against his conviction.

8 The defendant had no _____ _____.

▶ page 151 **VOCABULARYBANK**

I trained as a lawyer to free my brother

As a Hollywood film of her shocking story is released, Betty Anne Waters tells us what she went through to free her brother from prison.

My brother Kenny and I were best friends growing up. Although I was younger, he always looked up to me. When he was arrested for murdering his elderly neighbour, it was a total shock. He had an alibi, so we thought he would be coming home. But, although the evidence was fraudulent, he was given a life sentence. He was twenty-nine.

Shortly after his first appeal failed, Kenny tried to commit suicide. I was angry with him, but he said, 'I can't spend the rest of my life in prison for something I didn't do. I'm not going to make it.' I never doubted his innocence. He didn't start trouble and would never have killed this woman. We had no more money for lawyers, so it was then he asked me to go to law school and become his attorney. I was unemployed; I didn't even have a college degree. But I promised him I'd make it happen as long as he promised to stay alive.

Getting Kenny out of prison became my life. I enrolled at the local community college, then went on to law school. I was married with two sons, but home life became very difficult and, when the kids were four and six, my husband and I split up. It was hard, but I took it one hurdle at a time.

After Kenny had been in prison for sixteen years, I heard about the Innocence Project, an organisation that works to free innocent people using DNA testing – something that wasn't available when he was convicted. One piece of evidence at the trial was a bloodied curtain the perpetrator had wiped their hands on. But it was so long since his trial, finding it wasn't easy. By this point, I didn't trust anyone. So, I asked other students from law school to tell the police they were doing a project on the Waters case. Finally, a box with Kenny's name on it was found in one of the archives. My heart was pounding so hard as I opened it. As soon as I lifted the lid, I knew the curtain was in there.

Eighteen years after his conviction, Kenny was released. I remember taking him by the hand and walking out of the courtroom. The sense of freedom was amazing.

When I heard they were making a film of the story with Hilary Swank playing me and Sam Rockwell as Kenny, I was so excited. Watching the film and talking about it with the team was like being in therapy.

This experience has done a lot for me. I have grown in confidence and am proud to be involved with the Innocence Project. My brother was the eighty-third person to be released through DNA testing in the USA. Now there have been 259. I feel lucky to be a part of that.

SPEAKING

5A Work in groups. Choose one of the topics below and discuss it.

1 Why do you think the wrong people are sometimes sent to prison?

2 Is prison an effective deterrent against crime? Why/Why not?

3 Can the public do anything to help reduce crime? What can governments do to improve the situation?

4 Why do young people turn to crime? What is the best way to stop them? Who do you think should be responsible for this?

B Summarise your ideas and report back to the class.

7 Look at Exercises 6A and B again. Find examples of *it* used for the following purposes.

> Rules:
>
> Use *it* at the beginning of a sentence:
>
> a) to talk about the weather, a situation, dates, times, distances, etc.
>
> (*it* + verb)
>
> *It rains a lot in September.*
>
> b) to express opinion or emotion.
>
> (*it* + adjective/noun phrase)
>
> *It's extraordinary how often we have the same ideas.*
>
> c) to talk about what you understand from the evidence.
>
> (*it* + verb + clause)
>
> *It appears that someone broke into the office.*
>
> d) to report what someone else thinks or says.
>
> (*it* + *be* + past participle + clause)
>
> *It has been reported that the police decided not to pursue the case.*
>
> Use *it* in the middle of a sentence:
>
> e) as a substitute object for transitive verbs, to be expanded on later in the sentence.
>
> *I'd appreciate it if you would help with our enquiries.*
>
> f) as part of a set phrase.
>
> *I can't help it.*
>
> *We made it!* (succeeded)

⏩ page 134 **LANGUAGEBANK**

GRAMMAR introductory *it*

6A Look at the text. What does *it* refer to?

> *It* was the best of times, *it* was the worst of times, *it* was the age of wisdom, *it* was the age of foolishness, *it* was the epoch of belief, *it* was the epoch of incredulity, *it* was the season of Light, *it* was the season of Darkness, *it* was the spring of hope, *it* was the winter of despair …
>
> (From *A Tale of Two Cities* by Charles Dickens)

B Check what you know. Add *it* in the correct place(s) in sentences 1–10.

1 I could hardly believe when the policeman told me what had happened.

2 Has been reported that a number of people in the area were affected.

3 Is no use! I've looked everywhere for my wallet but I can't find anywhere.

4 We would appreciate if you didn't tell anyone about this.

5 Is surprising how quickly I was able to master the skill.

6 Is no wonder you couldn't find your bag. You left in the café.

7 A: How much further is? B: Is not far now.

8 Is a pity that you won't be able to make to the lunch.

9 Was a warm day for the time of year.

10 Appears that someone has made a mistake.

PRACTICE

8A Complete the sentences with the words in the box.

> difficult   help   fault   funny   shame
> appears   important   wonder

1 It's to believe he would have left all the money here.

2 It's no you were scared. That car nearly hit you.

3 It's not my we didn't finish on time. We started late.

4 I can't it if I keep making mistakes. Nobody's perfect.

5 It's that we clear up any misunderstandings.

6 It was a that we didn't see the beginning.

7 It to have been a mistake.

8 It's how things always turn out OK in the end.

B Complete the sentences to make them true for you.

> It's no wonder that …   I couldn't believe it when …

> I think it's important to …   It's pointless …

C Work in pairs and take turns. Compare your sentences and ask questions.

A: *I think it's important to find time to keep in touch with friends.*

B: *Why do you think that?*

VOCABULARY *PLUS* lexical chunks

9A Work in groups. Think of words which often collocate with *justice*.
a sense of justice, to demand justice

B Read sentences 1–6 and add any more phrases with *justice* to your list.

1 <u>Families of the victims</u> <u>demanded that</u> the killers be found and <u>brought to justice</u> <u>as soon as possible</u>.

2 Mr Jobe is <u>an experienced lawyer</u> who <u>specialises in this particular area</u> of <u>criminal justice</u>.

3 <u>It is imperative that</u> young people <u>on the streets</u> who are <u>committing crimes</u> should not <u>be allowed to escape justice</u>.

4 <u>It's up to</u> the courts <u>to uphold justice</u> – you can't <u>take the law into your own hands</u>.

5 <u>A surprising number of people</u> came to him <u>demanding justice</u> for how they had been treated.

6 Gangs <u>in the vicinity</u> <u>have been known to</u> practise <u>a kind of</u> <u>rough justice</u> on their members.

C Why do you think the other phrases in sentences 1–6 have been underlined?

D Which underlined phrases in Exercise 9B could be replaced with the following?

1 a sort of
2 it's the responsibility of
3 try to implement the law yourself
4 it is extremely important
5 in the area

❝ speakout TIP

A lexical chunk is a group of words commonly found together. They include collocations, but while collocations tend to consist of content words only, lexical chunks are more phrasal and may include grammatical words like prepositions and articles, e.g. *miscarriage of justice*. Lexical chunks may act as discourse markers or adverbials, e.g. *at that time, in her own way*. Find a lexical chunk in Exercise 9B which acts as a time adverbial.

10A Work in pairs. Look at the film posters opposite and read the synopses. What do the films have in common? Which would you prefer to watch? Why?

B ▶ 4.1 Listen to someone reading the first synopsis. Notice how they chunk the language, pausing between the chunks (marked 'I'). When we speak, we group words into meaningful chunks of language.

C Mark possible chunks in the second synopsis.

D ▶ 4.2 Listen to check. Listen again and shadow read the story.

HAVE YOU SEEN **The Wrong Man** -- ALFRED HITCHCOCK'S *NEWEST* ADVENTURE INTO TERROR!

HENRY FONDA · VERA MILES in ALFRED HITCHCOCK'S **THE WRONG MAN**
also starring ANTHONY QUAYLE · Screen Play by MAXWELL ANDERSON and ANGUS MacPHAIL · Music by BERNARD HERRMANN · Directed by ALFRED HITCHCOCK WARNER BROS.

The film | is based on the true story | of Manny Balestrero, | an honest, hardworking musician | who is unjustly accused | of armed robbery | when he goes to an insurance firm | to borrow some money, | and employees mistake him | for the armed robber | who had robbed them | the year before. | In classic Hitchcock form, | Balestrero vehemently protests his innocence, | but unfortunately | he acts guiltily, | leading a host of policemen | and witnesses | to identify him | as the thief. | The trial goes badly for Manny, | but things are even worse for his wife, | Rose, | who struggles to cope | with the strain of his ordeal.

A murdered wife. A one-armed man. An obsessed detective. The chase begins.

HARRISON FORD IS **THE FUGITIVE**

Dr Richard Kimble, a well-known Chicago surgeon, returns home one night to find that his wife has been viciously murdered in their own home. When police find Kimble at the scene of the crime, he is arrested, and later charged and convicted of his wife's brutal murder. However, on the way to the prison, a failed escape attempt by other prisoners gives Kimble his chance of freedom. While on the run from US Marshall Samuel Gerard, Kimble's only hope of proving his innocence and clearing his name is to find out for himself who was responsible for his wife's death, and to lead the team of detectives on his trail to the real perpetrator.

SOCIAL JUSTICE

▶ **GRAMMAR** | the perfect aspect   ▶ **VOCABULARY** | social issues   ▶ **HOW TO** | discuss social issues

LISTENING

1 **Work in pairs and discuss the questions.**

1 What do you know about the people in the photos?

2 What do you know about their humanitarian work?

2A ▶ 4.3 **Listen to three speakers talking about the people in the photos. Make a note of any information that is new to you. Tell your partner.**

B **Listen again and answer the questions.**

1 According to the speaker, how did Annie Lennox's humanitarian work start?

2 What does the speaker particularly admire about her?

3 Why, according to the speaker, didn't Al Gore get that much attention earlier in his career?

4 What did the speaker think after meeting him?

5 What is the speaker's personal connection with Sting?

6 What did Sting's example inspire the speaker to do?

GRAMMAR the perfect aspect

3A **Complete sentences 1–7 with the correct name: Annie Lennox, Sting or Al Gore.**

1 Since the 1990s, _Annie Lennox_ has been working as a human rights activist as well as a singer.

2 _____'s reputation as an activist appears to have overshadowed his fame as a politician.

3 Before becoming a global star in the 1980s, _____ had been a teacher.

4 _____'s work has helped raise awareness of the HIV epidemic in Africa.

5 By 2026, _____'s groundbreaking film will have been helping to educate people about global warming for twenty years.

6 For several years before _____ began working to save the rainforest, some estimates suggest that it had been declining at a rate of around 20,000 square kilometres per year.

7 It is estimated that, by 2020, _____'s *An Inconvenient Truth* will have become a part of school curricula in over thirty countries.

B **Which sentences above use the following tenses?**

- present perfect   4
- present perfect continuous
- past perfect
- past perfect continuous
- future perfect
- future perfect continuous
- perfect infinitive

Al Gore

Annie Lennox

Sting

4 **Read the description of perfect tenses. Look at the sentences in Exercise 3A and answer the questions.**

We use perfect tenses to create a link between two times: to look back from one moment in time to a time before that.

1 Which three sentences link the past and the present? *1,*

2 Which two sentences link the past to a time before that?

3 Which two sentences link a time in the future with a time before that?

4 Which three sentences focus on the action's duration?

▐▐▐➡ page 134 **LANGUAGEBANK**

PRACTICE

5 Work in pairs. Decide if there is a difference in meaning between the pairs of sentences. If so, what is the difference?

1. a) I've read that book.
   b) I've been reading that book.

Sentence a) focuses on the completed action. The speaker finished the book. Sentence b) focuses on the action of reading, but the speaker has not finished the book.

2. a) I hope to have finished my studies by the time I'm twenty-five.
   b) I hope I will have finished my studies by the time I'm twenty-five.

3. a) How long have you lived in your current home?
   b) How long have you been living in your current home?

4. a) Had you studied with Professor Robson before?
   b) Have you studied with Professor Robson before?

5. a) I've painted the kitchen.
   b) I've been painting the kitchen.

6A Find and correct the three mistakes in questions 1–5.

1. What do you hope to will have achieved by the time you're eighty?
2. Had you studied English before you came here?
3. By 2030, how long will you had been working?
4. What TV series have you been watching regularly in the last year or two?
5. How long have you been knowing your best friend?

B Ask and answer the questions with a partner.

VOCABULARY social issues

7A Work in two groups. Group A: look at the expressions in box A. Group B: look at the expressions in box B. What do the expressions mean? Write an example sentence for each.

A

> human rights   child labour   economic development
> intellectual property   capital punishment
> religious freedom

B

> environmental awareness   illegal immigration
> civil liberties   free trade   freedom of speech
> gun control

B Work in pairs with a student from the other group. Explain the meaning of your expressions using your example sentences.

C What other words/expressions do you know connected with social issues? Think about recent news stories.

8A What rhythm do the expressions in Exercise 7A have? Match them with the patterns below.

1. Oo Ooo   *civil liberties*
2. Oo O
3. O O
4. Oo o O
5. oOo Oo
6. oOo ooOo
7. ooOo Ooo
8. O oo
9. oOooo oOo
10. Ooo Ooo
11. Oooo oOoo
12. O Oo

B ▶ 4.4 Listen and check. Repeat the collocations slowly and tap your fingers at the same time (use both hands). Now say the collocations at full speed.

speakout TIP

The more ways you interact with new words, the better you will learn them. Research suggests that we need to use, see or hear new words six times (minimum) before we 'know' them. Use different methods: write sentences including the new word, teach the new word to someone else, pronounce the word many times and try to use the word in conversation. Which of these do you usually do?

⯈ page 151 **VOCABULARYBANK**

SPEAKING

9A Work in groups and discuss the questions.

1. What are the three most important social issues in your country and in the world at the moment? Think about the issues in Exercise 7A and add your own ideas.
2. What is being done about them? Do you know of anyone who is involved in tackling these issues?
3. What are the best ways of fighting for social justice?

B Work with other groups and compare your ideas.

WRITING a problem-solution essay

10A Which items in the box would you expect to find in a problem-solution essay?

> personal information   reference to research
> facts and figures   dialogue   anecdotes
> a description of a problem   a conclusion
> rhetorical questions   a plan of action

B Read the model essay and answer the questions.

1 What issue does it deal with?

2 What do you think of the writer's idea?

3 Which features in Exercise 10A does it contain?

1 How many people are killed with guns every year? Let's take a round number – one million – and look at the figures for gunshot deaths. In Japan, 0.7 people per one million inhabitants are killed by gunfire in a year. In South Korea it's 1.3; in England it's 4.6; in the Netherlands it's 7; in Spain it's 9; in Kuwait it's 12.5. In the United States, it's 152.2. That's not a misprint. The figure illustrates one of today's most important issues: gun control.

2 One of the causes of this figure in the US is the citizens' 'right to bear arms' (carry weapons) written into the US constitution. The country has an extremely violent past and this has resulted in an ingrained sense of the need to protect oneself and one's family. Another reason is the rate of gun ownership. Around forty-six percent of families in the US have a gun in the house.

3 How can countries – the United States in particular – reduce the number of gun deaths? A complete ban on guns is barely imaginable in the US. However, there are a number of other options. These include developing better systems for registering guns and ammunition, instigating background checks for prospective gun owners and introducing tougher prison sentences for people who own guns illegally. The problem is that these solutions have already been proposed, passed into law and denounced as failures.

4 One possible solution that hasn't been tried yet is 'ID tagging' on guns. Each gun would be registered to one person's fingerprint and only that person would be able to fire the gun. If someone else attempted to fire it, the gun wouldn't work. This would mean that stolen guns would be useless. Also, the police would have fewer problems identifying the killers.

5 In conclusion, the solution proposed here is one for the future. The idea would not bring an end to gun deaths. Until guns are completely banned, it is unlikely that anything could reduce that number to the magic zero. But the idea of using new technology (ID tags) to defeat the ills brought about by old technology (guns) is not just a shot in the dark. It could become reality sooner than you think.

11 Look at the expressions below for different parts of a problem-solution essay. Tick the expressions used in the model essay.

Introducing the problem

(This) illustrates one of today's most important issues …

This represents a growing problem.

Describing causes of the problem

One of the causes is …

This is largely due to …

Describing consequences of the problem

This has led to/resulted in/brought about …

One of the consequences of this is …

Suggesting solutions

One possible solution …

There are a number of (other) options. These include …

Concluding

In conclusion, …

To sum up, …

The purpose/aim of this essay was to …

LEARN TO use parallelism

12A Read two examples of parallelism from the essay in Exercise 10B. Find another example in paragraph 3.

> In South Korea <u>it's 1.3</u>; in England <u>it's 4.6</u>; in the Netherlands <u>it's 7</u> …

> These include <u>developing</u> better systems for registering guns and ammunition, <u>instigating</u> background checks for prospective gun owners and <u>introducing</u> tougher prison sentences …

B Why do you think writers use parallelism? Which idea below is **not** a good answer?

1 It gives symmetry and consistency to the writing.

2 It gives ideas equal weight.

3 It uses balance and rhythm to deliver the message.

4 It helps us write better introductions.

C Complete the sentences with the option that uses parallelism.

1 The protest against gun laws was led by a number of civil rights groups, social justice campaigners and _____.

   a) other people
   b) human rights activists
   c) those people who believe in fighting for human rights

2 In a few years, the powers-that-be may know everything about gun owners: the films they watch, the food they eat, _____.
   a) the air they are breathing
   b) and the air they breathe as they walk around
   c) the air they breathe

13 Work in groups and choose a topic. Use your own idea or a topic in Exercise 7A. Follow stages 1–5 below.

1 What exactly is the problem? Write it in one sentence.

2 Brainstorm possible solutions and make notes.

3 Discuss which solutions are the best.

4 Make an outline for your essay. Use the expressions in Exercise 11.

5 Write your problem-solution essay (300–350 words).

VOCABULARY decisions

1A Read the situation below. What would you do? Tell other students.

You are faced with a dilemma. Four friends buy you a lottery ticket for your birthday. The following week, you win €100,000 with the ticket. Your friends think you should share the winnings with them. You have spent some time thinking it through. You have tried to take all these things into consideration: how long you've been friends, how much your friends need the money, whether you should share the winnings equally and whether you think your friendships will survive if you keep all the money. Now you have weighed up the pros and cons, you need to make your decision.

B Underline expressions in Exercise 1A which have similar meanings to the expressions below.

1 in a predicament
2 assessing the situation
3 bear these points in mind
4 considered the benefits and drawbacks

C Discuss. What difficult decisions/dilemmas might the people below face?

- scientist
- teacher
- financial investor
- doctor
- soldier
- parent

A scientist would have to consider the pros and cons of his or her research.

2A Think of a real/imaginary dilemma you have faced. Describe it using some of the expressions in Exercises 1A and B.

B Work in pairs and compare your stories.

FUNCTION expressing hypothetical preferences

3 Read a true story and discuss questions 1–3.

1 What decision did Ann Timson have to make?
2 Do you think she was a hero?
3 What would you have done in her situation?

Supergran bashes burglars

A seventy-year-old grandmother became a hero when, armed with just a flimsy shopping bag, she defied six hammer-wielding jewellery thieves on motorbikes. Ann Timson was talking to a woman on the street when she heard a commotion. She looked across the road and saw six men smashing the windows of a jewellery store in broad daylight. Seeing that other bystanders were doing nothing, Ms Timson decided to act. She dashed across the road and started to hit one of the robbers with her shopping bag. He fell off his motorbike and was pinned down by several members of the public before the police arrived. Amazingly, all of this was captured on film by a freelance cameraman who happened to be nearby. The footage has since become a YouTube sensation. Asked later if she saw herself as a hero, Ms Timson said no, but 'somebody had to do something'. It turns out that Ms Timson has been 'doing something' for years. Residing in a poor area of Northampton, UK, she has confronted drug dealers and other criminals before, putting her own safety at risk in order to aid the community. Although she does not generally believe that the public should take on robbers – 'it's dangerous' she says – her actions have inspired countless numbers of people, and made at least a few would-be thieves think again.

4A ▶ 4.5 Listen to two people discussing the story. Would the speakers do what Ann Timson did?

B Listen again and try to work out what the expressions below mean.

1 a have-a-go-hero
2 [if/when] push comes to shove
3 jumped on the bandwagon
4 I take my hat off to her
5 I'd probably leg it
6 I'd do my bit

5A What words do you think complete the expressions for expressing hypothetical preferences?

If it was ¹_____ to me, I'd …

I'd sooner …

I'd just as soon … as …

Given the ²_____, I'd …

If I ever ³_____ myself in this situation, I'd …

Far better to … than …

This would be by ⁴_____ the best option.

My preference ⁵_____ be to …

Without a shadow of a ⁶_____, I'd …

No way would I …

B Read audio script 4.5 on page 168. Which of the expressions above can you find?

⟹ page 134 **LANGUAGEBANK**

6 Rewrite the sentences so the meaning stays the same. Use the words in brackets.

1 You should weigh up the pros and cons rather than deciding now. (far better)

2 Which of the two candidates would you choose? (up to)

3 I definitely think we can come up with some better ideas than these. (shadow/doubt)

4 If you had the choice, would you ban all web advertising? (given)

5 I would ask my boss for advice if I faced this kind of dilemma. (found myself/situation)

6 Instead of acting rashly, I'd prefer to put important decisions on hold. (sooner)

7 I'd rather buy a house now than wait until the economy gets better. (preference)

8 She'd quit her job rather than do something unethical. (just/soon)

LEARN TO add emphasis

7A Look at expressions a)–e) from the recording in Exercise 4A. Put them under the correct headings below.

a) It was totally wrong.

b) The fact is …

c) The thing is …

d) You're absolutely right.

e) I completely agree.

Adverbs for emphasis

1 _____

2 _____

3 _____

Fronting: expressions before the main verb

What you have to remember is …

4 _____

5 _____

Other expressions

That's out of the question.

No chance.

Not on your life.

B 4.6 Listen to the intonation of the phrases above. Repeat them using the same intonation.

speakout TIP

When we write, we can emphasise words by using *italics* or <u>underlining</u>. When we speak, we use intonation to emphasise the same words. The pitch is higher and we sometimes make the vowel sounds longer. When you hear people arguing, persuading, or getting excited, listen to the way they pronounce key words.

SPEAKING

8A Read the dilemmas below. Think about what you would do and complete the notes for each situation.

My first reaction is …

On the other hand, …

It depends on …

The best option …

1 Your friend's husband is supposed to be working late, but you see him in a bar talking in a friendly manner with another woman. You do not know the other woman. She could be a work colleague. Do you tell your friend what you saw?

2 You are in a hurry. You need to send a package urgently but the post office will close in two minutes. There are no parking spaces except in the Disabled section of the car park. You are not disabled. You think you will only be there five minutes. Do you park in the Disabled section?

3 A friend of yours stole something. You promise never to reveal this. Soon afterwards, an innocent person is accused of the crime. You tell your friend that she has to own up. She refuses and reminds you of your promise. It is possible that an innocent person will go to jail. Do you reveal the truth?

B Work in groups and compare your ideas.

DVD PREVIEW

1A Work in pairs. Do you remember what the words below mean? Explain them to your partner.

> the evidence   a courtroom
> a sentence   a trial

B Match the words in the box below with definitions 1–4.

> a witness   the defendant   the deceased
> the case (for the prosecution/the defence)

1 someone who has died, especially recently

2 someone who sees a crime or an accident and can describe what happened

3 the person in court who has been accused of doing something illegal

4 all the reasons that one side in a legal argument can give against the other side

2 Read the programme information. Why is Captain Blackadder on trial?

BBC Blackadder

Blackadder Goes Forth is a BBC comedy set during the First World War. Captain Blackadder is a British army captain who refuses to take orders from his generals. One day his assistant, Private Baldrick, finds a carrier pigeon* that has arrived with orders for Blackadder and his men to march to certain death. Captain Blackadder shoots it. Unfortunately for him, the bird belonged to Blackadder's superior, General Melchett, who had looked after it as a child. As a result, Captain Blackadder is put on trial with Melchett as the judge.

* **carrier pigeon** – a pigeon that has been trained to carry messages

▶ DVD VIEW

3A Work in pairs. What are the two worst things that could happen to you if you were on trial? Choose from the list below.

• The judge is biased against you before the trial starts.

• Your lawyer doesn't know what he is doing.

• The key witness for the defence is useless.

• A witness says you're guilty and identifies you.

• You are given a prison sentence.

B Watch the DVD. Which event in Exercise 3A <u>does not</u> happen to Captain Blackadder? What happens instead?

4A Who does the following things? Choose from the people in the box.

> General Melchett   Captain Blackadder
> George (defence lawyer)   Private Baldrick
> Captain Darling (prosecuting lawyer)

1 announces the charges against Captain Blackadder

2 acts as the first witness

3 calls a 'last and decisive' witness

4 denies everything

5 forgets to turn a page

6 asks about a pigeon called 'Speckled Jim'

7 puts on a black cap (signifying the death penalty)

8 asks for an alarm call

B Watch the DVD again to check.

5 Work in pairs and discuss the questions.

1 How would you describe the 'trial' in the DVD? Which bit did you think was the funniest?

2 Captain Blackadder is saved at the last minute. What do you think happens? Turn to page 162 to find out.

speakout a court case

6A Read about a court case and decide what you think should happen.

A Birmingham family has been torn apart by the father's will. When eighty-four-year-old James Holdicott died last April, it was widely expected that he would leave his successful clothing business to his sons, Chris (fifty) and Nicholas (forty-six). However, the company and all of Holdicott's assets were left solely to oldest son Chris, who had worked with his father as Chairman of Holdicott Clothing for two decades. Nicholas, a lawyer who has never been involved in the family business, got nothing. He immediately initiated proceedings to contest the will. He says his ailing father was pressurised by Chris Holdicott and other business associates into rewriting the will just before he died. The court case begins on Tuesday.

B ▶ 4.7 Listen to two people talking about the case. Why does the woman think Nicholas Holdicott will lose?

C Listen again and tick the key phrases you hear.

keyphrases

My first point is …

He doesn't have any proof that …

You have no case.

It's been claimed that …

But having said that, …

The question is …

An expert witness testifies that …

There's no evidence to suggest that …

7A Work in pairs and read your instructions. Student A: turn to page 159. Student B: turn to page 162.

B Argue the case with your partner.

writeback a case summary

8A Read a summary of another court case. Do you agree with the judge's decision?

Surprise Holiday

Lily Mason, twenty-eight, was overjoyed when she answered a question correctly on a radio quiz to win an all-expenses-paid 'dream holiday' at a surprise 'exclusive' destination. She was promised a week in a five-star hotel, complete with luxury suite and fine dining, while she would spend her days sunbathing on the hotel's private beach. Things didn't turn out quite like that. Instead, she was placed in a holiday camp on the windy south coast of England in April. The rocky beach was too dangerous for sunbathing, the pre-prepared food came from a canteen with plastic tables, and her 'suite' was a small room with a shared bathroom. The weather got so cold that Ms Mason went home after three days.

Within a week, Ms Mason's disappointment had turned to anger and she decided to sue. The owners of the radio station explained that they had fallen on hard times due to a drop in advertising revenues and couldn't afford to pay for a luxury holiday. They insisted, however, that they had done nothing wrong: the holiday was advertised as being in a 'surprise' destination and Ms Mason had certainly got a surprise. Nonetheless, after listening to a transcript of the broadcast, the judge ruled in Ms Mason's favour. He ordered the radio station to pay Ms Mason £1,500 – the value of the holiday.

After the hearing, Ms Mason expressed satisfaction that justice had been served. She said, 'It was one of the most disappointing weeks of my life. I think this sends a message. If you make a promise on air, you have to stick to it.'

B Write a summary of the court case that you discussed in Exercise 7B (250 words). Invent any additional details necessary.

CRIME COLLOCATIONS

1A Complete the sentences with a suitable word.

1 It is shocking the way that so many criminals are never b_____ to justice.

2 The convict was hoping for an early r_____ from prison for good behaviour.

3 Ali was sure she would never be found out. She had the perfect a_____.

4 The family is expected to make an a_____ against the ruling by the judge.

5 The case was reopened when f_____ evidence was discovered.

6 He was given a light sentence due to the fact that he had no previous c_____.

B Work in pairs. Test your partner on the collocations above.

A: This means you find new information which is relevant to the case.

B: You have fresh evidence.

THE PERFECT ASPECT

2 Complete the jokes with the phrases in the box.

> it will have been
> have you been feeling
> I've broken   have turned
> to have been ignoring

1 'Doctor, doctor, I keep thinking I'm a cat.' 'How long _____ like this?' 'Since I was a kitten.'

2 'Doctor, doctor, I appear to _____ into a dog.' 'Sit on the sofa and we'll talk about it.' 'I can't. I'm not allowed on the sofa.'

3 'Doctor, doctor, I'm in agony! _____ my arm in three places!' 'Well, don't go there any more.'

4 'Doctor, doctor, tomorrow _____ ten years since I last had my eyes tested. I think I need glasses.' 'You certainly do. You've just walked into a petrol station.'

5 'Doctor, doctor, people seem _____ me for years.' 'Next please!'

INTRODUCTORY *IT*

3 Use the prompts to make statements about yourself or people you know.

1 … would love it if …

I would love it if my husband surprised me by cooking dinner tonight.

2 … adore(s) it when …

3 … can't stand it when …

4 … find(s) it easy to …

5 It's pointless …

6 It's essential to …

SOCIAL ISSUES

4A What issues do the definitions describe?

1 _____ : the employment of children (especially in manual jobs) who are under the legal or generally recognised age

2 _____ : the movement of people across international borders in a way that breaks the immigration laws of the destination country

3 _____ : the notion of being free to practise and teach any religion you choose

4 _____ : basic freedoms that everyone should enjoy, e.g. freedom of thought and expression, the right to be free

5 _____ : when a country grows richer because of policies and/ or activity relating to business and money

6 _____ : something which someone has invented or has the right to make or sell, especially something that cannot legally be copied by other people

B Work in pairs. Complete the definitions.

1 freedom of speech: the right to …

2 free trade: a system of trade in which …

3 civil liberties: freedoms that protect …

4 gun control: efforts to regulate …

5 environmental awareness: an understanding of how …

HYPOTHETICAL PREFERENCES

5A Correct the word order in speaker B's responses.

1 A: I could have had a holiday on a beach or gone on a cruise.

   B: If it was to up me I'd have taken the cruise.

2 A: I don't know whether to read the book or watch the film.

   B: I sooner would watch the film than read the book.

3 A: We can either go to a posh international restaurant or eat at the street market.

   B: I'd as just soon eat local food as dine in a fancy restaurant.

4 A: So I was lost with a broken-down car in the middle of nowhere.

   B: If I myself found in that situation, I'd go to the nearest house and beg for help.

5 A: We decided not to give Christmas presents because there are thirty people in the family now.

   B: Better far to do that than buy presents for everybody!

6 A: We're thinking of taking trains around Europe rather than flying.

   B: That would be by the far best option if you want to see places.

7 A: I hated my job so I quit, even though I needed the money.

   B: I'd have done the same a without shadow of a doubt.

8 A: I got rid of my mobile phone. It was too expensive.

   B: Way no would I do that unless I really had to.

B Decide if you agree with speaker B. If not, change the response. Practise the conversations in pairs.

BBC VIDEO PODCAST

Watch people talking about legal and social issues on ActiveBook or on the website.

Authentic BBC interviews

www.pearsonELT.com/speakout

UNIT 5

SPEAKING
> Talk about secrets
> Debunk a myth
> Discuss freedom of information

LISTENING
> Listen to a radio programme about secrets
> Listen to a conversation about WikiLeaks
> Watch a BBC drama

READING
> Read a true story
> Read about everyday myths
> Read about investigative journalism

WRITING
> Write a narrative
> Write personal facts people don't know about you

BBC CONTENT
🎧 Video podcast: Are you good at keeping secrets?
⏺ DVD: North and South

UNIT 5

secrets

5.1 FAMILY SECRETS

GRAMMAR | modal verbs and phrases **VOCABULARY** | secrets **HOW TO** | talk about obligations

LISTENING

1 Work in groups and discuss the questions.

1 Why do people keep secrets? If someone tells you something in confidence, are you likely to keep their secret or to tell someone else?

2 Who would you talk to if you wanted to tell someone your innermost thoughts? Who would you definitely not talk to?

2A Read the radio programme listing. It says that society has become more 'confessional'. What does this mean? Do you agree?

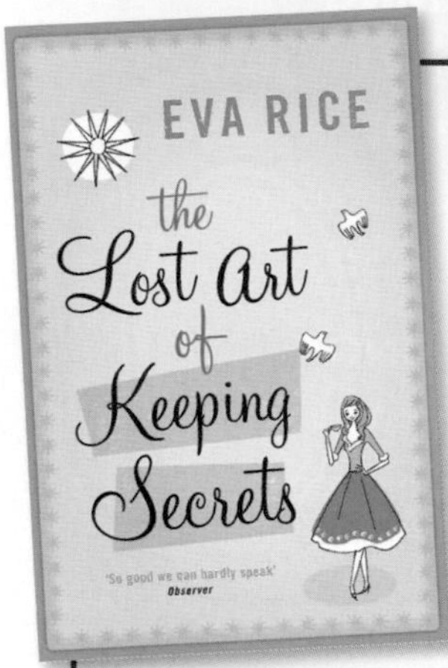

Everyone has a secret at some point in their lives and most of us will be told a secret and asked to keep it quiet. As society allegedly becomes more 'confessional', are we far too willing to talk about matters that should be kept hidden? Are we losing the ability to keep secrets? When is it appropriate to divulge a secret and how should it be done? Are there types of secret that should never be revealed?

In this BBC radio programme, Jenni Murray takes up the discussion with Eva Rice, whose new novel is called *The Lost Art of Keeping Secrets*, and Christine Northam, a relationship counsellor.

B 5.1 Listen to the programme. How many secrets do they mention? What are they?

C Listen again and answer the questions.

1 What would have made the presenter's father furious?

2 A girl revealed her friend's secret. Was she forgiven?

3 What secret did the wife want to know from her husband?

4 Is the woman who had another relationship still married?

5 What kind of secret would the author keep?

VOCABULARY idioms: secrets

3A Complete the sentences below with the words in the box.

cat	stay	game	beans	let	themselves	doors

1 We were raised in an atmosphere where families **kept themselves to** ________ and you told nobody your business.

2 We became more knowledgeable about the kind of dangerous secrets that might be held **behind closed** ________, and the damage they could do.

3 He almost ________ **it slip** where he was.

4 So when should you **spill the** ________ and be honest?

5 When is it better **to** ________ **schtum**?

6 It's a secret, so try not to **let the** ________ **out of the bag**.

7 We pretended we didn't know it was her birthday, but Sam **gave the** ________ **away**.

B Match the expressions in bold above with meanings a)–e). Some expressions have the same meaning.

a) deliberately disclose a secret (1 expression)

b) when something happens in private and the public are not allowed to know about it (1 expression)

c) tell something (possibly by mistake) that someone else wanted you to keep a secret (3 expressions)

d) remain silent, or say nothing (1 expression)

e) live a quiet private life, not doing things involving other people (1 expression)

page 152 **VOCABULARYBANK**

SPEAKING

4 Work in groups and discuss the questions.

1 When would it be important to keep a secret?

2 When might you have to reveal someone's secret? Explain why.

3 When is it important for people to speak openly rather than keep secrets?

4 When is it better for the public not to know a secret?

GRAMMAR modal verbs and phrases

5A Check what you know. Match the underlined forms in sentences 1–8 with the meanings in the box.

> it's possible   it's expected   I was obliged (strong)
> I was obliged (weak)   you did it but it was unnecessary
> it isn't a good idea   ~~I did it, but it wasn't a good idea~~
> it wasn't possible/I wasn't able

1 I <u>should never have</u> told her. It was my fault.
   I did it, but it wasn't a good idea.

2 I <u>couldn't</u> live with this secret.

3 I <u>had to</u> tell him.

4 Keeping a secret <u>can</u> be something that can bring about a more positive outcome.

5 You're <u>supposed to</u> tell everyone the way you feel twenty-four hours a day.

6 We<u>'d better not</u> start until everyone is here.

7 I felt that I <u>ought to</u> let her know.

8 You <u>needn't have</u> told him.

B Match each sentence with the correct meaning, a) or b).

1 We're supposed to catch the 8.30 train.

2 We have to catch the 8.30 train.

a) It's very important that we catch the 8.30 train as there are no more trains after that.

b) Ideally, we would catch the 8.30 train, but if we need more time, we can catch a later one.

3 You mustn't tell him about the relationship.

4 You don't have to tell him about the relationship.

a) It's definitely not a good idea to tell him about the affair.

b) Nobody is forcing you to tell him about it. It's up to you.

5 You shouldn't have called the hotel first.

6 You'd better call the hotel first.

a) It would have been better to call the airport first.

b) I think you should call the hotel before the airport.

C Find pairs of words/phrases in sentences 1–10 which have similar meanings.

1 allowed = 5 permissible

1 Dictionaries are **allowed** in the exam.

2 Alcohol is strictly **forbidden** in some countries.

3 It's **obligatory** for companies to provide details of their industrial processes.

4 At least she **had the courage to** tell him what had happened.

5 They reached the maximum **permissible** level of radiation.

6 She felt **compelled** to resign because of the scandal.

7 Cars have been **banned** from the city centre.

8 Only a few journalists **dared to** cover the story.

9 Maths and English are **compulsory** for all students.

10 Many companies have been **forced to** close.

⏩ page 136 **LANGUAGEBANK**

6A ▶ 5.2 Listen to some of the sentences from Exercise 5C. Notice how some sounds disappear or change in connected speech (elision).

1 A syllable containing an unstressed vowel is often lost.
   diction(a)ry   obligat(o)ry

2 /t/ and /d/ are often lost when combined with other consonants.
   compelle(d)_to   dare(d)_to

3 The sound /h/ is often omitted.
   tell him what (h)ad happened   cars (h)ave been banned

B ▶ 5.3 Listen and repeat the sentences.

PRACTICE

7 Choose the best alternatives to complete the text.

> ### Family secrets
>
> **Shari:** 'My grandmother disapproved terribly of smoking, so people [1] *were never allowed to | wasn't supposed to* smoke in the house. She didn't even realise that her own daughter, my mother aged sixty, was a smoker. We all [2] *ought to | had to* go outside and smoke on the balcony and my grandmother never realised what we were doing. She [3] *supposed to | used to* think we were hanging out the washing and things like that. I suppose we [4] *should have | ought have* told her really.'
>
> **Bob:** 'My dad, who's sixty-one, bought a second-hand Mercedes. He didn't spend loads of money on the car, but he thought he [5] *should have kept | ought to keep* it a secret from his father because he was sure he'd disapprove of his extravagance. We [6] *had to hide | should have hidden* the Mercedes in the garage whenever my granddad came round.'
>
> **Emma:** 'My uncle thought he [7] *'d better not | 'd not better* tell anyone when he decided to get married for the fi time at the age of sixty-five. He kept it a secret which nobody [8] *was supposed to | would supposed to* know. He [9] *would have | could have* told us – everyone [10] *should have | would have* been delighted for him. It wasn't as if he was marrying an eighteen-year-old. His bride was seventy-eight and was also marrying for the first time. '

8 Choose two or three of the topics below. Work in pairs and take turns to talk about them.

Talk about something:

• you would never dare to do.

• you ought to have done this week but you haven't.

• you weren't supposed to do as a child, but you did anyway.

• which is obligatory in your country, but not in other countries.

• you should never have done.

• you weren't allowed to do as a child, which you enjoy doing now.

• you'd better not forget to do.

WRITING a narrative

9A Read the true story below. What do you think was in the box? Turn to page 161 to find out.

1   As a child, my grandmother would often tell me stories. Stories of times gone by, of other eras. And I would listen with eager fascination, especially to the stories of her childhood. One story I will always remember was of my 'Auntie Madge', my great-aunt. She was a lovely woman, who I once met as a child. She was a quiet woman, unassuming. My grandmother told me how Auntie Madge had been a dazzling young lady. How all the boys in the neighbourhood had wanted to take her out on dates. But Auntie Madge only had eyes for one very nice young man, who she had fallen in love with.

2   Although the young couple planned to spend the rest of their lives together, there was a problem: my great-great-aunt Ada, Auntie Madge's mother. Ada had a reputation for being a bit of a dragon and wanting to control everything. Ada had decided that she didn't approve of the young man in question and she wasn't at all happy to let her daughter marry him.

3   After some persuasion, however, she reluctantly made a deal with Auntie Madge, saying, 'OK. If the two of you are determined to marry, then all I will ask is that you stay away from each other for one year. During that time, you shouldn't see each other, speak to each other, or write each other letters. And if, after a year, he writes to you and still wants to marry you, then I will accept. I'll consent.'

4   It was a long year, but the couple kept their promise. But, after a year, Auntie Madge never heard from the young man and had to assume that he'd found someone else. She subsequently married another man, but the marriage was very unhappy and eventually ended in divorce. From then on, Auntie Madge lived alone, and she never had children.

5   Years later, when her mother died, Madge found a box belonging to her mother …

B Work in pairs and discuss. What do you think of Ada's behaviour? Can you think of a good title for the story?

10A Which features 1–10 are often found in narrative writing?

1   an introduction to set the scene

2   detailed descriptions of people, places or objects

3   detailed statistics and evidence to support an argument

4   descriptions of feelings/actions to suggest mood or atmosphere

5   direct speech and a variety of adjectives and adverbs for impact

6   a summary of the main events

7   narrative tenses and time phrases in order to make the sequence of events clear

8   an unexpected end to the story

9   a conclusion which reflects on the consequences of what happened

10   a conclusion which includes details of all the main characters

B Read the story in Exercise 9A again. Which features in Exercise 10A does it contain?

LEARN TO use time phrases

11A Look at the extract from the story. Underline the time phrase.

During that time, you shouldn't see each other, speak to each other, or write each other letters.

B Underline the time phrases in paragraphs 4 and 5 of the story in Exercise 9A.

C Complete sentences 1–8 with the time phrases in the box. There may be more than one possible answer and you don't have to use all of the phrases.

after   as soon as   the moment   afterwards meanwhile   ever since   originally   while instantly   previously   subsequently   eventually immediately   in the meantime   from then on

1   _____ she entered the room, she knew there was something wrong.

2   The experience haunted me for years _____.

3   Cromwell, _____, picked up his hat and dusted it off.

4   They recognised him _____.

5   She knew she could never trust her boss again and _____ she left the job.

6   He _____ escaped and made his way back to France.

7   She has been terrified of the sound of aircraft _____ the crash.

8   They met in 1998, and _____ they were firm friends.

D Complete the sentences in any way you choose. Use the time phrases in Exercise 11C.

1   It was love at first sight. The moment …

2   He recognised her immediately. Previously, …

3   She arrived on a boat from Costa Rica. As soon as …

4   It was a long and tedious journey. Eventually, …

12A Follow stages 1–4 to draft a narrative of your own (200–250 words).

1   Identify an experience to write about (e.g. a childhood experience, a challenge, achieving a goal) and think about why it is significant.

2   Make notes about the experience, including details (sounds, colours, etc.).

3   Create an outline of the story.

4   Use the outline to write a first draft.

speakout TIP

After drafting your narrative, spend some time away from it. Then try reading it out loud. This helps to highlight any missing or repeated words or missing punctuation. Can you add any more detail to improve it? Are there any details you can remove because they distract from the main story?

B Check your draft. How many correct features from Exercise 10A did you use? Try to make some improvements and redraft your story.

▶ **GRAMMAR** | the passive ▶ **VOCABULARY** | truth or myth ▶ **HOW TO** | discuss whether something is true

READING

1A Read the introduction to the article below. Can you think of any commonly held beliefs that are actually myths?

B Work in pairs. Student A: read the myths below and answer the questions. Student B: turn to page 160.

1 What is the myth?
2 Which myths were disproved by experiments?
3 What is the truth about the myth?

C Tell your partner what you learnt. Then read your partner's section of the article quickly.

> Can you beat a speed camera and does cold weather *really* give you a cold? Conventional wisdom says 'yes', but what does science say? Are these commonly held perceptions of the world we live in really true or are they fallacies? We've spoken to experts to uncover the truth.

① You can beat a speed camera if you drive fast enough

Technically, this is true, but it wasn't easy to verify. As proven by *Top Gear*, a TV car show, to beat a speed camera you'd have to be travelling incredibly fast. The *Top Gear* Mercedes, which went past the camera at 148 miles per hour, was caught on film, but experimenters finally managed to do it at 170 miles per hour.

② Driving is safe with a hands-free mobile

This would seem to be intuitively true. Surely using a hands-free mobile is just like having a conversation with someone in the car? Research tells a different story. It's even worse for your concentration than alcohol, according to the Transport Research Laboratory. They tested drivers with or without alcohol, as well as with mobiles and hands-free mobiles. Afterwards, the drivers answered the experimenter's questions. Driving performance under the influence of alcohol was significantly worse than normal driving, yet better than driving with a phone – even one with a hands-free kit.

VOCABULARY truth or myth

2A Find the expressions below in the article on this page and answer the questions.

> conventional wisdom   a commonly held perception   a fallacy
> uncover the truth   verify   intuitively true   debunk a myth
> disprove a myth

1 Which expression means 'many people think it's true but it isn't'?
2 Which three expressions mean 'people think it's true but there's no scientific evidence'?
3 Which verb means 'reveal'?
4 Which two verbs mean 'prove something isn't true'?
5 Which verb means 'prove something is true'?

B Add the missing word in each sentence.

1 It is a held perception that no one can survive a plane crash.
2 Wisdom says you shouldn't swim soon after eating.
3 Scientists in Panama recently disproved myth that sloths are lazy.
4 The myth that you lose most of your body heat through your head has been.
5 It seems intuitively that long-distance running is bad for your knees, but recent research suggests otherwise.

C Work in pairs. Discuss other examples of common myths, using the expressions in Exercise 2A. Use your ideas from Exercise 1A.

③ Goldfish have short memories

A fifteen-year-old schoolboy has debunked this myth. Rory Stokes placed a piece of Lego (a small, plastic, coloured block) in the water of a fish tank at feeding time. Thirty seconds after placing it, he sprinkled food around it, so that the fish would start to associate it with eating. At the beginning of Stokes' experiment, it took the fish over a minute to swim over to the Lego. After three weeks, it took under five seconds. In the second part of the experiment, Rory removed the Lego from the feeding process and then reintroduced it after six days. It took the fish just 4.4 seconds to associate it with food again.

④ Owls have the ability to rotate their heads through 360 degrees

A bit of simple science allows us to disprove this myth. An owl's neck has fourteen vertebrae, which is twice as many as humans. Consequently, an owl can turn its head up to 270 degrees. In other words, they could start by facing 12 o'clock and turn their heads in a clockwise direction until facing roughly 9 p.m. – impressive, but not 360 degrees.

GRAMMAR the passive

3A **Read the statements. Are any of them true?**

1 The Great Wall of China is the only man-made object visible from space.

2 Caesar Salad is named after Julius Caesar.

3 Eskimos have over one hundred words for snow.

4 Chewing gum takes seven years to pass through the digestive system.

5 A sudden shock or great stress can suddenly turn your hair white.

B **Check your answers below.**

1 False. The Great Wall of China cannot be seen from space with the naked eye, but cities can be made out, especially at night.

2 False. Caesar Cardini, a restaurateur, invented the recipe in Tijuana, Mexico, in 1924. He had the dish named after him.

3 False. It is claimed by linguists that Eskimos actually have about as many words for snow as we have in English (sleet, blizzard, slush, powder, etc.) – nothing like one hundred.

4 False. Chewing gum is processed through the body like any other food.

5 False. Hair isn't expected to change colour suddenly, but some people's hair turns white quickly even in a stress-free situation.

C **Check what you know. Underline examples of passive forms in Exercise 3B. Why do we use passive forms?**

D **Which sentences contain examples of:**

a) a passive used when the important information in the sentence is the object of the verb? *4*

b) a passive used to show that we are not certain about a statement?

c) a pattern that uses *have/get* + object + past participle to describe something that is done to the subject?

d) a passive used because we do not know who performs the action (or it is not important), we are interested in the action itself?

e) a passive infinitive (*to be* + past participle + *to* + verb)?

➧ page 136 **LANGUAGEBANK**

PRACTICE

4 **Rewrite the sentences using passive forms.**

1 Some people believe that myths are spread easily on the internet.
It _____ that myths are spread easily on the internet.

2 Someone stole Jake's wallet.
Jake had _____.

3 Someone was fixing my car so I took the bus.
My car _____ so I took the bus.

4 I think people should take this matter seriously.
I think this matter _____ seriously.

5 They need to do more research on the topic of herbal medicine.
More research _____ on the topic of herbal medicine.

6 They say people have seen ghosts in the castle.
They say ghosts _____ in the castle.

5 **Work in pairs. Decide which phrases in italics would be better in the passive. Change the phrases as appropriate.**

One piece of conventional wisdom that [1] *people have passed on* throughout the generations is that Friday 13th is unlucky. [2] *No one knows* where this superstition came from, though [3] *some people have attributed it* to the fact that on Friday 13th October 1306, King Philip of France arrested the Knights Templar and [4] *began torturing them.* [5] *People know the fear of the number thirteen* as triskaidekaphobia, and [6] *people consider thirteen* unlucky in many cultures. [7] *We can see this superstition* in different contexts: in the United States, many skyscrapers don't have a thirteenth floor and several airports don't have a thirteenth gate. Hospitals and hotels regularly have no room number thirteen. In Italy, [8] *the organisers omit the number thirteen* from the national lottery, while on streets in Florence [9] *people give the house between number 12 and 14 the number 12½.* It's not just crazy Europeans; other countries are just as superstitious, although not necessarily about the same number. In Japan, [10] *people often omit the unlucky number four* from hotels, hospitals and apartment blocks.

SPEAKING

6A Prepare to debunk a myth of your choice. It can be about a person, a profession, a country or a belief. For ideas, turn to page 160. Complete the notes below.

The secret is out about ...
Many people think ...
They believe this because ...
The idea may have originated ...
They say ... but it's a fallacy inasmuch as ...
The truth is that ... / In fact ...
In order to really understand ... people would have to ...
This would happen if ...

B Work with other students and take turns to debunk your myths. Share your ideas with the class.

VOCABULARY *PLUS* multi-word verbs

7A Discuss. Which of the activities below have you done in the last twenty-four hours? Which do you do at least once every twenty-four hours?

• send a text message
• play a video game
• eat fast food
• go on a social networking website (e.g. Facebook)
• hang out in a shopping mall
• talk on a mobile phone
• listen to music/podcasts on an MP3 player

B Read the book review and answer the questions.

1 What is the message in Steven Johnson's book?
2 Do you agree with this idea?

The media is full of dire warnings about young people and modern life: too much technology, too many video games, too much fast food. Journalists and social theorists have looked back to the golden age before kids stood around texting and twittering and have decided enough is enough! Take away their iPods! Switch off their mobile phones! But writer Steven Johnson has thought it over and come to a different conclusion. His book, *Everything Bad is Good for You: How Today's Popular Culture is Actually Making us Smarter*, boils down to one message: kids can carry on facebooking, gaming and youtubing because as the world speeds up, these new skills are turning them into quick-thinking, multi-tasking, high-achieving citizens of the twenty-first century. Who's right? Could the doom-mongers be wrong? Read the book and find out for yourself.

8A Read the review again and underline multi-word verbs with *back, around, away, off, over, down, on, up* and *out.*

B Look at some common meanings of particles in multi-word verbs. Complete the table with the meanings in the box.

removal or disposal   think or talk about   ~~continue~~
remove, cancel or end something   with no direction or aim
~~increase or improve~~   return (to the past)   be in the open
decrease or reduce

preposition	meaning	examples
up	*increase or improve*	speed up, brighten up, jazz up
on	*continue*	go on, carry on, keep on
off		pension off, cry off, call off, switch off
out		find out, speak out, stand out, call out
down		slow down, narrow down, crack down
away		put away, blow away, take away
back		bring back, think back, look back, cast (your mind) back
around		mess around, stand around, hang around
over		mull over, pore over, look over, think over

C Which examples in the third column are new to you? Look them up in a dictionary and make a sentence with them.

speakout TIP

Knowing some general meanings of particles can help you to understand multi-word verbs when you read or hear them. However, many multi-word verbs have several meanings which depend on the context. It is a good idea to learn these and write them down as they arise.

9 Complete the sentences with the correct particles.

1 The Government cracked ____ on illegal immigration because the situation couldn't go ____.
2 We mulled ____ the candidates and narrowed them ____ to a shortlist of three.
3 We called ____ the game this morning, but the weather is brightening ____ now.
4 Stop standing ____ doing nothing and put ____ your stuff – it's all over the floor!
5 When I found ____ about the accident, it brought ____ memories of my grandfather.

10A Underline the correct alternatives.

1 *Cast your mind back/Narrow down/Talk over* to your childhood. Who taught you your most important lessons?
2 How do you *carry on/think back/find out* if a journalist or other writer is telling the truth?
3 When faced with many possible truths, how can we *call out/narrow down/speed up* our options to one?
4 Is it always useful to *mull over/mess around/speak out* difficult issues with other people?

B Choose two questions in Exercise 10A. Work in pairs and discuss your answers.

⫸ page 152 **VOCABULARYBANK**

DVD PREVIEW

1 Read the programme information. Which elements in the box do you think the drama involves?

> murder mystery   family saga   action
> fantasy   romance   comedy

BBC North and South

North and South is a BBC drama set in the North of England in the nineteenth century. In this episode the heroine, Margaret Hale, calls her brother Frederick back from Europe where he has been hiding from the law. Their mother is dying, so Frederick comes back secretly and at great risk. Meanwhile, John Thornton, a local mill owner and friend of Margaret's father, has fallen in love with Margaret, but he doesn't know about Frederick.

▶ DVD VIEW

2 Watch the DVD. What misunderstanding is resolved at the end?

3A Complete the descriptions of each scene.

Scene 1: Margaret tells her _____ that she wrote to Frederick.

Scene 2: _____ arrives at the house.

Scene 3: Frederick says he wants to stay for the _____ but Margaret and their father say he must leave.

Scene 4: At the train station, Margaret and Frederick are seen by _____.

Scene 5: Margaret tells _____ that she cannot explain what happened at the station because 'the secret is another person's'.

Scene 6: At the closed mill, Mr Thornton talks to a worker who explains that Margaret has a brother in _____ who got into trouble with the navy and made a secret visit.

B Watch the DVD again to check.

4 Work in pairs and discuss the questions.

1 Margaret says, 'The secret is another person's. I cannot explain it without doing him harm.' Was she right to keep her brother's existence a secret?

2 Mr Thornton says to Margaret, 'I have not the slightest wish to pry into the gentleman's secrets … I hope you realise that any foolish passion for you on my part is entirely over.' Was he right to be so angry with her? Could he have handled the situation differently?

3 How do you think the story will end?

speakout seven secrets about me

5A Read an extract from a website. What is the website asking for?

There are big secrets — like having a brother no one knows about — and little secrets — like the fact that you had an imaginary friend as a child. Secrethouse.com wants to read a list of seven facts that no one knows about you. These facts don't have to be world-shattering, just interesting, quirky and fun!

B ▶ 5.5 Listen to someone talking about their seven secrets. Work in pairs. How many of them can you remember?

C Listen again. Which key phrases does the speaker use to introduce information?

keyphrases

To start off with, …

(First/second/third) on my list is …

It's not what you'd call a big secret, but …

Something I've never told anyone is that …

A few close friends know this.

Last but not least, …

6A Decide on your seven secrets. Use the prompts below to help if necessary. Make notes.

- I worked …
- My favourite (film/song/book/person) is …
- If I wasn't … I'd …
- I nearly …

B Work in groups. Take turns to describe your secrets and ask follow-up questions.

writeback personal facts

7A Read the winning entry. What can you guess about the writer, e.g. nationality, age, personal and professional life?

Seven things you don't know about me

1 On my mother's side I'm related to a Shaolin monk. We don't know his name so we just call him 'the monk'. His brother, my great-grandfather, was the wild one of the family. He went out every night and partied his life away. His nickname was 'the bear'.

2 I nearly drowned when I was six. I fell off a boat in France and I suspect my family pretended not to notice. I made so much noise that the lifeguard finally took off his Walkman and jumped in to rescue me.

3 I worked in a cake factory every summer from the age of fourteen to eighteen. They paid peanuts but we ate like kings.

4 My favourite film is *Blade Runner* and I can quote the whole of Rutger Hauer's final speech before he dies. It goes like this: 'I've seen things you people wouldn't believe.' OK, I'll stop there.

5 If I wasn't studying marketing, I would be a photographer. I've got about thirty albums' worth of photos – idyllic sunsets, family get-togethers, cityscapes at night and arty black-and-whites snatched when people weren't looking.

6 I haven't lost at mahjong, a Chinese game that my mother taught me, for nearly ten years. I used to play at least twice a week, but now no one will play me. The world is full of sore losers.

7 I have a pet canary called Trill. My ex-flatmate emigrated to Argentina and left the bird behind, saying, 'he likes you more than me anyway'. Good excuse.

Kim Robinson

B Write your own list of seven secrets (250 words). Include as many details as you can.

C Read other students' lists. What unexpected information did you learn?

5.5 ◀◀ LOOKBACK

IDIOMS: SECRETS

1A Underline the correct alternatives.

1 A: What do you think of David, the new website designer?

B: He seems really nice and *keeps/stays* himself to himself.

2 A: Do you know what they decided during the meeting?

B: No. That kind of information is kept firmly behind closed *gates/doors*.

3 A: I don't know if I should tell you.

B: Oh go on. *Spill/Drop* the beans!

4 A: Do you think we should tell everyone?

B: No. I think it's best if we stay *schtum/shut*.

5 A: Why is your sister so angry?

B: I let *slip/lip* that she wasn't at Jo's house yesterday.

B Work in pairs. Write a short conversation using two phrases from Exercise 1A. Perform your conversation for other students.

MODAL VERBS AND PHRASES

2A Choose a suitable way to complete the second sentence. Use between two and four words.

1 I wish I hadn't gone to bed so late. I should _____ earlier.

2 We are expected to finish by Tuesday. We're _____ by Tuesday.

3 They didn't have the courage to argue. They _____ argue.

4 The restaurant was empty. We _____ booked.

5 We're not allowed to take mobile phones into class. Mobile phones _____ in class.

6 If you park here, you'll get a ticket. You'd _____ park here.

B Complete the sentences in any way you choose. Compare your ideas in pairs.

1 I was supposed to … but …

2 As a child, I was always/never allowed to …

3 I think we ought to …

TRUTH OR MYTH

3A Find and underline the incorrect word in each sentence. Then put the underlined words in the correct sentences.

1 The perception wisdom says you have to know grammar rules to learn a language.

2 People think it's possible to learn a language in a few weeks. This myth needs to be conventional.

3 It's believed that people have a 'language gene' but this is difficult to intuitively.

4 The truth has been debunked about translation: sometimes it can be useful to learners!

5 The idea that it's easier to learn foreign languages when you are young is verify true.

6 A commonly held uncovered is that bilingual children get confused learning two languages.

B Do you agree with the statements in Exercise 3A? Compare your ideas in pairs.

THE PASSIVE

4A Complete the text with the correct active or passive form of the verbs in brackets.

The story of maybe

It [1]_____ (believe) that this story comes from an ancient civilisation in the Americas. A farmer had a champion horse. One day, the horse [2]_____ (disappear). Everyone thought the horse [3]_____ (steal) and all the farmer's neighbours visited him. 'What terrible news,' they said. 'Maybe,' said the farmer.

A few days later, the horse [4]_____ (come) back with two magnificent wild horses. The neighbours visited again to offer their congratulations.

The next day, the wild horses [5]_____ (be) tamed by the farmer's son, when he [6]_____ (throw) off one of them and broke his leg. Again the farmer's neighbours visited. 'We are so sorry. This is awful news.' 'Maybe,' said the farmer.

The next day, an army captain came to recruit men for a war, but because the farmer's son had broken his leg, he [7]_____ (not recruit). He stayed at home and [8]_____ (help) to tame the wild horses, which became champions. The farmer's neighbours said, 'What wonderful news that your horses [9]_____ (recognise) as the best in the country!' 'Maybe,' said the farmer. And the next day the now famous horses were gone.

B What do you think the moral of the story is? Compare your ideas with other students.

MAKING A POINT

5A Add the missing words to the conversations.

1 A: If we carry on like this, there will be no fish left in the river.

B: Is there any evidence to that?

2 A: Sorry, I've lost you.

B: What basically saying is we can't afford to waste any more time.

3 A: If think about it, we'd be stupid to let this opportunity escape us.

B: Yes, I think you're right.

4 A: I don't how you can argue that economics doesn't have an influence on the situation.

B: I really don't see what that has got to do with the issue.

5 A: People aren't interested in buying organic food if it's too expensive.

B: Can we sure about that?

B Practise the conversations in pairs. Try to extend them.

BBC VIDEO PODCAST

Watch people talking about secrets and secret talents on ActiveBook or on the website.

Authentic BBC interviews

www.pearsonELT.com/speakout

SPEAKING
> Evaluate future inventions
> Discuss trends in language learning
> Describe changes in your country
> Talk about a decade

LISTENING
> Listen to a programme about global English
> Listen to descriptions of how trends started
> Watch a BBC documentary about a decade

READING
> Read about futurologists
> Read a report about languages on the internet

WRITING
> Write a report
> Write a review of a decade

BBC CONTENT
> Video podcast: Do you follow trends in music and fashion?
> DVD: History of Now: The Story of The Noughties

trends

BBC
speakout DVD

▶ **GRAMMAR** | future forms   ▶ **VOCABULARY** | trends and predictions   ▶ **HOW TO** | talk about future trends

SPEAKING

1 What types of predictions do you think the following people have to make?

- a weather man
- a stock market trader
- a businessman
- a fashion designer

VOCABULARY trends and predictions

2A Read sentences a)–j) below. Find expressions in bold which refer to:

1 predictions with a link to the past. (2 expressions)

2 a situation that is already true. (1 expression)

3 a fast change in the future. (2 expressions)

4 predictions that are highly possible. (3 expressions)

5 the evidence for a prediction. (2 expressions)

a) The trend for greener living **will gather pace**.

b) **The signs are** that the trend for outsourcing will grow.

c) **The days of** wasting water **are over**.

d) This trend for mobile offices **may well** grow.

e) Oil will **become a thing of the past**.

f) There'll **be an explosion in** non-synthetic materials.

g) This trend for reality TV **is bound to** end.

h) Plastic will be **a distant memory**.

i) The popularity of social networking sites **is likely to** fade.

j) The **figures point to** a major demographic change.

B Work in pairs. Think of examples of:

- something that was popular when you were younger, but is now a thing of the past.
- a social trend that is gathering pace.
- a worrying prediction that may well come true.

READING

3A Read the definition and discuss questions 1–3.

futurology /ˌfjuːtʃəˈrɒlədʒi/ n [U] the activity of trying to say correctly what will happen in the future — **futurologist** n [C]

1 Who do you think futurologists work for?

2 How do you think they come up with their ideas?

3 What difficulties do you think they face?

B Read the article to check your ideas.

4A Look at answers 1–5 about the article. Think of the questions. There may be several possibilities.

1 big companies *Who do futurologists work for?*

2 good judgement and instincts *What …*

3 to conferences

4 intelligent homes and jet packs

5 They have to connect with people's emotions.

As everyone from business moguls to football managers to weather forecasters knows, predicting the future is not easy. History is packed with mistaken ideas about the future. Among the more famous are record company Decca's excuse for rejecting The Beatles: 'Guitar music is on the way out', and Ken Olson's prediction made at the Convention of the World Future Society in 1977: 'There is no reason for any individual to have a computer in their home'. Despite thousands of similar errors, big companies still employ futurologists, the men and women whose job is to guess correctly what will happen tomorrow, next year and in ten years' time. So how do these modern-day Nostradamuses do it?

1 It turns out that the job of a futurologist is less mystical than commonsensical. To be a futurologist, you need good judgement and strong instincts, but mainly you need to do lots of research. By and large, the companies that employ futurologists aren't interested in solving the world's problems. They want to find out about business opportunities, risks, threats and changes in society that may affect sales.

2 According to futurologist for British Telecom Ian Pearson, people in his profession look at patterns in research and development – what is being researched and by whom – and they attend conferences and read technical magazines. Then they apply common sense, rooting out ideas that seem illogical. For example, a few years ago there was the idea of the intelligent home. Using a computer to organise every aspect of a home that is constantly changing (new owners, growing children, changing circumstances) just doesn't make sense. Another

B Work in pairs and answer the questions.

1 What does *rooting out ideas* mean? (paragraph 2) What is a root? Why do you think the writer uses *to root out* here?

2 What is the pun (a play on words) in this sentence? *The jet pack … failed to take off.* (paragraph 2)

3 Dr Patrick Dixon says the past is '*full of graveyards of bits and pieces of gadgets*'. (paragraph 4) What is a graveyard? Why do you think he uses this metaphor?

4 What does the expression *give someone a buzz* mean? (paragraph 5) Why do you think the writer uses this expression? What is the pun?

C Work in groups and discuss the questions.

1 What do you think of the job of a futurologist: would it be enjoyable, stressful, difficult?

2 Do you agree that the future is about emotion – about how people feel about technology?

great idea, the jet pack – a battery-powered backpack that allows you to fly – also failed to take off.

3 The fact that most predictions fail presents a problem for futurologists. They simply have to think big: radical and revolutionary rather than minor and minuscule. But radical, revolutionary ideas rarely become reality. Faced with this, one alternative for futurologists is to look at today's technology and find new ways in which it can be applied to everyday life.

4 Trends analyst Dr Patrick Dixon says the past is, 'full of graveyards of bits and pieces of gadgets which form no particularly useful function' and that the key will be how technology can work with human emotions. 'It's about how people feel about technology ... how people actually want to live.'

5 He may have a point. Recent innovations include toys that respond emotionally to the tone of a child's voice (happy, sad, etc.), as well as musical bath tiles that 'read' your emotions and play mood-enhancing music. Another new product is a pair of bracelets that send signals across the mobile phone network. They can vibrate or heat up so you can send your partner a warm glow or literally give them a buzz. But don't bet on these becoming bestsellers. The future, as we know, doesn't always turn out as we expect it to. Just ask Decca or Ken Olson.

GRAMMAR future forms
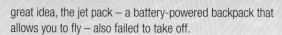

5 Check what you know. Match sentences 1–5 with rules a)–e).

1 Radio stations **will play** personalised streams of music based on your tastes.

2 By 2020, we **will have been using** portable medical tools for nearly a decade.

3 'Nutrition pills' full of vitamins **are going to be** the main diet in non-farming areas.

4 Within ten years, self-service shops **will have become** the norm.

5 In the near future, **we'll be using** specialised glasses that contain books and internet functions.

Rules:

a) Use *be going to* + infinitive to make a prediction based on current evidence.

b) Use *will* + infinitive (without *to*) to make a prediction.

c) Use the future continuous to describe an activity that will be in progress at some time in the future.

d) Use the future perfect to describe something that happens before a time in the future.

e) Use the future perfect continuous to describe something in progress for a period up to a specified time in the future.

6 Read about three other ways to talk about the future. Look at sentences 6–8 and choose the correct option to complete rules f)–h).

6 The government **is to introduce** new laws making health insurance compulsory.

7 According to some, robot intelligence **is due to surpass** human intelligence in the next thirty years.

8 Time travel **could be** a reality by 2075, but it might only be available for the rich.

Rules:

f) Use *be* + *to* + infinitive to describe *an informal plan / an official arrangement or order*.

g) Use *be due to* + infinitive to describe something that is *expected to happen or arrive at a particular time / unlikely to happen in the foreseeable future*.

h) Use *could / might / may* + infinitive to describe a prediction that is *not certain / certain*.

7A ▶ 6.1 Tick the sentences you hear.

1 She'll be running. / She'll have been running.

2 I'll see him later. / I'll be seeing him later.

3 I'll be there. / I'll have been there.

4 We're going to be there at 1.00. / We're to be there at 1.00.

B Notice how some grammar words (e.g. auxiliary verbs) are pronounced in connected speech. Listen again and repeat.

She'll have been running. /ʃɪləvbɪn/

⟫ page 138 **LANGUAGEBANK**

PRACTICE

8A Are both alternatives in sentences 1–8 possible? If so, is the meaning different?

1 By 2020, eighty percent of city dwellers *will be working / are to work* from home.

Both are possible. We use 'will be working' to make a prediction. We use 'are to work' to describe an order from an authority.

2 Europe *might / will* become a united state in the next ten years.

3 Families *will be / will be being* racially very mixed.

4 By 2030, scientists *are finding / will have found* cures for most illnesses.

5 Cars *will / are due to* be banned from city centres.

6 In fifty years' time, most rich people *will live / will have been living* until they are over 100.

7 By 2030, English *is going to be / will have become* the world's third language.

8 By 2050, it's possible that governments *will censor / will have been censoring* the web for years.

B Say the correct sentences out loud, using shortened forms of auxiliary verbs.

C Do you agree with statements 1–8? Discuss with other students.

SPEAKING

9 Read about some ideas of the future and discuss the questions.

1 Which ideas do you like?

2 Which do you think will come true?

3 What problems would the inventions solve?

4 What would the consequences be if these ideas became reality?

Black box

A personal 'black box' that records everything you do, see and hear every day and which allows you to watch, hear and feel any sensation from any time in your past.

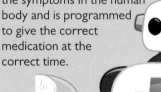

iPillow

A pillow that reads your audiobook while you're in bed, gradually lowers the volume and switches to soothing sounds as you drift off to sleep.

Robot nurse

A robot that cares for sick patients twenty-four hours a day, can automatically 'read' the symptoms in the human body and is programmed to give the correct medication at the correct time.

Hand-held water purifier

A €1 contraption the size of an aerosol can that purifies any liquid that you put into it and turns it into drinkable water.

VOCABULARY **PLUS** prepositional phrases

10A Work in pairs and read about a futurologist's ideas for the future. Complete the paragraphs with suitable prepositions (one or two words). Use one preposition for each paragraph, once in every sentence.

India is *on* track to surpass China as the most populated country by 2035. In India, 48,000 babies are born every day *on* average. In future, India's resources such as schools and hospitals will be permanently *on* trial as they try to keep up with rising demands.

Millions of children are risk of contracting diseases from dirty water. Only sixty percent of the world's population has easy access to drinking water present. In the future, it is hoped that least ninety-five percent of people will have running water at home, but there are no guarantees of this.

As humanity's need for resources and industries has grown, it has become clear that man is far the most destructive animal on Earth. We are, nature, extraordinarily prolific polluters of the planet. In future, everyone will have to monitor their pollution law.

While the number of humans has risen, the number of wild animals such as lions and buffalo has been decline for decades. We are now preserving the genetic codes of animals that are danger of extinction. In future, we hope to be able to, effect, 'recreate' these animals.

In the early twenty-first century, corruption in business has started getting control. Corporations have tried to keep a number of scandals sight. In future, necessity, stricter anti-corruption laws will be passed.

B Look at all the prepositional phrases you completed in Exercise 10A and try to work out what they mean.

❛❜ speakout TIP

Prepositional phrases are short, fixed phrases (usually two or three words) that begin with a preposition. They are often followed by a noun, e.g. *at war*, *by accident*. When you notice prepositional phrases, write them down in a complete sentence. This will help you to remember them.

11A Replace the underlined words below with prepositional phrases from Exercise 10A. Then use your own ideas to complete as many of the predictions as you can.

1 In the future, people will be <u>vulnerable to</u> catching a new disease called … *at risk of*

2 Birth rates are <u>falling fast</u>, so soon …

3 Inflation will get <u>completely crazy</u>, which will lead to …

4 A new energy form will replace oil, <u>because we really need it</u>, and as a result, …

5 In 2040, <u>easily</u> the most important change in the world of work will be …

6 By 2040 there will be <u>a minimum of</u> ten billion people alive, and this will cause …

7 In future, <u>legally</u> people will have to register their …

8 In order to protect animals that are <u>close to becoming extinct</u>, we will …

9 People will, <u>generally</u>, have only one …

10 <u>Right now</u>, robots aren't very intelligent, but by 2040, …

B Think of three predictions on any topic, their consequences and what should be done about them. Make notes.

C Work in groups and share your ideas.

▶ page 153 **VOCABULARYBANK**

VOCABULARY language

1A Check you understand the meaning of the phrases in bold.

1 Why do you think English has become a '**lingua franca**', used by people around the world to communicate? What factors contributed to its rise as a **global language**?

2 Think of three ways to improve your **command of a language** and one situation where you need to **mind your language**.

3 What happens when you experience a **language barrier**? Do you think these will still exist in the future? Why/Why not?

4 Can you name a **dead language**? Can you name a country where the **official language** is different from the **everyday language**? Do you think this is a problem?

B Discuss the questions above.

▸ page 153 **VOCABULARYBANK**

LISTENING

2 Work in pairs. Read the radio programme listing and answer the questions.

1 What do Stephen Fry and David Crystal discuss in the programme?

2 What are the two main reasons given for why English is changing?

3 What kinds of changes are mentioned?

Stephen Fry's English Delight

As the use of English as a lingua franca continues to grow and spread around the world, the language itself is changing – adapting to how its speakers use it. The number of people who speak English as a second language has now grown to far outweigh the number of native speakers. Professor David Crystal, a world authority in language change, thinks sounds which some speakers find difficult to pronounce might disappear. And the vocabulary will certainly change, too.

The other huge influence on the way English will change relates to technology. With computers that 'read' text and automatic person-to-person translators, will computers soon be joining the swelling billions who use and change English? In this BBC radio programme, Stephen Fry and Professor David Crystal discuss the evolution of English.

3A ▶ 6.2 Listen to part of the programme. Tick the topics that are mentioned.

• culture and identity

• new Englishes

• the type of English spoken by computers

• local languages/local brands of English

• changing pronunciation

• English as a mother tongue

• English as a second or foreign language

B What do they say about each point?

Language is linked to your culture and identity because everything that makes up your identity (plants, animals, history etc.) has to be expressed with language.

4A Two of the sentences below are incorrect. Listen to the programme again and correct them.

1 The way English continues to move across the globe gives us a whole range of Englishes.

2 In the beginning, there was just British English and American English, and then came Australian English, South African English, Indian English and so on.

3 When a country adopts a new language, it changes it to suit its local needs.

4 English has been adopted by more than sixty countries around the world.

5 There are about 400 million first language speakers of English.

6 Around the world, one fifth of the population speaks English as a second or foreign language.

B Discuss. How do you think English will change in the next 200 years? Do you think it will continue to be a global language? Do you think other languages will become more important?

GRAMMAR concession clauses

5A Check what you know. Read the predictions about the future of English. Underline the correct alternatives.

1 *While/Despite* English is still the dominant language on the internet, other languages (like Mandarin, Russian, Spanish and Portuguese) will become increasingly important.

2 *In spite of/Although* 27.3 percent of internet users are English speakers, this number is closely followed by Chinese speakers (22.6 percent). *Though/Despite* we may find it hard to believe, the global language of the future might be Chinese or Arabic.

3 *Difficult though it may be/Strange as it seemed* for students, in the future many school and university subjects are likely to be taught in English, using English materials.

4 *However/Whichever* way you look at it, children need to start learning English when they are as young as possible.

5 *Even though/In spite of* increasing numbers of English speakers, the global predominance of English is likely to change.

6 *Even if/Despite* being able to use simultaneous translation on their phones to speak to each other, there will always be people who want to learn another language.

7 *Whilst/Whichever* people continue to use English to communicate on the internet, the language itself will continue to change.

B Work in pairs. Do you agree or disagree with the statements above? Why?

C Use the rule below to help you identify the main clauses and concession clauses in sentences 1–7 above.

Rule:
Concession clauses are used to introduce information which contrasts with information in the main clause.

D Answer the questions.

1 What punctuation separates the clauses?

2 Do the linkers in italics introduce the main clause or the concession clause?

3 Most of the linkers in italics are followed by a verb clause. Which two are followed by a noun/-ing form?

▶ page 138 **LANGUAGEBANK**

PRACTICE

6A Write one sentence to connect each pair of ideas. Use the words in brackets. Think carefully about the punctuation.

1 I always try to speak to people in their local language / I don't speak it very well (even if)

*I always try to speak to people in their local language, **even if** I don't speak it very well.*

2 I spend a lot of time studying grammar / I still make mistakes (though)

3 It is difficult / I always try to believe what people tell me (difficult though)

4 It doesn't matter which way you look at it / technology is changing education (however)

5 I agree that English is important / I think students need to learn several languages (while)

6 It may seem strange / I find it hard to remember facts and figures (strange as)

7 It is a fact that I enjoy travelling / I don't get the opportunity very often (despite)

8 Learning a language is difficult / it doesn't matter which method you choose (whichever)

B Choose three of the linkers in italics from Exercise 5A (*even if*, *while*, *although*, etc.) and write sentences which are true for you. Compare your ideas in pairs.

SPEAKING

7A Work in groups of three and read about three ideas for language learning. Student A: read the text below. Student B: turn to page 159. Student C: turn to page 163. Take turns to explain the ideas you read about.

Robot teachers
English-teaching robots, called 'Engbots' have been introduced in schools in Korea.
It is expected that by 2018 these robots should be able to teach on their own, so that there will be no need for English teachers in the classroom.

B Discuss the pros and cons of each idea. What language learning ideas do you think are likely to be popular in the future?

WRITING a report

8A Look at the graph. What does it tell you about which languages will be important in the future? Can you make any predictions based on the evidence provided?

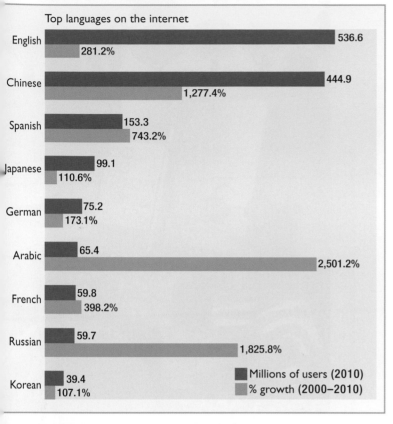

Top languages on the internet

English 536.6 / 281.2%
Chinese 444.9 / 1,277.4%
Spanish 153.3 / 743.2%
Japanese 99.1 / 110.6%
German 75.2 / 173.1%
Arabic 65.4 / 2,501.2%
French 59.8 / 398.2%
Russian 59.7 / 1,825.8%
Korean 39.4 / 107.1%

■ Millions of users (2010)
■ % growth (2000–2010)

B Read the first part of a report about languages on the internet. Answer the questions.

1 Which language does the writer think may become the dominant internet language of the future? Why?

2 Which other languages do you think are important to mention in the report? Why?

This report will look at the changing importance of various languages on the internet and draw conclusions about the implications for language learners around the world. The graphic shows the top ten languages used on the internet, and gives information about the rate of growth of each language and the total percentage of users.

It is quite clear from the data that languages other than English are becoming increasingly important on the internet. There has been a huge surge in demand for Mandarin Chinese, for example, which has increased by 1,277.4 percent in the last ten years and is now not far behind the use of English in terms of total numbers of users. Whilst there are 536.6 million users of English on the internet, Chinese is fast catching up, with 444.9 million users. If the current trend continues, Chinese will soon become the most dominant language on the internet.

Another popular language on the internet is currently Spanish, with 153.3 million users, making it the third most dominant language. Spanish users have also shown a steady increase in growth (743.2 percent) over ten years, indicating the continued importance of Spanish as an internet language.

However, there are other languages which show an increasing influence. In particular, …

9 Read the guidelines for writing a formal report. Which guidelines 1–6 are followed in the report in Exercise 8B? What would you expect to find in the remaining part of the report?

1 Introduce the report so that its purpose is clearly demonstrated.

2 Organise your report into paragraphs or sections under different headings/subheadings.

3 Refer to statistics, graphs and other data.

4 Give recommendations or draw conclusions about the information in your report.

5 Use formal language (objective structures like the passive, full forms rather than contractions, formal vocabulary and register).

6 Use linking words and phrases to help support your ideas.

LEARN TO describe trends

10A Look at sentences 1–6. Which alternative is <u>not</u> possible according to the graph in Exercise 8A? Cross out the incorrect alternative.

1 The importance of Mandarin as a global language has *increased dramatically/risen sharply/dropped alarmingly*.

2 There has been *a surge/a drop/an increase* in the use of Chinese on the internet.

3 Numbers of people using Arabic on the internet have *plummeted/soared/grown* in recent years.

4 There has been a relative *surge/decline/drop* in the percentage of people using English online, as numbers of people using languages such as Chinese, Russian and Arabic have *declined/increased/grown*.

5 Numbers of Chinese speakers with access to the internet have *rocketed/exploded/collapsed*.

6 There has been a *steady/sharp/gradual* increase in the use of Spanish online.

B Use the prompts to write sentences describing trends in education. Use the present perfect tense.

1 explosion / demand for / mobile technology/ language learning

2 number / people / communicating regularly / use / blogs / increase / dramatically

3 number / students / attend / private language schools / study English / plummet

4 sharp increase / ability / learners / access / learning materials / internet

5 gradual decline / appeal / traditional teaching methods

11 Complete the report in Exercise 8B by continuing the last paragraph and adding a conclusion (150 words). Use the language in exercise 10A to help.

VOCABULARY fashion

1A Discuss the questions.

1 How would you describe the people and things in the photos?

2 Are there any images that you think look out-of-date?

3 How do trends start and spread?

B Read the text about how trends spread. What is the main idea of the text? What is <u>your</u> answer to the question at the end of the text?

The best way to understand how trends take off might be to think of them as epidemics. How is it that unknown books suddenly become bestsellers, TV programmes become instant classics, toys that were adored by generations suddenly lose their appeal? The answer is that trends spread like viruses. Somehow they capture the imagination and strike a chord with the public. Take the rise of the shoe brand, Hush Puppies. Sales of Hush Puppies had stagnated to just 30,000 pairs a year. Suddenly, the shoes became the latest thing in Manhattan clubs and stylists began to use them as accessories in fashion photo shoots. It turned out to be more than just a passing trend. In 1995, Hush Puppies sold 430,000 pairs, and in 1996, 1,700,000 pairs. Or look at the technology revolution led by Apple Computers. The number of Apple users has risen dramatically in the last ten years. How do these changes happen? Some say it's a combination of word of mouth and pure luck, while marketers think it's something we can control. Who is right?

2A Read the text again and find the words that complete the phrases in bold.

1 When trends suddenly become popular, they **take** ...

2 When a product goes out of fashion, it **has lost its** ...

2 One way that fashions spread is that they **capture the** ...

4 When people like and identify with something, it **strikes a** ...

5 When a product or trend is suddenly popular, we say it **becomes the latest** ...

6 When something is popular for just a short time, we say **it's just a passing** ...

7 When there is more of something now than before, we say **the number has** ...

8 When something becomes trendy because people tell each other about it, it spreads **by word of** ...

B Work in pairs. Think of examples of:

• something that was a passing trend.

• something that has captured the public imagination.

• something that has taken off recently.

FUNCTION describing cause and effect

3A ▶ 6.3 Listen to people describing how two trends started and answer the questions.

1 What trends do they talk about?

2 How did the trends start?

3 How/Why did the trends spread?

B Read the expressions below for describing cause and effect. Can you remember which expressions the speakers in Exercise 3A used?

	informal and neutral	formal
cause	It all started ... It originated in/from ... It's because of ...	It has its origins/roots in ... It can be traced back/attributed to ... It stems from ...
effect	It led to ... It has caused ... Because of this, ...	It resulted in ... It gave rise to ... It brought about ...

C Listen again to check.

▐▐▶ page 138 **LANGUAGEBANK**

4 Rewrite the sentences using the words in brackets. Change the verb tenses as necessary.

1 Reggae comes from Jamaica. (have/roots)

2 The Mohican haircut, in the UK, was originally from the punk era. (have/origins)

3 Technology has led to new types of crime, such as hacking. (give rise)

4 Some say football started in China. (can/trace)

5 Global warming is the reason for many recent environmental disasters. (cause)

6 Better healthcare and diet, plus fewer babies per family, mean the population is ageing. (because of)

7 The rising number of female world leaders can be attributed to the women's liberation movement. (stem)

8 The growth in online publishing has necessitated new laws. (lead to)

9 It's thought that chess began in India over a thousand years ago. (originate)

10 Medical procedures for disfigured soldiers later helped the development of cosmetic surgery. (resulted)

11 The recent popularity of tattoos is because of celebrities who have them. (can/attributed)

12 Globalisation has meant big changes to the way businesses are run. (bring/about)

LEARN TO summarise your views

5A Look at the expressions in the box. When do you think we usually use these expressions? What is their purpose?

> So overall, …   To sum up, …   All in all, …   Basically, …
> In conclusion, …   So what I'm really saying is, …

B Which expressions did the speakers in Exercise 3A use? Check your answers in audio script 6.3 on page 170.

speakout TIP

When we are finishing a long 'turn' (a long explanation, story, description, etc.) we often try to summarise it using different words from the original turn. We may add a moral to a story or repeat the main points. This helps our listener to capture the message.

6A Complete the sentences in any way you choose.

1 People now expect to download music for free and CD sales are at their lowest ebb. Basically, …

2 We saw some great presentations at the conference. The hotel was wonderful and we loved the food. So overall, …

3 Bloggers take news from real reporters and write comments. They do hardly any reporting themselves. So what I'm really saying is …

4 Sales of the game soared in May, jumped again in July and rose dramatically at the end of the year. To sum up, …

5 This report says young people believe in openness. They share details of their private lives enthusiastically online. In conclusion, …

6 We had developed a great product, so logically it should have been a success. However, we had technical problems. Then we ran out of money and a competitor stole the idea. All in all, …

B Compare your answers in pairs.

C Which two sentences are in a formal context? Which two expressions for summarising do they use?

7A ▶ 6.4 Listen to completed sentences 1–6 in Exercise 6A. Are any of the endings similar to yours?

B How many vowel sounds do the words in the box have? When we say these words in connected speech, one sound in each word gets 'swallowed'. Which one?

> basically   dramatically   enthusiastically   logically

C ▶ 6.5 Listen to check. Cross out the swallowed sounds.

D Practise saying the words, omitting the swallowed sounds.

SPEAKING

8A What has changed in your lifetime in your country? Think about fashion, awareness of green issues, cost of living, the media, etc. Choose one issue. Make notes about the causes and effects of the changes.

B Work in groups and present your ideas.

DVD PREVIEW

1 Look at the words in the box. How do you think these factors have influenced the world since the start of the twenty-first century?

> climate change   globalisation
> Google   credit crunch   Web 2.0
> carbon footprint

2 Read the programme information. What is the key trend that this episode focuses on?

BBC History of Now: The Story of the Noughties

History of Now is a BBC documentary series which aims to identify key cultural and social trends which have defined recent decades. This programme, *The Story of the Noughties*, looks at the inexorable rise of 'youth culture' during the first decade since the turn of the millennium. It examines how 'youth' is now enjoyed by those unwilling to relinquish it until well into their forties, fifties or even sixties. It describes how the noughties became the decade of the childish adult, or 'kidult', and of those who tell you they're in 'middle youth' not middle age.

▶ DVD VIEW

3A Which of the following statements do you think are true?

1 The generation gap between young people and old people is getting bigger.

2 Increasingly, old people are afraid of young people and young people do not appreciate older people.

3 The concept of being a teenager only really started in the 1960s.

4 The market for selling toys to adults is larger than the market for selling toys to children.

B Watch the DVD to check your ideas.

4A Complete the extracts.

1 The first decade of the new millennium saw waves of massive and, at times, _____.

2 Age is to the twenty-first century what social class was to the twentieth century. It's one of the _____ in our society.

3 We had a situation where everybody wanted to be young, but the only people who could afford _____ were the old.

4 Adults and young people are probably more divided now than they ever were in the past, partly because of the _____ and the role that youth culture has in dominating society.

5 People say, 'Well, in the 1950s, you know, there was a transition. You went from having _____ to wearing _____.'

6 Why not have toys, why not _____, why not carry on behaving like you might have behaved when you were eighteen, nineteen, or twenty?

B Watch the DVD again to check.

5 Work in groups and discuss the questions.

1 Do you agree that we are living in a society which is dominated by youth culture? Can you think of examples?

2 How do old and young people treat each other in your country? Do you think this is different in other countries?

speak**out** talk about a decade

6A ▶ 6.6 Listen to someone talking about a decade. Which decade does she describe? What does she say about the following topics?

- historical events
- mobile phones/technology
- economics
- music/clubbing
- fashion

B Listen again and choose the correct alternatives to complete the key phrases.

key**phrases**

The nineties was when the internet first *went downhill/took off*.

Generally though, the nineties was quite a *poor/prosperous* time.

I think one of the most *memorable/terrible* things about the 1990s has to be the music.

I remember *wanting to go/going* to the Take That concert in '93.

Clubbing was generally really *big/cool* too.

Thinking about *fashion/music* back then makes me cringe.

(It) was a great decade to *grow up in/be a teenager in*.

7A Work in groups and choose a decade to discuss. Make notes about three factors which you think helped to define the decade. Think about music, fashion, politics, news events and social or cultural trends.

B Present your ideas to the class.

write**back** a review of a decade

8A Work in pairs. Read the review of the noughties. Think of other examples to add to each section.

Portrait of a decade: high points of the noughties

Is it really possible to sum up a decade? We asked readers to send in their ideas of events, people and cultural highlights which they thought defined the last ten years. Twitter, Xbox, Ugg boots and *Big Brother* … these were just some of the highlights of the noughties.

Technology: The noughties was definitely the decade during which the internet really took off, and began to significantly change our world. With the success of companies like Google, video-sharing sites like YouTube, and social networking sites like Facebook, MySpace and Twitter, the noughties was a time of information explosion.

Television: There was a profusion of reality TV shows and popularity contests like *Big Brother*. This was perhaps driven by a demand for more realistic television than was being provided by the classic soap operas, and also by the increase in the use of home-made video recordings, which meant that people were getting used to watching each other on television.

Games: The Xbox, the Playstation and later the Wii all became household names, and there was a move from computer gaming being an individual pursuit towards it becoming a family activity. Internet gaming also became popular with the success of games like *Warcraft*.

People: The list of famous faces included Presidents, like George Bush, or Prime Ministers, like Tony Blair or Silvio Berlusconi, as well as sportsmen such as David Beckham and Roger Federer, and singer celebrities like Beyoncé and Eminem.

B Write a short review of a decade of your own choice (250–300 words).

TRENDS AND PREDICTIONS

1 Complete the text by adding one word in each gap.

The idea of resurrecting extinct species used to be science fiction, but this development [1]_____ well come true. The science already exists. The recent explosion [2]_____ genome research tells us that the recipe for making a creature lies in its DNA. Creating animals from a genome sequence is impossible now, but the [3]_____ are it will happen soon. When an animal dies in a dry cave or in ice, we can find intact genome sequences. We then need a surrogate species to give birth to the animal. If we wanted to bring back a mammoth, the surrogate would be an elephant. As a result of this development, fears about the extinction of some species could become a [4]_____ memory. As the science [5]_____ pace, conservationists are getting ready; they have begun freezing tissue samples of these animals. The days of campaigns to save the whale and so many other species could [6]_____ over, as extinction becomes a [7]_____ of the past!

LANGUAGE

2A The phrases in italics are in the wrong sentences. Put them in the correct place.

1 It's useful to study Latin, even though it is a *lingua franca*.

2 A *language barrier* is a language that is used to communicate between speakers of many different languages.

3 A simplified version of English, sometimes called 'Globish', will become the dominant *dead language*.

4 I wish teenagers would *global language*. I hate to hear them swearing.

5 It's important for global economics that people can communicate without a *mind their language*.

B Work in pairs. Do you agree with the rewritten statements above? Compare your ideas.

FUTURE FORMS

3A Work in pairs. Student A: you are an optimist. Student B: you are a pessimist. Complete the sentences according to your role.

1 By the time I'm old, I hope I will have done many things, such as …

2 Tomorrow I'm going to …

3 By 2020, I will have been …

4 If everything goes to plan, I will …

5 If my plan falls through, I might …

6 I'm due to …

7 I will be visiting …

8 Apparently, I am to …

B Compare your sentences. Now compare with another pair. Who was the most optimistic and who was the most pessimistic?

CONCESSION CLAUSES

4A Match the sentence halves.

1 I'm planning to join a gym,

2 I love travelling. I always enjoy meeting people,

3 However hard I try to be organised,

4 I get tempted to buy things,

5 In a relationship, you need to be able to forgive people,

6 No matter how early you get up in the morning,

a) whatever they do.

b) wherever I go.

c) I still forget things all the time.

d) there are never enough hours in the day.

e) although finding the time to go is difficult.

f) even though I can't really afford them.

B Use the prompts to write your own sentences. Compare your ideas in pairs.

1 I'm good at … even though …

2 I'd like to … whatever …

3 As hard as I try, …

4 No matter what happens, …

5 Despite feeling … I …

DESCRIBING CAUSE AND EFFECT

5A Correct the mistakes in sentences 1–7. What trends do they describe?

1 These can be tracing back to the 1700s, when a Dutchman attached tiny wheels to strips of wood and nailed them to his shoes.

2 This fashion item is often attributed by British designer Mary Quant in the 1960s, but ancient Roman soldiers wore a similar garment!

3 This musical style was popularised in New York in the 1970s, but it has the origins in the 'talking' style of West African musician-poets.

4 These have their rooting in ancient China, though they were popularised in the USA in the early 1900s when actors wore them to avoid being recognised in public.

5 When an American engineer, Sherman Poppen, invented a toy for his daughter by fastening two skis together and attaching a rope to one end in 1965, it lead to a new sport.

6 The first type was produced in the 1960s for the University of Florida's American football team, nicknamed 'the Gators' (short for alligators). This resulted on the brand name Gatorade.

7 The term 'weblog' was first used in 1997, but Peter Merholz divided this word into two and gave rise of one of the most popular forms of electronic writing.

B Check your ideas. Match the trends below with sentences 1–8.

roller skates   blog   sunglasses
mini-skirt   hip-hop
snowboarding   energy drinks

BBC VIDEO PODCAST

Watch people talking about their interest in music and fashion trends on ActiveBook or on the website.

Authentic BBC interviews

www.pearsonELT.com/speakout

UNIT 7

freedom

READING

1A Look at the photos and read the story. What do you think really happened?

B Answer the questions.

1 Why do you think John Darwin was tanned?

2 What might have happened to his canoe?

3 Where do you think Mr Darwin had been during those five years?

4 What do you think happened next?

C Turn to page 161. Read part two of the story and check your ideas.

2A Work in pairs. Complete the sentences using information from part two of the story.

1 The circumstances that led John Darwin to consider faking his own death were …

2 John Darwin managed to live secretly at home by …

3 In Panama, the Darwins had hoped to …

4 The deception was uncovered by …

5 As a punishment for their crime of fraud and deception, the Darwins …

B Work in pairs and discuss the questions.

1 What do you think of what John Darwin did?

2 What do you think was the most difficult part of the deception for the Darwins?

3 Do you think it was right for the Darwins to go to prison?

4 What do you think Anne Darwin should/ shouldn't have done?

The case of the disappearing man

When a man walked into a police station in London, claiming to be suffering from amnesia, he told officers, 'I think I am a missing person.' He apparently had no recollection of his whereabouts or events over the previous five years. What police didn't initially realise was that the man in front of them was in fact John Darwin, 'the missing canoe man'.

When John Darwin, a married father of two, initially went missing five years previously, a massive search and rescue mission was launched along the northeast coast of the UK, near to where he was last seen. Prison officer John Darwin had been spotted paddling out to sea with his kayak early in the morning on 21st March, but it was only when he failed to arrive at work for a night shift that evening that the alarm was raised. The rescue teams searched extensively, but to no avail.

Several weeks later, when the shattered remains of John's kayak were found washed up on the beach, John Darwin was presumed dead. More than a year later, his wife threw flowers into the sea to mark the anniversary of her husband's disappearance. At an inquest, the coroner recorded an open verdict, which allowed the family to 'move on'. However, no trace of Mr Darwin's body was ever found.

On his reappearance in London, his family were informed. His two sons, Mark and Anthony, were thrilled to be reunited with their father. And his wife Anne – who had sold up her properties in England and moved to Panama three months before his reappearance – expressed surprise, joy and elation at the return of her missing husband.

However, nobody could have predicted what would come to light over the following days. When John Darwin appeared at the police station, he claimed memory loss, but otherwise he appeared both fit and well, and he was also suntanned (a little unusual for December in the UK). An investigation was immediately launched into his disappearance.

GRAMMAR cleft sentences

3A Sentences 1–4 express ideas in the story, but are phrased slightly differently. Rewrite them using the prompts in italics.

1 Police didn't initially realise that the man standing in front of them was John Darwin, 'the missing canoe man'.
What police …

2 The alarm was raised only when he failed to arrive at work for a night shift.
It was only when …

3 He spent the next few years hiding inside the house and rarely leaving.
What he did then …

4 A colleague of Anne Darwin's eventually put the pieces of the puzzle together.
It was a …

B Check your answers in the stories on pages 80 and 161.

C What is the effect of starting the sentences with the phrases in italics? Read the rule to check.

> Rule:
>
> To add emphasis or focus attention on one part of a sentence, we can add certain words or phrases to the beginning of the sentence using another verb (e.g. *It was … / What he knew was … / The reason why … is … / The person who … is …*, etc.). This is called a 'cleft sentence'.

page 140 LANGUAGEBANK

PRACTICE

4 Rewrite the sentences using the prompts.

1 I don't understand why Anne Darwin didn't tell her sons about their father.
What I don't understand …

2 They planned to start a new life in Panama.
The place where …

3 The photograph of the couple buying a house in Panama revealed the deception.
It was …

4 She couldn't understand why Anne had decided to emigrate to Panama.
The thing that …

5 John Darwin flew back to the UK from Panama because he was missing his sons.
The reason …

6 He found it difficult coming to terms with what his parents had done.
What he found …

5A Complete the sentences to make them true for you.

1 Something I have always wanted to do is …

2 The reason why I enjoy … is …

3 The place I would most like to visit is …

4 What I enjoy/dislike most about living where I do is …

5 One thing I would like to change is …

B Use your sentences to start conversations with other students.
A: One thing I would like to change is my job.
B: Really? Why's that?

VOCABULARY escape

6A Match the sentence halves.

1 Sometimes I feel so **trapped**
2 The car broke down and we were
3 Don't you sometimes just want to **escape**
4 They packed up their belongings and
5 The couple were **released**
6 Suspecting the police were after him, he decided to
7 The prisoners spent much of their time together
8 During the frequent air raids, people took

a) **fled** the country.
b) by the life I am living.
c) **refuge** in their cellars.
d) **stranded** on the side of the road for hours.
e) hatching **an escape plan**.
f) the boredom of everyday life?
g) **make a break for it**.
h) from prison after serving only three years of their sentences.

B Complete the sentences with words/phrases in bold from Exercise 6A.

1 Flights were cancelled and I was _____ in Rome with no money.

2 I don't like going in lifts. I always worry that they will malfunction and we'll be _____.

3 The police stopped the car to arrest the robbers, but the young men tried to _____.

4 I've been working on _____. All we need to do is dig a tunnel at night when the guards are sleeping.

5 When I saw the shoplifter, I called out. He looked up, then turned and _____.

6 In the book, he describes his experiences of being kidnapped and how he was eventually _____.

C Work in pairs and answer the questions.

1 If you had to plan an escape route from your classroom which didn't use the door or windows, what would it be?

2 If you were captured by kidnappers, what would your plan be?

3 Have you or anyone you know ever been stranded? What happened? What did you/they do?

SPEAKING

7A What would you do if you were stranded on an island? Would you try to raise the alarm or make a break for it yourself? Turn to page 159 and read the rules of a game.

B Work in groups. Decide on a list of five things which you think would be useful to you in this situation. Work out an escape plan.

C Tell other students about your plan. Which group has the best plan?

VOCABULARY *PLUS* suffixes

8A Check what you know. Add the headings in the box to the correct columns in the table.

adjectives	nouns	adverbs	verbs

emigrate	emigration / emigrant		
deceive	deception	deceptive	deceptively
pretend	pretence	pretend	
suspect	suspicion	suspicious	suspiciously

B Underline the suffixes in the words in the table.

9A One word in each sentence is incorrect. Change or add the suffix to correct it. You may need to change some letters in the original word.

1 When she finally managed to emigrant, they bought a £200,000 tropical estate.

2 They travelled to Panama, looking for opportunities to start a new life together, while Mrs Darwin kept up the pretend that her husband was dead.

3 He apparently had no recollect of his whereabouts or events over the previous five years.

4 In the meantime, in the UK, several people had become suspicion.

5 A massively search and rescue mission was launched along the northeast coast of the UK.

6 What police didn't initially realisation was that the man in front of them was in fact John Darwin.

7 The rescue teams searched extensive, but to no avail.

8 When visitors came, Mr Darwin supposed hid in the neighbouring house.

B What parts of speech are the corrected words? Find two verbs, two nouns, two adjectives and two adverbs.

10A Add the corrected words from Exercise 9A to the groups below.

To form verbs

-*ate*:	motivate, hesitate, renovate, ¹_____
-*en*:	darken, strengthen, brighten
-*ise*/-*ize* (UK/US):	prioritise, legalise, modernise, ²_____
-*ify*:	glorify, electrify, exemplify

To form nouns

-*tion*/-*ation*:	exhaustion, production, ³_____
-*cy*:	immediacy, accuracy, tendency
-*ity*:	clarity, stupidity, opportunity
-*ment*:	embarrassment, enjoyment, harassment
-*ness*:	loneliness, unhappiness, tiredness
-*er*/-*an*/-*or*:	engineer, musician, professor
-*ant*:	applicant, attendant, disinfectant
-*ance*/-*ence*:	clearance, reappearance, ⁴_____

To form adjectives

-*ant*/-*ent*:	dominant, redundant, independent
-*ous*/-*ious*:	scandalous, rebellious, ⁵_____
-*able*/-*ible*:	capable, edible, visible
-*ive*:	persuasive, elusive, evasive, ⁶_____
-*ful*:	respectful, helpful, resourceful

To form adverbs

-*ly*:	deeply, financially, dramatically, ⁷_____, ⁸_____

> **speakout TIP**
>
> Some suffixes, especially adjectives, have a clear meaning, e.g. -*less* indicates 'without' – hope**less**, use**less**, meaning**less**; -*proof* indicates 'resistant to the effect of' – child**proof**, water**proof**, sound**proof**. These can help you to guess the meanings of words you do not know. Think about the meaning of these suffixes: -*like* (child**like**, looka**like**), -*worthy* (trust**worthy**), -*ible*/-*able* (incomprehens**ible**, habit**able**).

B Work in pairs. Take turns to choose words from Exercise 10A. Use them to make questions for your partner.

A: *Have you ever hesitated before doing something?*
B: *Yes! I hesitated before I did my first parachute jump.*

➡ page 154 **VOCABULARYBANK**

▶ **GRAMMAR** | participle clauses   ▶ **VOCABULARY** | relaxing   ▶ **HOW TO** | talk about your leisure time

VOCABULARY idioms: relaxing

1 Look at the photos. What are the people doing? How do you think they feel?

2A Look at the phrases in the box. They are idioms for relaxing. Work in pairs and answer the questions.

> hang out   take it easy   have a breather
> slow down   take your mind off (something)
> switch off   let your hair down   unwind

Which expression:

1 means to stop thinking about anything?

2 do we use when someone is living life too fast?

3 describes the process of relaxing, usually after work?

4 might we use if someone has been focusing on something bad?

5 means 'spend lots of time in a particular place while not doing much'?

6 means 'relax and enjoy yourself without worrying what other people will think'?

7 might we use when someone is out of breath after physical exercise?

8 might we use if someone is working too hard and should stop for a while?

B Replace the words in italics with phrases from Exercise 2A. There may be more than one possibility.

1 OK, run around the field one more time, then you can *take a rest.*

2 If you're free tonight, we can *spend time relaxing* at my house.

3 I'm a workaholic, but in recent years I've been trying to *do a little less.*

4 If I've been working a sixteen-hour stint, I usually go to the bar to *relax.*

5 Why don't you go to that party and *go wild for a bit*?

6 I find it hard to *stop focusing on my work* in the evening.

7 Try to *think of something else besides* your exam.

8 I'm just going to put my feet up and *relax* this evening.

3A ▶ 7.1 Listen to the phrases from Exercise 2A and answer the questions.

1 Which expressions have two syllables? Which syllable is stressed?

2 Where is the stress on phrases with three or more words? Is it on the verb or on another word e.g. noun/ adjective?

B Listen again and repeat the expressions.

C Choose three of the expressions in Exercise 2A and write true sentences about yourself. Compare your sentences in pairs.

⫸ page 154 **VOCABULARYBANK**

LISTENING

4 Discuss the questions in groups.

1 What do you do to get away from your day-to-day routine?

2 How long have you been doing it?

3 How does it help you to switch off?

5A ▶ 7.2 Listen to three people talking about how they switch off from their day-to-day routine. Which questions from Exercise 4 does each speaker answer?

B Listen again and note down the answers.

C Which person's method of relaxation would you most like to try? Why?

GRAMMAR participle clauses

6A Read about someone who found true freedom by learning a new skill. What did she learn and how did she do it?

Feeling jaded from life at a desk and armed with nothing but a love of Argentinian culture, I decided to learn the tango. Having listened to the music as a child, I already knew the rhythms, so I felt excited walking into my first tango class. However, the tango was harder than it looked and after the first class, my feet were sore and my knees ached. Not wanting to give up, I decided to take matters into my own hands (and feet!). Using a CD lent to me by a friend, I practised at home and after a while, I improved. Encouraged by my teacher, I went to a café where you could hear the music and eventually, having struggled with it for months, I got the hang of it. People looking for something a bit different always love the tango. When you're doing it you feel completely free: the world disappears – it's just you, your partner and the music.

B Check what you know. Underline the present and past participles in the text. The first two have been done for you.

7A Match example sentences 1–4 with rules a)–d).

1 **Encouraged by my teacher**, I went to a café where you could hear the music.

2 **Not wanting** to give up, I decided to take matters into my own hands.

3 a CD (that was) **lent** to me by a friend

4 I felt excited **walking into my first tango class.**

Rules:

Participle clauses can:

a) replace relative clauses.

b) have an active meaning (when they begin with a present participle).

c) have a passive meaning (when they begin with a past participle).

d) describe actions happening around the same time or one immediately after another.

B Read rules e) and f). Find an example of each in the text.

Rules:

e) *Having* + past participle can be used to give background information or show the cause of a second action.

f) The past participle can be used as an adjective to add extra information.

IIII▶ page 140 **LANGUAGEBANK**

PRACTICE

8 Make one sentence from two. Use participles and the words in brackets. You will need to omit some words.

1 She was staying in Toulouse. This is where she learnt French cooking. (While)

2 I honed my technique. Then I spent all my free time painting. (Having)

3 I didn't know how to relax. I always felt tense until I discovered pilates. (Not)

4 Paul was given the chance to go to a dance school in Colombia. He learnt salsa. (Given)

5 As experts have proven, jogging is a stress buster. It's great exercise. (Proven by / to be)

6 My rollerblades are a great way for me to get around. They were bought for me by my brother. (Bought)

7 He wasn't a 'natural' at sports. He had to work incredibly hard. (Not)

8 Alternative lifestyles are practised by many people. These people are looking for freedom from modern life. (looking)

SPEAKING

9A Discuss. Where would you go to get away from your day-to-day routine and what would you do?

B Work with other students. Look at the list of activities below and answer the questions.

1 What types of people might be interested in these activities? Who are they for?

A survival course is probably for people who like nature and spend a lot of time outdoors.

2 Which activities might be good for people you know? Who? Why?

3 Which would be good for you? Why?

• a survival course

• a spa retreat

• an extreme experience weekend, e.g. F1 racing

• a pottery course

• a film-making course

• a cooking holiday

• a dance course

• a kids' camp

WRITING a leaflet

10A What is the purpose of leaflets, brochures and information sheets? What are their typical features?

B Read the guidelines to check.

1 Leaflets, brochures and information sheets inform us about something. They can also advise, warn or persuade. Businesses and organisations use them to promote events, places, services and products.

2 The title must be bold, eye-catching and give a clear idea of the topic.

3 Use short, clear subheadings. They must stand out in a different font.

4 Break the text up into short sections in a logical order.

5 Don't use language that is too complex. The message must be clear and easy to understand.

6 Lay the text out using spaces between sections. Use bullet points for lists of features and include illustrations, charts and photos if appropriate.

11 Read a leaflet about a place to relax and answer the questions.

1 Who is the intended audience?

2 Does the leaflet follow the guidelines above?

3 Would you like to go there?

Sparngall Spa Retreat
Relax, Rejuvenate, Recharge

 WELCOME
Sparngall Spa Retreat welcomes you to a place of natural beauty, where you can recharge your body and mind. Our mission is to provide the highest quality environment, accommodation, food and activities, so that you can relax completely during your time with us. Our highly qualified staff will provide you with a warm welcome and ensure that you get the most out of your stay.

 ACCOMMODATION
Sparngall Spa Retreat boasts eighteen luxury double bedrooms with large en-suite bathrooms and views of Sparngall Mountain. All bedrooms come with stocked refrigerators, fresh flowers that are changed daily, fruit, and spring water from our very own Sparngall Reservoir.

FACILITIES AND ACTIVITIES
The spa retreat includes a sauna, jacuzzi and swimming pool, all of which are open from 0500 until midnight. We are located minutes from Sparngall Mountain and Lake, and we offer seasonal Nordic walking, hiking and fishing. Our other services and activities include:

* massage therapy
* facials
* aromatherapy
* yoga classes
* beauty treatments

 DINING
The Sparngall restaurant includes high quality, healthy dining with the freshest ingredients. These are grown and harvested on the 4,000 acres of land that surrounds the spa retreat. Our chefs will be delighted to prepare meals to order, including full vegetarian and vegan fare.

 RATES
Rates vary according to the month. Please go to our website for current rates: www.sparngallspa.net

SPARNGALL SPA RETREAT, SPARNGALL, SA2 7ND
PHONE: 01567 887254
EMAIL: SPARNGALL97@COM

LEARN TO use subheadings

12A Which of the following are subheadings in the leaflet in Exercise 11?

a) Sparngall Spa Retreat

b) Relax, Rejuvenate, Recharge

c) Welcome

d) Facilities and activities

e) Rates

B Find a heading and a slogan in the leaflet. How are they different from subheadings? Think about the types of words that are used and their purpose.

C Why do you think subheadings are useful? Tick the ideas you agree with.

1 They help the writer, when he or she is planning the piece, to see what to include and what to leave out.

2 They show the reader how the piece is organised.

3 They allow the reader to jump to the specific information he or she is looking for.

4 They reveal the writer's opinion of the topic.

5 They visually break up blocks of text so that the piece is easier to read.

D Read the additional information about Sparngall Spa Retreat. Think of a suitable subheading.

Sparngall Spa Retreat is accessible by car or train. The nearest railway station is Sparngall Station. From there it is a ten-minute taxi ride to the retreat. We are happy to arrange transport to and from the station for you.

13A Read the scenario and think of an idea you can write about. Make notes and think of subheadings.

You own a place where people go to switch off from their daily routine. What type of place is it? Do people go there to learn something or just to relax? What services and facilities do you offer? Is food and accommodation included? How expensive is it?

B Write a promotional leaflet for your idea (250 words).

▶ **FUNCTION** | exchanging opinions ▶ **VOCABULARY** | risk ▶ **LEARN TO** | convince someone

e blogspeak ||||||||||||||||||||||||||||||||||||||||||||||||||||||||||||||||||||||||||||

Kids and freedom

When a New York journalist, Lenore Skenazy, wrote about how she had **deliberately** left her nine-year-old son in central New York and let him take the subway home alone, she unleashed a media frenzy. Her son, Izzy, whose idea the expedition had been, was happy with the experience. He had arrived home safely, ecstatic with independence. He had been nagging his mother for weeks to be allowed out on his own and to travel **unsupervised**. She had given Izzy a subway map, twenty dollars and a few quarters in case he needed to make a phone call. She hadn't given him a mobile phone (in case he lost it). But Ms Skenazy's actions landed her in a huge row. Although many came out to support her, she was labelled 'crazy' and 'America's worst mom' by others. 'My son had not climbed Mount Fuji in flip-flops,' she wrote subsequently. 'He'd simply done what most people my age had done routinely when they were his age: gone somewhere on his own, without **a security detail**.' She now runs a blog called Free Range Kids, which advocates **encouraging independence** in children and says, 'The problem with this everything-is-dangerous outlook is that **over-protectiveness** is a danger in itself. A child who thinks he can't do anything on his own eventually can't.' So, are we living in a **risk-averse culture** where we stifle our children's ability to **deal with danger** by never allowing them to **take reasonable risks? Does Western society mollycoddle its children?** Or did Ms Skenazy's actions **expose her son to real and unnecessary danger**? What do you think?

||||||||||||

VOCABULARY risk

1 Work in pairs and answer the questions.

1 Do you think that, as a society, we have become afraid to take risks?

2 If so, why do you think this is? Can you think of any examples?

3 When is it OK to break the rules (at work, driving, at school, etc.)?

2A Read the article and answer the questions.

1 What did the journalist let her son do?

2 What was her reason for doing this?

3 What kinds of reactions did she receive when she wrote about the experience?

4 What does Ms Skenazy think is the problem with protecting children too much?

B What do you think the words/phrases in bold in the article mean? Use some of them to complete the sentences below. You may need to use just part of the phrase, or adapt it to fit the context.

1 It's a good idea to get children to cook for themselves from an early age, because it encourages _____.

2 If parents _____ their children by indulging them all the time, the children will never learn to look after themselves.

3 No rational parent would _____ try to _____ their child to unnecessary danger.

4 Children should be encouraged to take _____ _____, like learning how to use sharp knives. This way, they will learn to do things _____.

5 The problem with _____ parents is that the child doesn't learn to deal with problems they will face in the real world.

6 The fact that your coffee cup is labelled 'Caution: contents hot' shows that we are living in a _____ society.

C Do you agree with the statements in Exercise 2B? Why/Why not?

FUNCTION exchanging opinions

3 ▶ 7.3 Listen to people talking about the story in Exercise 2A. Who agrees with the following statements, the man (M) or the woman (W)?

1 It was a brilliant idea for the mother to leave her son to go home alone.

2 The boy could have got lost, or been attacked.

3 As parents we have to take a stand against mollycoddling.

4 Doing things by yourself at a young age teaches you how to protect yourself and be streetwise.

5 Children should be thrown in at the deep end.

6 New York is one of the most dangerous cities in the world.

7 It's too dangerous to leave a nine-year-old alone in a city without a mobile phone.

8 We're in a hurry to push our kids to grow up too soon.

4A Listen again and complete the phrases you hear.

a) Oh come on! You must be _____.

b) That's absolutely _____.

c) Well, I agree with you up to a _____.

d) Surely you don't _____ that …

e) That goes against my better _____ because …

f) How can you _____ that?

g) It just doesn't make _____ to me.

h) Oh that's _____!

B Put phrases a)–h) under the correct headings.

B Put phrases a)–h) under the correct headings.

Agreeing

1 _____

I couldn't agree more.

Absolutely! I'm with you 100% on that.

Agreeing in part

2 _____

I suppose you've got a point, but …

Questioning someone's opinion

3 _____

4 _____

5 _____

6 _____

Where's the logic in that?

You can't honestly think that…

Strongly disagreeing

7 _____

8 _____

▥▶ page 140 **LANGUAGEBANK**

speakout TIP

In order to disagree politely, ask questions, for example: *Do you really think so? Don't you think it's a bit long? Isn't that rather extreme?* To make your disagreement seem less forceful, use *Well, Right,* or *Yes, but* at the start of the sentence.

Look at audio script 7.3 on page 171 for examples of these devices.

LEARN TO convince someone

5A ▶ 7.4 Listen to the speakers trying to convince the listener of their opinion. How does the speaker try to sound polite?

1 **The point is** that he was only nine years old.

2 **Surely you don't think** he should never be allowed out?

3 **That's the whole point.** We need to encourage independence.

4 **All I'm trying to say is** New York is a dangerous city.

5 **I just think** we're too risk-averse.

6 **Oh come on!** You can't really think that.

B Listen again and repeat the phrases, copying the intonation.

6A Use the prompts in brackets to write responses which try to change A's opinion.

1 A: Everyone should be a vegetarian.

B: _____?
(surely/think/people/never/eat/meat)

2 A: Children shouldn't be allowed to hold knives.

B: _____.
(all/say/children/need/learn/some stage)

3 A: Nobody should have to take exams.

B: _____.
(point/exams/useful way/measure progress)

4 A: Young drivers shouldn't be allowed to drive with other youngsters in the car.

B: _____!
(come/not make sense)

B Practise the conversations in pairs. Focus on polite intonation.

SPEAKING

7A Look at the situations below. Who do you think should decide in each case? Why? Think of arguments to support your case.

B Work in groups and discuss the situations. Try to convince others of your opinion.

The state versus the individual
Who should decide:

• whether you are allowed to smoke in a public place?

• whether you should be allowed to eat junk food?

• how much exercise an individual should do?

• whether you should be allowed to keep a gun in your house?

• the age at which a child should go to school?

• how often you use your car or how fast you can drive in certain areas?

• the minimum age that someone can start work?

DVD PREVIEW

1 Work in pairs and look at the photo. Where do you think the man is? What is his mood?

2A Read the programme information. Were your predictions correct? What do you think the good news might be?

BBC Little Dorrit

Little Dorrit is a BBC adaptation of a novel by Charles Dickens set in the nineteenth century. Although once prosperous, William Dorrit loses his fortune and is confined in Marshalsea Prison for Debt for many years. His children grow up in the prison with him, although they are free to come and go as they please. One day, his daughter Amy and Arthur Clennam, a friend, come to the prison. Mr Clennam tells William to compose himself. Clennam then announces two pieces of good news.

B Find words/phrases in the programme information with the following meanings.

1 rich and successful
2 a very large amount of money
3 kept in a place which you cannot leave
4 try to remain calm

▶ DVD VIEW

3 Watch the DVD. What are the two pieces of good news?

4A Who says each sentence? Write Amy (A), William (W), Mr Clennam (C) or the prison worker (PW).

1 There's something up, John. I feel it in my bones.
2 If he had not prepared me for it, I do not think I could have borne it.
3 Compose yourself and think of the best surprise that could possibly happen to you.
4 You are heir to a great fortune.
5 And you can be as you were again.
6 'Tis but a few hours, sir.
7 How long do you think an hour is to a man who is choking for want of air?
8 Perhaps it's for the best.

B Watch the DVD again to check.

5 Work in pairs and discuss the questions.

1 What is the best surprise that could happen to you?
2 If you suddenly came into a lot of money, would it change your life? If so, how?

speakout develop a plot

6A Work in pairs. Look at the pictures and think of three questions to ask about the story shown.

B ▶ 7.5 Listen to someone telling part of the story. Does he answer any of your questions?

C Listen again and tick the key phrases you hear.

keyphrases

Once upon a time, …

After this, he …

No sooner had he … than …

Once he'd … , he …

Having … , he …

And the moral of the story is …

And he lived happily ever after.

D Which of the key phrases usually go:
- at or near the beginning of a story?
- in the middle of a story?
- at or near the end of a story?

7A Work in pairs. Prepare to tell your own version of the story in the pictures. Try to use some of the key phrases and include one of the sentences below. Make notes.

The map was wrinkled but still intact.

Among the bones a diamond glistened.

Wrapped in newspaper was a pair of rough leather boots.

B Practise telling the story.

C Tell your version of the story to other students. What similarities do your stories have? Whose is the most original?

writeback a story

8A Read one person's continuation of the recording in exercise 6B. Which sentence from exercise 7A do you think comes next?

He'd been looking forward to this moment for twenty years. Having waited so patiently, he knew his moment was close. He glanced out of the car window and saw, by the light of the moon, what he had been looking for. He pulled the car over and got out. He stretched for a moment, stiff from driving, and walked over to the tree. He ran his hand over the rough bark. 'This is it,' he said. Sitting down at the foot of the tree he was suddenly overcome with tiredness, so he lay down and slept.

When the sun came up, he stirred gradually as the songs of the birds rang out from the branches overhead. He went to the car, pulled out the shovel and began to dig. Within minutes his shovel hit upon something hard. It was a wooden box. He scrabbled in the ground and picked it up, holding it to his heart. With trembling hands he opened it.

B Write your version of the whole story (300–350 words).

CLEFT SENTENCES

1A Complete the sentences with the phrases in the box.

> What most impresses me
> What you should do is
> The reason I've come
> All I want to say
> One thing I've learned is that
> It was when I was reading that book
> The person who
> What they do

1 _____ is to talk about what we need to do.

2 _____ that I realised what I wanted to do with my life.

3 _____ is his ability to fix any problem.

4 _____ it's generally better to keep your thoughts to yourself.

5 _____ works harder than any of the other students is Kristina.

6 _____ call your manager to discuss the options.

7 _____ is that I think it's too expensive for students.

8 _____ is ask you lots of questions about your preferences and choose a product for you.

B Work in pairs. Make your own sentences using the prompts.

1 All I want to say about … is …

2 One thing I'd like to try is …

3 It was … who taught me …

4 What I think we should do is …

IDIOMS: RELAXING

2A Complete the sentences with one suitable word.

1 To _unwind_, I usually _play tennis_.

2 The last time I _____ my hair down was _at a New Year party_.

3 What helps me to take my _____ off work is _dancing salsa_.

4 I like hanging _____ _in the shopping centre_.

5 I need to slow _____ because _I work too much_.

6 _Exercise_ helps me when I want to switch _____ from work.

B Work in pairs. Make the sentences in Exercise 2A true for your partner by changing the pronouns and the sections in italics. If you don't know, guess.

To unwind, Davide goes swimming.

C Check your sentences with your partner.

ESCAPE

3A Complete the sentences with the words in the box.

> made a break   refuge   fled
> stranded   escape   released

1 Air travellers were left _____ because of icy conditions.

2 He was arrested, but managed to _____ from the police cell.

3 He was _____ by his captors after his family paid them a large sum of money.

4 Two of the prisoners _____ for it, but were soon recaptured.

5 After the floods, many villagers took _____ with friends higher up the mountain.

6 His attackers turned and _____ when the police arrived.

B Work in pairs. Use phrases from Exercise 3A to say what you would do in the situations below.

1 There is a serious crisis in your country. Your brother lives overseas and has offered to help you and your family leave.

2 You have been kidnapped by an armed gang. The person guarding you has fallen asleep. You think you might be able to steal one of their motorbikes.

3 You are walking along the coast when a huge storm strikes. You can see a small cave in the side of the cliff.

PARTICIPLE CLAUSES

4A Imagine your perfect day. Write a paragraph about it using the participle clauses below in any order.

- Refreshed by a good sleep, I …
- Having eaten, I …
- Not wanting to …
- Offered a choice of …
- Walking to …
- Having been taken to …
- Having met up with …

B Work in pairs and compare your paragraphs. Are they very different? How do they reflect your personalities and lifestyles?

EXCHANGING OPINIONS

5A Correct the mistakes in speaker B's responses.

1 A: Everyone has the right to freedom of expression.

   B: I agree with you up a point.

2 A: Freedom of speech means the media are allowed to publish absolutely anything.

   B: That ridiculous! There need to be controls.

3 A: The most important freedom we have is the right to vote.

   B: I could agree more.

4 A: People should be free to choose the country they live in.

   B: I suppose got a point, but there are obvious problems with what you're suggesting.

B Write your own responses to speaker A's statements. Discuss your ideas with other students.

BBC VIDEO PODCAST
Watch people talking about what makes them feel free on ActiveBook or on the website.

Authentic BBC interviews

www.pearsonELT.com/speakout

SPEAKING
> Choose objects that represent you
> Talk about memories
> Discuss ways to save time
> Describe a turning point in your life

LISTENING
> Listen to a programme about memory and smell
> Listen to people brainstorming ideas
> Watch a BBC documentary about the universe

READING
> Read about time capsules
> Read a personal story
> Read time-saving tips

WRITING
> Write a personal story
> Describe a major decision

BBC CONTENT
- Video podcast: What is the best time of life?
- DVD: Wonders of the Universe

UNIT 8

time

READING

1A What objects would you choose to put in a time capsule to represent your culture?

B Read the article about time capsules. Are any of your ideas mentioned?

2A Reread the article quickly to find out who, what or when the underlined words refer to.

1 <u>He</u> must be a famous Brazilian singer.

2 Maybe there's a lot of hunting in <u>that place</u>.

3 <u>It</u> is probably a really well-known restaurant in the area.

4 Maybe there's a lot of surveillance <u>there</u>.

5 The recordings were put <u>there</u> because it was probably safer than the Paris Opera House.

6 <u>He</u> believed his capsule would survive over 6,000 years.

7 <u>They</u> collaborated to create time capsules.

8 Only <u>at that time</u> will his grandchildren know exactly what Davisson put in the capsule.

B Discuss. What do the contents of the time capsules tell us about the different societies in the text?

VOCABULARY time expressions

3A Read extracts a)–f) from the article and answer the questions. Which phrases in bold describe:

1 the beginning of something? (2 expressions) Which one is more literary and used only for very big occasions?

2 a long time in the future? (1 expression)

3 something that was very close to happening? (2 expressions)

4 a situation that will continue far into the future? (1 expression)

a) **On the verge of** a fresh start, people get nostalgic.

b) … what objects and images represented us **at the dawn of** the new millennium?

c) … a new air conditioning system **was about to** be installed …

d) His capsule was to remain hidden **for the foreseeable future** …

e) … **in years to come** someone would find such glories of our time …

f) From **the outset**, it was to have been the world's biggest time capsule …

B Complete each sentence with two words.

1 In years, we will remember this as a golden age.

2 Scientists are the verge finding a cure for AIDS.

3 Humanity probably won't exist at dawn the next millennium.

4 We are enter an age of natural disasters.

5 From, the internet was able to unite people around the world.

6 Poverty will be with us for foreseeable.

C Do you agree with statements 1–6? Compare your ideas in pairs.

On the verge of a fresh start, people get nostalgic. The end of the millennium saw an unprecedented number of objects packed into boxes and buried in the ground, where later generations would find them and reflect on us, their ancestors. So what objects and images represented us at the dawn of the new millennium?

1 People in Curitiba, Brazil, chose a recording of the songs of Antonio Carlos Jobim, processed, packaged meat, an indoor toilet, a pair of jeans and a local tree with yellow flowers.

2 People in Bulawayo, Zimbabwe, chose a bottle of soil, a plastic cup used by beggars, an akierie (a walking stick used for hunting), and a pair of Bata 'Toughees' school shoes.

3 People in Fountain, Colorado, USA, chose a piece of barbed wire, a packet of cigarettes, a brick, a high school code of conduct, an issue of *Girl's Life*, a hearing aid, a recording of a high-speed car chase, Prozac, Valium, a TV remote control and a menu from Ralph's Fine Dining.

4 People in Bharatpur, India, chose a bag of soil, a closed-circuit TV camera, a chillum, a gold nose ring and a pair of flip-flops.

5 Arguably, the idea of 'history in a box' dates back to ancient Egypt, when the pharaohs were buried with their possessions. Since then, there have been numerous examples of time capsules, all with their own stories attached.

6 On Christmas Eve 1907, members of the Paris Opera placed twenty-four musical recordings into two containers made of iron and lead. They were going to leave these untouched in the opera house's basement for 100 years, but in 1912 they added more recordings, plus a gramophone with instructions on how to use it. The time capsule was supposed to be opened in 2007. However, in 1989, when a new air conditioning

system was about to be installed, it was discovered that one of the capsules had been broken into and the gramophone was missing. The remaining recordings were taken to France's National Library and opened eighteen years later.

7   Another time capsule was devised by Professor Thornwell Jacobs of Oglethorpe University, Georgia, USA, in 1940. While researching ancient history, he realised historians' lives would be easier if there were more artifacts available, so he created the Crypt of Civilization. He gathered hundreds of objects and sealed them in a waterproof room with a stainless steel door welded shut. His capsule was to remain hidden for the foreseeable future: Jacobs optimistically stipulated that the crypt wasn't meant to be opened until 8113.

8   In 1968, two Japanese companies, Panasonic and Mainichi Newspapers, worked together to create two identical time capsules. One of them would be opened regularly to check the condition of the contents, but the other wasn't going to be touched for five thousand years. Inside the capsules were 2,090 items, ensuring that in years to come someone would find such glories of our time as a glass eye, false teeth, dead insects encased in resin, an origami instruction book, fake money and handcuffs.

9   It isn't just big organisations that do it. Harold Keith Davisson, from Nebraska, USA, made a time capsule in 1975 because he wanted his grandchildren to know what life was like in the 1970s. He put it on his front lawn. Of approximately 5,000 items inside it, there was a suit and even a car. From the outset, it was to have been the world's biggest time capsule, but then Davisson learned that other people were building bigger ones. Deciding that actions speak louder than words, in 1983 he built a second capsule on top of the first, including a second car! The capsule will be opened in 2025.

GRAMMAR future in the past

4A Find sentences a)–d) in the article. Answer questions 1–3.

a) The time capsule was supposed to be opened in 2007. (paragraph 6)

b) His capsule was to remain hidden for the foreseeable future. (paragraph 7)

c) The other wasn't going to be touched for five thousand years. (paragraph 8)

d) It was to have been the world's biggest time capsule. (paragraph 9)

1   Which grammatical structures in sentences a)–d) talk about plans or intentions in the past? Underline them.

2   Which three structures suggest that the plan did not become a reality?

3   How many other examples of the 'future in the past' can you find in paragraphs 6–8 of the article? Which two describe plans that did not become reality?

B How do we make the 'future in the past'? Complete the table.

future	future in the past
am/is/are going to	1 _____ going to
am/is/are to + infinitive	2 _____ to + infinitive OR 3 _____ to + have + past participle
am/is/are meant to	4 _____ meant to
am/is/are supposed to	was/were supposed to

⟶ page 142 **LANGUAGEBANK**

PRACTICE

5 Rewrite the sentences using the words in brackets.

1   We planned for the opening of our time capsule in 2020. (to be) Our time capsule …

2   The document was secret. No one could see it until 2050. (not / be) The document …

3   The plan was for the safe to be locked for ten years, but someone opened it. (supposed) The safe …

4   The idea was to visit Montevideo, but we didn't have time. (going) We …

5   They expected it to be the world's biggest outdoor festival, but then the rain came. (have) It was to …

6   Jim went to Peru on holiday. He ended up living there for twenty years. (would) Jim went to Peru, where …

6A Complete the sentences for you, with two true and two false statements.

1   Recently, I was planning to … but …

2   When I was younger I was going to … but …

3   A few years ago I was supposed to … but …

4   A friend and I were thinking about … but …

B Work in pairs. Take turns to read your sentences. Guess which of your partner's sentences are true.

SPEAKING

7A Look at the photo. What kind of person do you think she is? Why?

B What objects represent you? Choose some items for a 'Museum of Me'. Include clothing, food or drink, books, magazines or DVDs. What stages of your life do they represent?

C Explain your ideas to other students. How many objects do you have in common?

The first idea on my list is an iPod. I chose this because …

VOCABULARY *PLUS* proverbs

8A Look at the extract from the article on page 93 and underline the proverb. Do you have a similar saying in your language?

Deciding that actions speak louder than words, in 1983 [Davisson] built a second capsule on top of the first …

B What are proverbs? Think of a definition and compare your ideas.

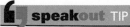 **speakout TIP**

Proverbs are short, simple statements that express a general truth or give advice. They often come from literary sources or refer to ways of life in the past, so may use some old vocabulary. They often have a strong rhythm. It is essential to use proverbs at the right moment and with the exact words. Do you know any proverbs in English? Tell other students.

9A Work in two groups. Group A: when would you use the proverbs below? Match proverbs 1–6 with situations a)–f). Do you have equivalents in your language? Group B: turn to page 162.

1 A picture is worth a thousand words.
2 Better safe than sorry.
3 Out of sight, out of mind.
4 Home is where the heart is.
5 Practise what you preach.
6 Rome wasn't built in a day.

a) I've enjoyed this trip, but I've had enough now.
b) You should leave home an hour early. There may be heavy traffic.
c) You always say it's important to arrive on time, but you were late!
d) The photo of the melting ice caps sent a powerful message.
e) I'd been away only two days, but I'd already forgotten my ex-girlfriend.
f) If you want to fulfil your ambitions, you'll need to study for six years.

B Work with a student from the other group and take turns. Show your list of proverbs to your partner. Explain them in any order. Can your partner guess which proverb you are describing?

10 ▶ 8.1 Listen to the proverbs. Notice the rhythm and repeat. Many proverbs have two or three main stresses. Listen again and underline the stressed syllables.

11 Work in pairs and discuss. Which of the proverbs do you generally agree with? Think of examples from your own life and tell your partner.

I agree with 'practice makes perfect'. I learnt the piano for twenty years. I'm not perfect, but I got much better by practising.

▮▮▶ page 155 **VOCABULARYBANK**

► **GRAMMAR** | ellipsis and substitution   ► **VOCABULARY** | memories   ► **HOW TO** | describe a memory

LISTENING

1 Work in pairs. What do the smells in the box make you think of?

> candles   cigarettes   vinegar   fresh bread
> coffee   perfume   disinfectant   sun cream
> lemons   petrol   paint

2A Read the radio programme listing. What kinds of memories are often evoked by particular smells? What is this phenomenon called?

> What does the smell of sun cream remind you of? Does it evoke strong memories of blue skies and happiness? Then perhaps you have experienced what psychologists have termed the Proust phenomenon. Why is it that particular smells bring back powerful childhood memories? In this BBC radio programme, Claudia Hammond explores the link between smell and memory.

B ▶ 8.2 Listen to the programme. Which smells from Exercise 1 are mentioned? What do the speakers say about each smell?

3A Which sentences are incorrect? Correct the mistakes.

1 The smell of mint sauce reminds one speaker of Sunday lunches in his childhood home.

2 One man remembers his nursery school when he smells privet (a type of hedge).

3 Psychologists think memories associated with photos are stronger than those evoked by smells.

4 Professor Chu uses unfamiliar smells to trigger autobiographical memories.

5 The woman used mints (polos) and perfume to cover up the smell of cigarettes.

6 When the man smells candles, he is reminded of when he played the church organ.

B Listen again to check your answers.

4A Complete the extracts with the phrases in the box.

> evocative smell   evoking memories
> takes me back in time   carried back in time

1 Now, ever had that feeling of being suddenly _____ by a particular odour?

2 There is, it seems, something special about smells when it comes to _____.

3 The smell that always really _____ is the smell of disinfectant.

4 For me, the most _____ is that smell you get when candles have just been snuffed out.

B Check your answers in audio script 8.2 on page 171.

C Work in groups and discuss. Which smells bring back strong memories for you?

GRAMMAR   ellipsis and substitution

5A Check what you know. Read the conversations and answer questions a) and b).

a) What words have been left out where you see ▲? Why is this?

b) Look at the words in bold. What do they refer to? What words do they replace?

1 A: ▲ Remember any special smells from your childhood?
   B: Yes, I **do** actually. ▲ The smell of my grandmother's perfume.

2 A: The smell of pine trees reminds me of holidays in Greece.
   B: Does it ▲? I've never been **there**.

3 A: ▲ Got any photos of your family?
   B: Yes, ▲ **lots**.

B Read the rules and answer the questions.

> **Rule:**
> Use ellipsis to leave out a word, or words, when the context is obvious. In informal speech, we often leave out the beginnings or endings of common phrases.

1 Which words have been left out of the phrases/questions below?

Ever been to Spain?

See you.

> **Rule:**
> Use substitution to replace a word or phrase with a single word (e.g. *so, do, many, one, these, some, it, them, there, this, that*) in order to avoid repetition.

2 What does *so* replace?

A: Got everything you need?

*B: I think **so**.*

〰➡ page 142 **LANGUAGEBANK**

PRACTICE

6A Underline the correct alternatives.

1 A: Are you coming to the party?
  B: Yes, I think *do/so/not*.

2 A: Did you just delete the file?
  B: I hope *not/such/do*.

3 A: Do you want to try this perfume?
  B: No, but I'll try that *some/much/one*.

4 A: Do you think we'll have enough time to discuss this later?
  B: We'll have *so/a little/one* time.

5 A: Are you going away on holiday this year?
  B: No. Ann Marie doesn't have enough money and *more/nor/so* do I.

6 A: Are you sure you've got enough copies for everyone?
  B: Yes, I've got *none/one/lots*.

B ▶ 8.3 Cross out any words which could be left out of the conversations in Exercise 6A. Listen and check your answers.

7 Work in pairs. Student A: turn to page 161. Student B: turn to page 162. Take turns to read out your sentences and choose the correct responses.

VOCABULARY memories

8A Complete the sentences. Choose the correct word in brackets and put it in the appropriate place.

1 This place lots of memories for us. (gets/holds)

2 When I hear those old songs it back a lot of memories. (brings /takes)

3 It's one of my memories. (oldest/earliest)

4 I have very memories of my time at primary school. (vague/slim)

5 I only have a very recollection of what my grandparents' house looked like. (light/hazy)

6 It was a long time ago, but I remember it. (strongly/vividly)

7 I remember her dress. It was blue with a red belt. (distinctly/heavily)

8 Every time I go there, the memories come back. (flooding/running)

B Which words from Exercise 8A can you use to talk about memories which are not very strong? Which words can you use to talk about memories which are very strong or clear?

▶ page 155 **VOCABULARYBANK**

SPEAKING

9A Read about the website and choose a stage of your life to talk about.

talkingmemories.com

Do you have vivid memories of your childhood or is it just a hazy blur? At talkingmemories.com you can record your memories of particular stages or events in your life, adding photos and videos. It allows you to preserve meaningful memories of your life, record important milestones and share memories of special events with friends, family and future generations.

B Prepare to talk about memories from that stage of your life. Make notes using the prompts below.

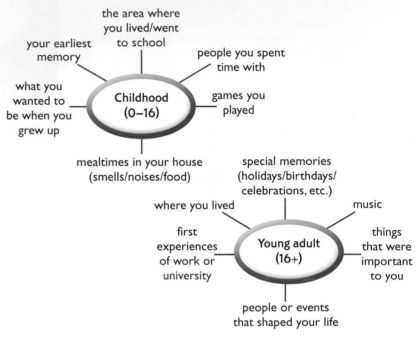

Childhood (0–16): your earliest memory, the area where you lived/went to school, people you spent time with, games you played, what you wanted to be when you grew up, mealtimes in your house (smells/noises/food)

Young adult (16+): where you lived, special memories (holidays/birthdays/celebrations, etc.), music, first experiences of work or university, things that were important to you, people or events that shaped your life

C Work in groups and take turns. Talk about the special memories you have. Do others in the group have similar memories from that time?

WRITING a personal story

10A Read the personal story on page 97. Answer the questions.

1 Why was the fig tree so important?

2 What happened to the house?

B Read the advice for writing a story for a magazine. Does the writer of *The Fig Tree* follow the advice?

1 Remember your audience (who is going to read this?) and use a range of structures and vocabulary.

2 Use an informal, chatty style. It makes your article sound more personal, so the reader can identify with you.

3 Capture the reader's attention with an anecdote, something surprising or a strong image.

4 'Close the circle': the ending could echo the beginning or refer to the wording in the task.

LEARN TO improve descriptive writing

11 Read guidelines a)–d) for descriptive writing and follow instructions 1–4 below.

a) Include precise language. Use specific adjectives and nouns and strong action verbs (verbs that carry a specific meaning) to give life to the picture you are painting in the reader's mind.

The lion ate (weak) *the antelope.*
The ravenous (specific) *lion devoured* (strong) *the antelope.*

b) Include all the senses. Remember to describe sounds (using onomatopoeia – where the sound of the word imitates the meaning being described), smells, tastes and textures.

The car <u>screeched</u> to a halt.
The <u>murmuring</u> of innumerable bees.

c) Make use of contrasts. Describe how someone's mood changed from good to bad, or describe a location at different times of year.

d) Use figurative language (metaphor, simile, personification). Imagery can help to engage a reader.

The stars danced playfully in the sky.
(personification – giving human qualities to something which is not human)

Her home was a prison.
(metaphor – when you say one thing is another thing)

She felt as free as a bird.
(simile – when you say one thing is like another thing)

1 Find examples of specific adjectives and strong action verbs in the story of *The Fig Tree*.

2 Find an example of onomatopoeia. Where does the writer describe a texture?

3 How does the writer use contrast in this story?

4 Find an example of personification of an object and an example of metaphor.

speakout TIP

It's important that you communicate to your reader exactly what you mean in the clearest possible way. Using strong verbs and adjectives helps you to paint accurate pictures of what you mean in the reader's mind. How do the verbs change the meaning of the following sentences? '*I love you,*' *he said.* / '*I love you,*' *he screamed.* / '*I love you,*' *he whispered.* / '*I love you,*' *he mumbled.* Keep a list of strong verbs.

12 Read the instructions and write a personal story.

1 Work alone. Think about any particular people, objects or places which hold special memories for you. Can you remember particular sights, sounds, smells or textures associated with them?

2 Make some notes about the memory, including personal details (how you felt, why it was special, etc.).

3 Write your story (220–250 words). Add a title.

4 Check your writing. Try to improve the description by using more precise language.

THE FIG TREE

I remember we used to visit my grandmother's house at weekends. It was a huge house with gardens leading down to a field, and it seemed almost like a palace to me. At the bottom of the field was an orchard, planted with apples, and twenty-one walnut trees. In the middle of the field stood an ancient fig tree. It was here, in the tree, that my cousins and I would sit and play for hours on end. I can remember the smell of the green leaves, the sticky sap that would leak from the leaves and the figs as they ripened. We each had our own special branch and we would climb up and then sit looking out over the countryside. I can almost feel the warmth of the sun on our faces and the feeling of safety and security as we hid among the branches. In that tree, we would sit and chatter about life, feast on the sweet, crunchy apples, hold meetings, tell jokes, read books, make plans, have fig fights and discuss what we wanted to be when we grew up. The fig tree knew all our secrets.

When I was twelve, my grandmother moved into a small flat and we stopped going to the house. But a few years ago, I was in the area, so I drove back there to see if it was how I had remembered it. The house was almost unrecognisable. It had been turned into a doctor's surgery, with signposts all around and cars parked all over the drive. The gardens had been redesigned, and there were pathways to walk along and benches to sit on and enjoy the views. Gone was my grandmother's wild flower garden. But behind the house, in the middle of the field, just as if time had never passed, stood the fig tree, full of lush green leaves, and juicy figs. Its branches hung heavily towards the ground, almost beckoning me to climb up. Just standing in the field brought all the memories of my grandmother and our life there flooding back to me. And touching the smooth bark on the trunk, it was all I could do to resist sprinting to the end of the field to pick an apple or two and then back to the fig tree to enjoy the rest of the warm afternoon.

VOCABULARY collocations with *time*

1 Work in groups. Look at the photos and discuss which activities are the biggest time-wasters. Which waste your time? What other things waste time?

2A Complete the expressions in bold below with the words in the box. What do the expressions mean?

| in | pushed | the | to | ~~world~~ | spare | hands |

1 What would you do if you had **all the time in the** *world*?
2 Are you ever _____ **for time**? When?
3 When was the last occasion you had lots of **time on your** _____?
4 Do you wish you had more **time** _____ **yourself**?
5 When you're bored, how do you **pass** _____ **time**?
6 In your work/studies, do you usually finish tasks **just** _____ **time** or **with time to** _____? What does it depend on?

B Discuss questions 1–6 with other students.

FUNCTION discussing ideas

3 Work in pairs. Read the list of ways to save time. Which do you think are good ideas? Which are not serious?

Five time-savers that will put years on your life

Prioritise
Some tasks are important and urgent. Others are important but not urgent. Most are neither. Forget about them until they become important <u>and</u> urgent.

Don't multi-task
You think you're doing lots of things well at the same time. You aren't. You're doing lots of things badly at the same time, which will need re-doing later once you realise you've made a bad job of them. Focus on one thing at a time and do it properly.

Kill distractions
Ignore email, leave the mobile in your car, unplug the phone and remove all TVs within sight. If you want to work, work.

Don't have children
This means you won't need to change nappies, prepare baby food or deal with tantrums. When they're older, you won't waste time being a taxi service.

Be creative
Take gifts: instead of traipsing into town to buy flowers for your partner, just pick them from the local park. Or entertainment: don't waste two hours watching the latest Bond film on DVD; read the synopsis on the back of the box and imagine the film.

4A ▶ 8.4 Listen to people brainstorming ways to save time in their daily lives. Tick the ideas they mention.

| read only the conclusion   take a short cut   phone first
| divide up your day   have a routine   take the lift
| bring in an expert   use the microwave   do it yourself
| make lists   read the instructions first

B Are the statements true (T) or false (F)? Listen again to check.

1 The student sometimes makes notes from a text.
2 Two of the women use microwaves to save time.
3 One man says lists help him divide up the day.
4 One woman saves time by always reading the instructions on how to assemble furniture.
5 One woman says it's a waste of time to call a technology expert to fix your problems.
6 One man says using the phone often wastes time.

5A Read audio script 8.4 on page 172. Find expressions for acknowledging an idea or introducing an alternative. Write them in the correct column of the table below.

acknowledging an idea	introducing an alternative
Right, OK.	Mind you, …
Sure.	

B Work in pairs. Add the expressions in the box to the correct column of the table.

| But looking at it another way, …   Alternatively, …
| Definitely.   (Although) having said that, …
| I know what you mean.   I never thought of that.
| On the other hand, …   Yes and no.

8A Here are five more expressions for soliciting information. Which words do you think are missing?

1 What ___else___?
2 Can you tell us _____?
3 Can you go into more _____?
4 Is there anything we've _____?
5 Anyone managed to _____ up with other ideas?

B The answers are below but in the wrong order. Complete the expressions.

detail   missed   more   come   ~~else~~

speakout TIP

We use expressions with *any*: *any* ideas, *anything*, *anyone*, etc. when we don't want to be specific. It means that it doesn't matter which or who. Which word beginning with *any* could be replaced by *anybody*?

9A ▶ 8.5 Listen to the expressions in Exercise 8A and choose the correct answer.

1 Which words are stressed in these expressions?
a) the first word in each expression
b) the last word in each expression
2 What type of words are stressed?
a) 'content' words, which tend to be nouns, verbs, adjectives and adverbs
b) grammar words such as prepositions and auxiliary verbs

B Listen again and repeat.

10 Put the words in the correct order to make questions. Add capital letters.

1 A: tell / more / us / you / can /?
   B: Well, for example, we could put a 'To Do' list on the wall.
2 A: you / go / detail / can / more / into /?
   B: Yes. Every Wednesday, we could spend an hour discussing the issue.
3 A: missed / there / is / we've / anything /?
   B: No, I think that's everything.
4 A: else / of / think / can / anything / you /?
   B: Yes, we haven't mentioned homework.
5 A: ideas / come / anyone / with / to / managed / other / up /?
   B: Sorry, nothing else from me.

SPEAKING

11A Work alone. Think of as many ways as possible to save time while working, studying, travelling or doing housework.

B Work in groups and follow the instructions.
1 Choose one facilitator to lead the discussion, solicit ideas and make sure everyone has a chance to speak.
2 Choose one scribe to write down all the ideas.
3 Share your ideas.
4 Divide the ideas into: a) really good, b) interesting but not always practical, c) too difficult to implement.
5 Present your group's best ideas to the class.

6 Cross out the incorrect alternative in each sentence.

1 Shopping online is quicker. *On the other hand, / Mind you, / That's true,* you're taking a risk because you don't see the product or the vendor in the flesh.
2 So you think we should bring a map? *I know what you mean; / But looking at it another way, / I'm with you there;* it's easy to get lost in these parts.
3 Eating fast food saves time, but *I never thought of that, / looking at it another way, / on the other hand,* it's not very healthy.
4 So you think we should leave early in the morning? *That's a good idea. / Yes and no. / That makes sense.* The traffic gets really bad later in the day.
5 Do you really think I should delegate more? *Having said that, / I never thought of that. / That's interesting.* I thought I had to do everything myself.
6 I'm always pushed for time. *Having said that, / Mind you, / Alternatively,* my time management is terrible! I do everything at the last minute.

▶ page 142 **LANGUAGEBANK**

LEARN TO solicit more information

7 Read an extract from the recording in Exercise 4A. Underline three expressions for soliciting more information.

'Yeah. Okay, well anything to add? I mean to sum up, we've talked about the idea that you use the microwave, you make lists, you read the instructions first properly and divide up your day so you have things sort of more organised. Can you think of anything else? Any other suggestions?'

DVD PREVIEW

1A Complete the sentence below with two words in the box.

science   universe   nature   art

Whilst _____ seeks to understand reality through the observation of emotions and the sharing of human experience, _____ relies more on logical reasoning and detailed analysis.

B Compare your answers in pairs. In general, which approach do you tend to accept?

2 Read the programme information. What concept is discussed in this episode?

BBC Wonders of the Universe

Who are we? Where do we come from? For thousands of years, humanity has turned to religion and myth to answer these questions. But in this BBC series, Professor Brian Cox presents a different set of answers – answers provided by science. In this episode, Brian seeks to understand the nature of time and its role in creating both the universe and ourselves. Using the Perito Moreno glacier in Patagonia, Argentina, Brian explores the concept of the arrow of time, describing how time is characterised by irreversible change, and why sequences happen in the order they do.

▶ DVD VIEW

3 Watch the DVD. Number the ideas in the order they are mentioned.

a) There's a scientific reason for why the world doesn't run in reverse.

b) It's human nature to want to find the answer to these fundamental questions.

c) Permanent change is a fundamental part of what it means to be human.

d) The glacier has been moving down the valley for tens of thousands of years.

4A Complete the extracts.

1 Events always happen in the same order. They're never _____ and they never go backwards.

2 We never see waves travelling across lakes, coming together and bouncing chunks of ice back _____.

3 We are compelled to travel into the _____.

4 And that's because the arrow of time dictates that as each moment passes, things _____.

5 I suppose it's kind of the joy and _____ of our lives.

6 In the life of the universe, just as in our lives, everything is _____.

B Watch the DVD again to check.

5 Work in pairs and discuss the questions.

1 What do you think about the point Professor Cox is trying to explain? Do you think the glacier is a useful metaphor for the arrow of time?

2 Are you someone who relishes or resists change?

speakout a turning point

6A ▶ 8.6 Listen to someone talking about major turning points in her life. Answer the questions.

1 What were the three important decisions?

2 Does she regret the decisions she made?

3 How is her life different from her sister's?

B Listen again and choose the correct alternatives to complete the key phrases.

> ### keyphrases
>
> My parents gave me the option to *go to a specialised theatrical school/stay at home*.
>
> There was *a lot of pressure on me to …/no pressure either way*.
>
> I made the decision to *go to a theatre school/go to a comprehensive school*.
>
> Luckily for me, *it's panned out/it's turned out OK*.
>
> I found myself faced with *a dilemma/another decision*.
>
> The next major decision … was whether to *move house/have children or not*.
>
> I … wonder *what would have happened if … /if I made the right decision*.

7A Prepare to talk about a turning point in your life. Think about the questions and make notes.

1 What was the decision? Who was involved? Did anyone or anything influence your decision?

2 How did the decision affect what happened afterwards?

3 How might things have been different now had you made a different decision?

B Work in groups. Discuss your decisions and how they have affected your lives.

writeback a major decision

8A Work in pairs and read the forum entry. Do you think Jason made the right decisions?

Tell us about a pivotal moment in your life

Jason, Australia: I'd say that the major pivotal moment of my life early on was when I was eleven years old and my parents decided to divorce. It was up to me to decide who I wanted to live with. At that time, my dad was living in a completely different part of Australia to me and my mum. After some deliberation, I chose to go and live with my dad.

Looking back, it was a hard decision to make for an eleven-year-old, and I do sometimes wonder if I made the right choice. If I could turn back time, I wonder if my relationship with my mother would be any better now had I made a different choice. I suppose I have a sense of regret about that.

However, if I hadn't gone to live with my dad, I wouldn't have met my girlfriend at the time. We were together for over three years and when she wanted to move to England I gave up a really good career in Australia to move with her. That was fine for a while, but we eventually split up and then there was nothing to keep me in the UK.

I came back to Australia, but it hasn't been easy to rebuild my career. At the end of the day, I think your guiding principle should be that blood is thicker than water, and it's usually best to put your family first.

B Write about a major decision in your life (250–300 words).

TIME EXPRESSIONS

1A Write sentences about your classmates.

1 For the foreseeable future, _____ will probably …

2 _____ is about to …

3 From the outset of the class, we all realised _____ was …

4 We will all remember _____ in years to come because …

B Work in groups. Read some of your sentences aloud, but don't say the name of the person. Can the others guess who you wrote about?

FUTURE IN THE PAST

2A Underline the correct alternatives.

Here are some excuses made by absent or late employees.

I [1]*meant to/supposed to* be in the office at 8.00, but my dog was stressed out after a family reunion.

I [2]*was on the verge of/was to have* written the report at the weekend, but my finger got stuck in a bowling ball.

My husband and I [3]*were meant/were for* to go away for the weekend, but we had car trouble. It's now fixed so we're going today (Monday).

And some excuses for bad behaviour in relationships:

I was [4]*to go to/going to* call you, but my three-year-old niece dropped my phone in a swimming pool.

I [5]*had been/was planning* to break up with you in person, but I thought you'd prefer this email.

And finally, two excuses for neglected homework.

I read the questions, but I didn't realise we [6]*were supposed/were suppose* to answer them.

I [7]*meant for/was going* to do it, but I started worrying about the oil crisis and I couldn't focus.

B Write excuses for the situations below. Use the future in the past. Compare your ideas. Who has the best excuses?

- You were absent from work.
- You forgot to meet a friend.
- You didn't do your homework.

ELLIPSIS AND SUBSTITUTION

3A Complete the sentences with a suitable word.

1 A: Do you think we're going to be late?
   B: No, I hope _____.

2 A: Are you enjoying the fish?
   B: My husband hasn't tried it yet, but I _____ and it's delicious.

3 A: Do you expect your decision to have repercussions?
   B: Yes, I expect _____.

4 A: It's a spectacular part of the country.
   B: Is it? I've never been _____.

5 A: Will we see you on Saturday?
   B: No, we'd hoped to be able to come, but I'm afraid we _____.

6 A: Do you mind if I borrow one of these umbrellas?
   B: Of course _____! Take _____.

B Cross out words in sentences 1–6 above that could be omitted in casual conversation.

C Practise the conversations in pairs.

MEMORIES

4 Complete the sentences with the words in the box.

| vague | flooding | earliest |
| holds | distinctly | brings |

1 My grandmother's house _____ lots of memories for me.

2 Looking at photos _____ back wonderful memories of happy times.

3 I have a very _____ recollection of my great-grandfather, who was an artist, but I can't really remember him well.

4 I _____ remember telling you to leave the key for me.

5 As soon as I walked into the room, the memories came _____ back.

6 One of my _____ memories is of my parents and me on a beach in France.

DISCUSSING IDEAS

5A Use a word from each box to complete the conversation.

makes	I'm	another	mind
thought	other	that's	having
a	know		

| said | you | what | true | with |
| of | perfect | hand | good | way |

A: University students should spend their first day getting to know the buildings and staff. This will save them time in the long run.

B: That's [1]____ ____ idea. I'd never [2]____ ____ that.

A: They should also attend a seminar on ways to save money.

B: That [3]____ ____ sense. Although [4]____ ____ that, aren't there advisors to help them with that?

A: Yes, there are, but often students don't know where to find them.

B: Yes, [5]____ ____. But looking at it [6]____ ____, shouldn't students take responsibility?

A: I [7]____ ____ you mean. But on the [8]____ ____, university is the first time they have had to fend for themselves. Many of them just aren't prepared.

B: [9]____ ____ you there. I remember how naïve I was when I first left home. [10]____ ____, I soon learned!

B Work in pairs. Think of things that students at your school/office should do on their first day. Write a conversation using the phrases in Exercise 5A. Practise your conversation and perform it for other students.

UNIT 9

SPEAKING
> Choose sculptures to suit clients' needs
> Ask creative questions
> Rant or rave
> Recommend a cultural place

LISTENING
> Listen to people talking about where they get their ideas
> Listen to rants and raves
> Watch a BBC documentary about an art gallery

READING
> Read about living statues
> Read a review of a television programme

WRITING
> Write a review
> Write a recommendation

BBC CONTENT
▯ Video podcast: Do you do anything creative in your life?
◉ DVD: The Culture Show: Tate Modern is 10!

UNIT

9

inspiration

▶ **Living art**   p104

▶ **Feeling inspired**   p107

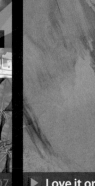

▶ **Love it or hate it**   p110

▶ **Tate Modern is 10!**   p112

VOCABULARY   adjectives: the arts

1A Look at three works of art that have been displayed in Trafalgar Square, London. What do you think of each 'statue'?

B Work in two groups. Group A: look at box A. Group B: look at box B. Answer questions 1–4 below.

A

> unconventional   thought-provoking   moving   bleak
> impressive   compelling   charming   well-received
> poignant

B

> overrated   offbeat   stylish   amusing   striking
> dramatic   stunning   heart-breaking   subtle

1 Which words do you know? Use a dictionary to check the meaning of unknown words.

2 Which art forms do you think these words usually describe?

3 Which words can be used about people?

4 Can you use any of the words to describe the art in the photos?

C Work with a student from the other group. Teach them your words. Think of films, books, music or works of art that fit the adjectives in Exercise 1B. Think of as many as you can in two minutes.

The film Avatar was stunning.

D ▶ 9.1 Say the words in Exercise 1B aloud. Which three words are spelt differently from their pronunciation? Listen and repeat.

thought-provoking ...

❝ speakout TIP

In English, many words look different from the way they sound. Sometimes, combinations of letters in the middle of words aren't pronounced in the way we expect. What are the silent letters in the following words: *whistling, cupboard, foreigner, mosquito*? Now say the whole word.

READING

2A Read the title of the article. What do you think it is about?

B Read the article to check your ideas.

3 Match paragraphs 1–6 with headings a)–f).

a) The first and the last

b) Amusing or thought-provoking? What the 'artists' did

c) Up on the plinth – the artists' viewpoint

d) Antony Gormley's 'One and Other'

e) What to do with the fourth plinth

f) The computer's choice: art for everyone by everyone

4 Find words/expressions in the article with the following meanings.

1 show (paragraph 1)

2 leading to (paragraph 1)

3 organise (paragraph 1)

4 worries or concerns (paragraph 2)

5 people who are watching (paragraph 2)

6 unsystematically (paragraph 3)

7 range (paragraph 3)

8 went on longer than (paragraph 4)

9 calming (paragraph 6)

10 as if someone enjoys watching other people's private lives (paragraph 6)

5 Discuss. What do you think of the project? Have there been any similar projects in your country?

Sixty minutes of fame: living statues

1 In London's Trafalgar Square stand three statues. These depict old soldiers – British heroes who helped build its empire. The fourth plinth (the base on which a statue stands) stood empty for years, engendering a national debate about what should go on it. Should it be a statue of another British hero – Winston Churchill, for example, or John Lennon? Should it be a striking piece of modern art or something representative of modern multicultural Britain? While the debate went on, Antony Gormley, one of Britain's best-known sculptors, was asked to orchestrate a project to fill the plinth for 100 days.

2 Gormley decided to offer the plinth to members of the public, who would stand, sit or lie on it in their own piece of performance art. While there, they could speak of their preoccupations, stand up (literally) for their beliefs, reveal their fantasies, or simply enact their everyday lives in front of onlookers. It was an unconventional project, bringing the world of reality TV onto the street. It was called 'One and Other' and would have a different person occupying the plinth every hour for twenty-four hours. The plan was to develop a compelling portrait of the UK in the twenty-first century. Gormley also seemed to be challenging the idea that only famous old soldiers or politicians should be depicted in statues.

3 Gormley invited the public to submit their names for a spot on the plinth. They didn't need to say what they were planning to do once they were there. Rather than select from the 14,500 entries according to artistic skill or ambition, participants were chosen at random by a computer. They ranged in age from sixteen to eighty-three and their professions covered the full spectrum of British life, from professors to blacksmiths to rubbish collectors.

4 The first 'living statue' was housewife Rachel Wardell, who took her place on the plinth on Monday 6 July, 2009. She did it 'to show my kids that you can do and be part of anything'. The last was a medical photographer, Emma Burns, who read out a moving short story about the ninety-six victims of a disaster at a British football stadium in the 1980s. She overran her hour, but as there was no one to take her place, she was allowed to finish.

5 In between Wardell and Burns, there were 2,398 others. They came up with wildly different ways to spend their sixty minutes of fame, some thought-provoking, some poignant, some amusing. Darren Cooper performed a silent disco for an hour, while fifty of his friends stood below, listening to the same music at the same time on their headphones. Jane Clyne dressed up as a bee to highlight the decline in the numbers of bees due to environmental damage. Heather Pringle, a student, marked her twentieth birthday on the plinth, and celebrated with a solo birthday party. David Rosenberg, a forty-one-year-old designer from London, used a folding pink bicycle to generate electricity to light up his suit.

6 And what was it like up on the fourth plinth? Did the performers have to put up with nerves and noisy onlookers? Cooper said, 'I was quite nervous at first, but once I started dancing, the nerves went away and I had the best time.' Rachel Lockwood said, 'It felt very peaceful and serene on the plinth looking down at everyone living their lives. All I could hear was the noise of the fountains and the traffic below. I felt like I was isolated and in a bubble.' Martin Douglas said, 'It was strangely voyeuristic watching people go about their daily lives. Not many people look up, you know!'

GRAMMAR verb tenses for unreal situations

6A Read some comments on the 'One and Other' project. Which ones do you agree with?

1 This is great. It's about time people realised that art is for everyone.

2 These are normal people acting as if they were artists, but what they're doing isn't art.

3 I wish I was brave enough to do something like that in front of everyone. I admire them for their courage.

4 Imagine you had sixty minutes to perform in public. I think it would be hard.

5 I'd rather nobody noticed me in public. I'd hate to be up there.

6 What if I had been on the plinth? I'd have done something about world peace.

B Look at the underlined clauses in the comments above and answer the questions.

1 Which tense are the final verbs in each underlined clause? One of the verbs is a different tense. Which one?

2 Do these situations refer to a) the past, or b) an imaginary/hypothetical situation?

➠ page 144 **LANGUAGEBANK**

PRACTICE

7 Complete the sentences with the words in the box.

| time | rather | would | imagine | if | had |
| was | hadn't | | | | |

1 He walked in here as though he _____ a hero.

2 If only I _____ lost my lottery ticket, I'd be rich!

3 It's _____ you stopped complaining and did something!

4 Supposing you _____ seen her! What would you have said?

5 I'd _____ nobody knew about my plans.

6 Hey, _____ you could speak twenty languages! Wouldn't that be amazing?

7 What _____ you could retire right now? Would you?

8 I _____ sooner do a research paper than take the exam.

8 Answer the questions. Then compare your answers with other students.

1 Would you rather somebody took you to a film or to the theatre? A rock concert or a ballet?

2 Imagine you could own any painting or sculpture in the world. Which would you choose?

3 Supposing you were asked to act in a soap opera. Under what conditions would you accept?

4 If someone from your home town said, 'It's time we did something cultural,' what would you suggest?

SPEAKING

9A You are an art dealer. Read about your clients 1–3 and look at the sculptures on this page and on page 162. Decide which sculpture to recommend to each company.

1 Icontech.com is an internet start-up run by twenty-one-year-old twins. There is no one over thirty in the company and everyone wears jeans and shorts. The company recently relocated to a stylish one-storey office. The owners want a dramatic sculpture for the roof. It must fit their company motto: Live for Now.

2 Daniels and Stone is a conservative, traditional law firm. The new boss wants a more exciting image for the firm, but doesn't want to offend old clients. He is looking for a sculpture to go outside the main entrance of the building.

3 Green Tuesdays Ltd is a company that sells organic food. It is run by fifteen ex-hippies who live in a multi-coloured bus. In two years, the company has expanded by 180 percent and now has a stunning new office building surrounded by trees and hills. The owners want a striking sculpture to go in reception.

B Work in groups and discuss your choices.

VOCABULARY *PLUS* three-part multi-word verbs

10A Read three extracts from the article on page 105 and answer the questions below.

a) While there [on the plinth], they could stand up for their beliefs.

b) They came up with wildly different ways to spend their sixty minutes of fame.

c) Did the performers have to put up with nerves and noisy onlookers?

1 Underline the multi-word verbs. What do they mean?

2 Is it possible to split three-part multi-word verbs? (Can we say: *he came up with an idea* and *he came up an idea with*?)

3 Where is the main stress on three-part multi-word verbs?

B Read the advice for learning multi-word verbs. Which pieces of advice do you agree with?

1 Write full examples of multi-word verbs in your notebook because they are best understood in context.

2 Learn all the meanings of the most common phrasal verbs by heart. The top ten are *go on, carry out, set up, pick up, go back, come back, go out, point out, find out, come up*.

3 Never use phrasal verbs in formal English.

4 Don't learn long lists of multi-word verbs because there are too many and they have different meanings. Instead, 'discover' them in texts.

5 Learn the general meanings of some particles (see page 61) because you can sometimes guess the meaning of the multi-word verb from the particle.

6 Group the multi-word verbs either by topic (e.g. friendship: *get on, fall out*), main verb (e.g. *get up, get over*), or particle (e.g. *come up, eat up*) in your notebook.

11 Choose the correct multi-word verb to complete each sentence.

1 You stole the money, but you'll never *get away with/get round to* it!

2 I've been meaning to write to Sally but I never *get away with/get round to* it.

3 I don't really *go along with/go in for* dangerous sports; I prefer golf.

4 I'm happy to *go along with/go in for* your plans.

5 Because of the price, I don't know if we'll buy the flat; it'll all *come up with/come down to* money.

6 We have twenty-four hours to *come up with/come down to* a plan to save this company!

7 I'm not going to *put down to/put up with* this noise for one minute longer!

8 He had problems reading, which he *put down to/put up with* his poor education.

9 You have to *stand up for/stand up to* that bully, or he'll walk all over you.

10 My father taught me to *stand up for/stand up to* my beliefs.

11 I hope to *catch up with/catch on to* you at the party next month.

12 The police will never *catch up with/catch on to* this little scam!

12 Choose three questions to answer. Compare your answers in pairs.

1 Is there anything you've wanted to do for a long time but haven't **got round to**?

2 When you need ideas desperately, how do you **come up with** them?

3 What irritations of modern life do you find difficult to **put up with**?

4 Is there anyone from your past you'd love to **catch up with**?

5 Do you **go in for** any dangerous sports or do you prefer a quiet life?

6 Can you think of a time when you **stood up for** your beliefs?

▶ page 156 **VOCABULARYBANK**

▶ **GRAMMAR** | adverbials   ▶ **VOCABULARY** | ideas   ▶ **HOW TO** | give a review

VOCABULARY ideas

3A Write a list of all the phrases you can think of which use the words *idea or ideas.* You have two minutes.
have an idea, think of an idea …

B Look at the list of common collocations below. Does it include any of the phrases on your list? Can you think of other ways to express the phrases in bold?

1 He's always **coming up with novel ideas.**
2 I'm **toying with the idea of** going back to college.
3 What **gave you the idea for** the book?
4 **The idea came to me** while I was having a bath.
5 We had a meeting **to brainstorm ideas for** the new advertising campaign.
6 We **hit on the idea of** renting a cottage.
7 **Whose bright idea was it** to leave the washing out in the rain?
8 The company is looking for people who can **come up with original ideas.**
9 **It seemed like a good idea** at the time.
10 Camping in the middle of winter was **a ridiculous idea.**

C Answer the questions.

a) Which phrase is often used ironically (to mean the opposite of what you say)?
b) Which phrases talk about having new ideas?
c) Which phrase is used when you're considering something?
d) Which phrases refer to bad ideas?

4A Which phrases in Exercise 3B could you use to talk about the following situations?

1 Your younger brother is thinking about going to university, but isn't sure if he wants to.
2 Your business has a new product and is looking for some new ideas for ways to sell it.
3 You've been wondering what to do for your birthday, and when you were out today you suddenly had an idea.
4 You convinced your family to go out for a walk, but the weather turned bad and now everyone's in a bad mood.

B Choose two or three phrases in Exercise 3B. Write sentences to describe situations in which you might use the phrase. Read your sentences to a partner. Try to guess the phrase.

LISTENING

1A Work in pairs and discuss the questions.

1 Where do you think people in different jobs might find inspiration, e.g. musicians, artists, writers, designers, chefs, architects?
2 Write a list of six ways to find inspiration.

B ▶ 9.2 Listen to four people talking about where they get their ideas. Make notes about what their job is and where they get their inspiration.

C Did the speakers mention any of the ideas from your list in Exercise 1A?

2A Answer the questions.

1 Why does the writer like to do the washing up?
2 Why does the artist like photos? What does she do with them?
3 Why does the chef enjoy using old recipe books that he has had for a while?
4 What kinds of things does the fashion designer put on her inspiration board? How does it work?

B Listen again to check your answers.

C Discuss. What do you think of the ideas suggested? What kinds of things do you do when you're looking for new ideas/inspiration?

▌ **speakout** TIP

The collocations in Exercise 3 were taken from the *Longman Advanced Dictionary of Contemporary English.* Most good dictionaries will show lists of common collocations. Use a good dictionary and find some common collocations for the word *creativity.* Write them in your notebook.

⟹ page 156 **VOCABULARYBANK**

GRAMMAR adverbials

5A Read the six suggestions for finding inspiration. Tick any ideas you like.

B Work in pairs. Cover the text and try to remember the six ideas.

6A Look at the underlined adverbials in the text. Replace them with the words/phrases in the box.

> most probably   alone   at the same time
> to keep track of his observations   willingly   annually

B Read the rule and answer the questions.

> **Rule:**
>
> An adverbial gives us additional information about a verb, an adjective or another adverb. It can be a single word (*frequently, eventually*) or a group of words (*on your own, for his ideas*) which act together to give detail.

Which adverbials in the text describe:

1 how something happens/should happen? (adverbial of manner)
2 when something happens? (adverbial of time)
3 how often something happens? (adverbial of frequency)
4 the probability of something happening? (adverbial of probability)
5 why something happened? (adverbial of purpose)

C Find at least three other examples of adverbials in the text.

▶ page 144 **LANGUAGEBANK**

PRACTICE

7A Expand sentences 1–6 using the adverbials in a)–f). Make sure you put each adverbial in the correct position.

1 I ¹*totally* forgot to call you ²*yesterday* ³*to tell you about this great idea I've had*.
2 We ¹_____ go walking ²_____ ³_____.
3 I can ¹_____ change the appointment ²_____ ³_____.
4 I ¹_____ like to facebook friends ²_____ ³_____.
5 I ¹_____ like to take things easy ²_____.
6 I'll ¹_____ try to visit my family ²_____.

a) to make it more convenient / easily / for you
b) to find out what they've been doing / generally / in the evenings when I'm at home
c) next time I'm in the area / probably
d) ~~totally / to tell you about this great idea I've had / yesterday~~
e) at the weekends / usually
f) in the mountains near our house / regularly / during the holidays

B Choose two sentences from Exercise 7A. Expand them in a different way to make them true for you. Compare your sentences in pairs.

1 Cultivate your imagination. Write everything down. Charles Darwin kept a rigorous system of notebooks <u>for his ideas</u> and he reread them frequently. These days, we have Google Docs. Use a 'spark file' to keep track of interesting ideas and websites you come across.

2 Create a 'coffee house' culture in your brain by extending your sphere of interest with hobbies. Many great inventors worked on several projects <u>simultaneously</u>. Darwin had no fewer than sixteen hobbies.

3 Take a reading sabbatical. Bill Gates takes two weeks off <u>a year</u> just to read. This isn't practical for most people, but you can adopt the principle. Save up everything you want to read around a topic and then take a long weekend to do nothing but read.

4 Learn to share. George Bernard Shaw said, 'If you have an apple and I have an apple and we exchange these apples then you and I will still each have one apple. But if you have an idea and I have an idea and we exchange these ideas, then each of us will have two ideas.' Share your ideas <u>readily</u>, both online and offline.

5 Spend time <u>on your own</u>. Every once in a while, find space and time to just relax and be by yourself. Solitude bears surprising fruit.

6 Try new things. Doing the same thing every day does little to spark your creative genius. Put yourself in new situations and try new experiences. This will <u>almost certainly</u> allow your brain to make new and interesting connections.

SPEAKING

8A Work in groups. Write a list of 'creative' questions you could ask a stranger in order to get to know them. Try to think of questions you have never been asked before.

If you were a colour, what colour would you be?
If you could change the world, where would you start?

B Work with a different group. Ask and answer your questions, making your answers as interesting as possible.

C Use your answers to tell the class two things they didn't know about you.

WRITING a review

9A Read the review of a television programme and answer the questions.

1 What kind of programme is this?

2 Who is it suitable for?

3 Is the review positive or negative?

4 Would you watch this based on the review?

B Read the guidelines for writing a review. Which ones does the Wallace and Gromit review follow? How could it be improved?

1 Try to be both informative and entertaining.

2 Give an account of the subject in question (the book, film, play or event) and offer a reasoned opinion about its qualities. Report on the content, the approach and the scope of the work.

3 Your audience may or may not have heard about the work in detail. Make sure your review caters for those who have and those who haven't.

4 Even with a short review, try to follow a clear structure. Include:

- a brief introduction.
- a description of contents.
- an assessment of value.
- a comparison with others.
- a conclusion.

LEARN TO use a range of vocabulary

10A Work in pairs. Think of synonyms for the words/phrases below.

1 unusual/peculiar

2 very clever

3 very pleased

4 extremely interesting

5 at first

6 unusual adventures

7 happily

8 funny and enjoyable

9 extremely attractive or beautiful

B Find synonyms for words/phrases 1–9 in the review. Compare them with your own ideas.

speakout TIP

Make your review interesting by using a variety of adjectives, e.g. *good = excellent, superb, top quality, terrific, exceptional*, etc. Qualify the adjectives you use in a review with adverbs, e.g. *absolutely gripping, completely credible, quite heavy-going*. Find examples of adverb + adjective combinations in the review in Exercise 9A.

Wallace & Gromit's World Of Invention

Wallace and Gromit hit the world stage in 1993 when their short film *The Wrong Trousers* won an Academy Award. Since then, the animated duo – an eccentric cheese-loving inventor Wallace, and his quiet but highly intelligent dog, Gromit – have become some of the best known and best loved stars to come out of the UK. I was absolutely delighted to discover they are back on our screens with a new BBC series, *Wallace & Gromit's World of Invention*.

In the series, Wallace and Gromit explore the wonders of the natural world and look at inventions inspired by Mother Nature. They travel to various locations around the world to meet inventors working on some really fascinating projects. Among them are a robot that takes its inspiration from a Venus fly trap and an artificial gill which allows a person to breathe under water.

I had initially expected the whole show to be animated. Much though I am a fan of this comic duo and their extraordinary escapades, I was pleasantly surprised to find that Wallace, in his animated form, just plays host to the show, introducing the inventors and their ideas. The rest of the filming is live, on location, and it is this combination of humorous animation mixed with stunning action segments that gives the show its appeal, both entertaining and truly educational for adults and children alike. Don't miss it.

11 You have been asked to write an exhibition review for a magazine. Read the exhibition description below. Then turn to page 163 and read some notes about it. Write a review based on the notes (200–250 words).

Exhibition: Inventing the 21st Century

Folio Society Gallery, The British Library   **Price: FREE**

In a celebration of British ingenuity, this exhibition explores the stories behind some of the most iconic inventions of the century's first decade. Whether they are changing the world of sport, fighting climate change, or just making life a bit easier, each inventor has challenged the established way of doing things. From Dyson's revolutionary bladeless fan to President Obama's favourite dog bowl, trace the journey of an idea from that first spark of inspiration to the development of a business. See original drawings, patent specifications and the finished products.

▶ **FUNCTION** | ranting/raving ▶ **VOCABULARY** | express yourself ▶ **LEARN TO** | use comment adverbials

VOCABULARY express yourself

1A Read the website extract and discuss the questions.

1 What kind of website does it talk about?

2 What kinds of things can you read about on this site?

3 Do you know of any other websites like this?

4 Do you think they are a good/bad idea? Why/Why not?

LOVE IT OR HATE IT?

Do you ever find yourself hating something which everyone else raves about? For me, it's football and Coca Cola. For my husband, it's Marmite. Now you have the chance to celebrate your individuality on rantrave.com. This website claims to have a community of independent thinkers who crave a fresh perspective and are always willing to speak their mind. You can find more than just reviews here – this is a place for people to rant and rave about anything that's on their mind, whether it's paying for an overpriced ticket, raving about a new album you've bought, or simply complaining about football results. Sign up to rantrave.com and start to let your feelings fly. Why not give the world a piece of your mind, whether they like it or not?

B What do you think the following words/phrases from the extract mean?

1 rave (v, n)   4 speak their mind

2 rant (v, n)   5 let your feelings fly

3 crave a fresh perspective   6 a piece of your mind

C Complete the sentences with words/phrases in Exercise 1B.

1 Everything I read in the newspapers is the same. I really _____.

2 He went on a _____ about the evils of modern society.

3 That's not acceptable. You should give the manager _____.

4 Don't tell them they are wrong all the time. Let them _____.

5 I've never seen you so animated before. You really _____.

6 Rick loves to _____ about how wonderful life is in Australia.

FUNCTION ranting/raving

2A Choose three of the topics below. What do you think people would rant or rave about for each one?

- arts and entertainment
- culture and lifestyle
- economy
- food
- news and politics
- people
- products
- science and technology
- sports
- travel *speaker 1*

B ▶ 9.3 Listen to people ranting and raving about different things. Match each rant/rave with a topic in Exercise 2A.

C What did each person say about their topic?

3A Listen again and complete the phrases below.

Raving

It was the most wonderful/amazing/awesome …

It was absolutely [1]_____ /incredible.

It's really the best (show) [2]_____.

There's (absolutely) nothing [3]_____ than …

(It was) one of the most [4]_____ (sunsets) I've ever seen.

I couldn't believe my [5]_____ when …

It was idyllic.

It's an all-time [6]_____.

Ranting

If there's one thing I can't [7]_____, it's …

It drives me up the [8]_____.

It was absolutely [9]_____.

It was a total [10]_____ of money.

It's not my style/kind of thing/cup of tea at all.

B ▶ 9.4 Listen to the phrases. Notice how the intonation changes for the positive and the negative comments. Repeat the phrases.

4 Match the sentence halves.

1 If there is one thing I can't

2 We went to an exhibition at the Tate Modern, but I'm afraid

3 The hotel had great reviews, but the service was

4 It was most definitely one of the funniest films

5 There's nothing better than

6 It's one of the most

a) absolutely horrendous.

b) a really well-made coffee, in a friendly and welcoming café.

c) stand, it's having to read a boring book.

d) spectacular shows ever. That's why it's been such a raving success.

e) I've ever seen. I was on the floor with laughter.

f) it wasn't my cup of tea.

page 144 LANGUAGEBANK

LEARN TO use comment adverbials

5A ▶ 9.5 Listen to extracts from the rants/raves in Exercise 2B and complete the sentences.

1 _____, it drives me up the wall.

2 I have, in the past, _____ raised my voice at tourists.

3 I'd _____ go back there again.

4 She was _____ good, honestly.

5 The restaurant was _____ overpriced.

6 _____ it's hard to cook for a lot of people.

speakout TIP

Listen out for comment adverbials (*absolutely, definitely, obviously, totally, simply, undoubtedly, completely, surprisingly, incredibly*, etc.) to help you understand someone's viewpoint. Also, when you are talking, comment adverbials which come at the beginning of the sentence can give you thinking time (*Honestly, Basically, Seriously*, etc.).

B Choose the correct alternatives.

1 *Honestly/Undoubtedly*, I have no idea where you could possibly find more delicious chocolates!

2 *Incredibly/Basically*, he's just lazy.

3 *Clearly/Completely*, this was one of the more luxurious hotels.

4 Not *clearly/surprisingly*, with high unemployment young people are struggling to find jobs.

5 It's quite *basically/simply* the most ridiculous idea I've ever heard.

6 *Undoubtedly/Completely*, this is one of the top bands of the moment.

C Work in pairs. Are the sentences in Exercise 5B rants or raves? Choose one of the sentences and develop it into a short conversation. Include two more comment adverbials.

SPEAKING

6A Choose two or three topics from the list below. Prepare to rant or rave about each topic. Make notes and try to use comment adverbials.

• a restaurant you've enjoyed/been disappointed by

• a spectacular/ugly place you have visited

• an item of clothing you love/hate

• an actor or film you love/hate

• a piece of music/album you love/hate

• something you bought recently which was a success/disaster

B Work in groups. Take turns to talk about your topics.

DVD PREVIEW

1 Work in pairs and discuss the questions.

1 How much do you know about famous art galleries, museums and other cultural places in your city or region? Which have you visited and why?

2 Are there any galleries, museums or cultural places you would like to visit in other countries?

2 Read the programme information. What question will the programme attempt to answer?

BBC Tate Modern is 10! A Culture Show Special

The Culture Show is a BBC programme that looks at different aspects of the arts, such as books, film, art, music and fashion. In this episode, presenter and art critic Matthew Collings celebrates the tenth birthday of one of the world's most popular art galleries, London's Tate Modern. The programme asks why the gallery has been so popular and examines how it has changed the public's perception of art.

DVD VIEW

3 Watch the DVD. Tick the works of art that you see.

1 a giant slide

2 a mechanical sun

3 a metal container that is completely dark inside

4 a giant spider

5 a work by Henri Matisse called *The Snail*

6 a portrait by Pablo Picasso

7 an animation of a cartoon girl

8 an old van with sledges coming out of the back door

4A Answer the questions.

1 How many people visit Tate Modern each year?

2 What is the impressive thing about Tate Modern even when it's empty?

3 The presenter shows us two areas of Tate Modern: the Turbine Hall and the higher floors. How are the two areas different?

4 What years does the permanent collection cover?

5 What comparison does the presenter make between modern artists like Henri Matisse and contemporary artists like Gerhard Richter?

6 What is the final question that the presenter asks?

B Watch the DVD again to check.

5 Work in pairs and discuss the questions.

1 The presenter describes one area of Tate Modern as a 'make-you-think' theme park and a 'philosophy fairground'. Do these 'happenings' make you think, or are they just for amusement?

2 The presenter says 'this temple of the far-out [crazy or strange things] has become a fixture in ordinary people's lives.' Why do you think so many people go to art galleries like Tate Modern? Is it because of the art or are there other reasons?

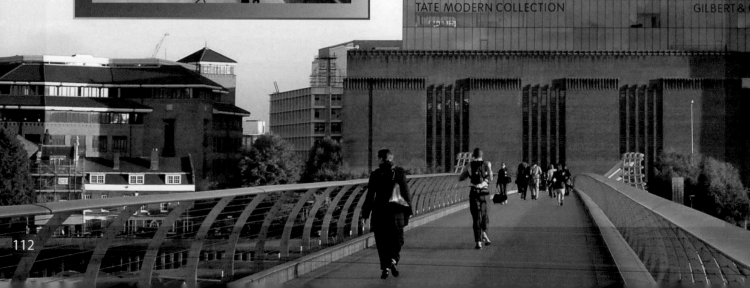

speakout recommend a cultural place

6A ▶ 9.6 Listen to someone recommending a cultural visit to a group of students. What is impressive about the place? What subject do you think the students are studying?

B Listen again and tick the key phrases you hear.

keyphrases

It's one of the world's most recognisable landmarks.

It's an absolute must-see.

The most striking thing about it is …

The best time to go is …

What makes it so breathtaking is …

The building itself is obviously admired all over the world.

It's also been very influential in …

It makes an impression on you because …

7A Read the instructions and think about questions 1–3.

A group of students is coming to your city. You have been asked to recommend a place for them to visit. This place must be relevant to their studies. You will also need to provide a short oral introduction to the place, saying why it is important today or how influential it has been.

1 What are your visitors studying? Choose from: architecture, art, fashion, engineering, design, music, sport, business or history.

2 What place in your city will you recommend? It could be a building, stadium, museum, street, etc.

3 In your introduction to the place, what will you tell the students? Why are you recommending it?

B Work in groups and take turns to introduce your cultural places. Listen to other students' recommendations and ask questions.

writeback a recommendation

8A Read one post and one reply from a travel forum. Why does the writer recommend this place?

We are going to Cairo next month. Is there anything we should particularly see or do apart from the Great Pyramids and the Sphinx? We are interested in culture and history.

Molly

Go to Khan el-Khalili, the downtown bazaar. This is a wonderful place to browse. The bazaar is huge so you'll need several hours if you want to see everything. You can buy all kinds of things here, but it's particularly good for hand-made jewellery, precious stones, pottery, rugs and all kinds of textiles. Don't be shy about haggling, either. The locals expect it and they are very friendly and open. As soon as you arrive, you're hit with a sensual explosion – noise, colour, smells, people everywhere. This can get a bit overwhelming, but fortunately there are several restaurants and coffee shops where you can take refuge. The most famous of these is El Fishawy, where the great writer Naguib Mahfouz used to go. While in Khan el-Khalili you should pause to appreciate the architecture. For those who look closely enough, there are many wonderful archways, engraved doors and ornate decorations on the walls. Overall, I'd say Khan el-Khalili is unmissable for any visitor to Cairo. Just make sure you take your camera and some money for souvenirs.

Kim Hae-Jeng

B Write a comment for the forum about somewhere you know (200 words). Recommend the place, explaining why visitors should see it.

WWW.TATE.ORG.UK

ADJECTIVES: THE ARTS

1 Underline the correct alternatives.

1 The exhibition was very *impressive/ overrated*. No wonder it was sold out.

2 What a *compelling/ well-received* film. I couldn't stop watching.

3 The song is very *poignant/ subtle*. It reminds me of some hard times.

4 I don't think this book is that good. It's *stunning/ overrated*.

5 The movie was quite *bleak/ offbeat*. It was full of bizarre surprises.

6 That actress is extremely *stylish/ thought-provoking*. She always dresses well.

TENSES FOR UNREAL SITUATIONS

2A Read about a wish list for the arts. Find and correct the six mistakes.

It's high time art forms like opera are made accessible to the public. Tickets should be cheap, and free for children. Opera and theatre are treated as though they're for the elite, but they're about the same things that are in the papers every day: jealousy, passion, murder and blood feuds, and it's about time the public is having a chance to enjoy them.

I'd sooner TV isn't overtaken by sites like YouTube. The do-it-yourself culture has its benefits, but people talk as if anyone can make a masterpiece on camera. They can't and that's why TV will survive.

Finally, it's time schoolteachers will think outside the box. What if circus skills were taught in schools? Supposing kids having a chance to learn how to juggle, swing on a trapeze and be real clowns? I'm sure millions of kinaesthetic learners would rather they are spending their days doing this than sitting at desks doing worksheets.

B Write three sentences to describe your own wish list for the arts. Remember to use language for unreal situations.

IDEAS

3A Choose the correct option to complete the sentences.

1 Oh no! The whole bookcase has fallen over now. Whose _____ idea was it to move it?
a) toy   b) novel   c) bright

2 We were completely at a loss until we _____ on the idea of renting out the office.
a) hit   b) had   c) held

3 What _____ him the idea of becoming a circus performer? I have no idea.
a) hit   b) gave   c) had

4 If we don't know what to do, I suggest we _____ a few ideas.
a) toy   b) original   c) brainstorm

5 I've never heard of that before. What an _____ idea!
a) original   b) origin   c) originate

6 I've never heard of such a _____ idea in all my life.
a) ridiculous   b) ridicule
c) ridiculously

B Work in pairs. Test each other on the phrases above.

A: We thought it was a good idea at the time …

B: It seemed like a good idea.

A: Correct.

ADVERBIALS

4A Work in pairs. Try to expand the sentences as much as possible by adding different adverbials.

1 I eat chocolate.

A: I always eat chocolate.

B: I always eat chocolate at the end of the day.

A: I always greedily eat chocolate at the end of the day.

2 I like music.

3 He left the office.

4 We agreed to pay.

5 We went there.

6 I love the way she speaks.

7 He cooks.

B Compare your sentences with other students.

RANTING/RAVING

5A Complete the conversations with the words in the box.

| horrendous | amazing | ever | idyllic |
| luck | all-time | waste | thing |

1 A: What did you enjoy about the film?
   B: The most _____ thing about it was the cinematography. It was spectacular!

2 A: Did you like his latest book?
   B: Yes, it's an _____ classic. It's his best one yet.

3 A: Did you enjoy your holiday?
   B: Yes, it was the best holiday _____.

4 A: Did you enjoy the exhibition?
   B: I'm afraid I didn't. It's not my kind of _____.

5 A: Did you manage to get tickets?
   B: Yes, I couldn't believe my _____ when I saw there were still some available.

6 A: It's a four-star restaurant.
   B: I can hardly believe that. The service was absolutely _____.

7 A: What was the island like?
   B: Oh it was _____. The beaches were sandy and deserted and the sea was a beautiful turquoise blue.

8 A: Is that new computer game you bought good?
   B: No, it was a total _____ of money because it was the wrong version for my computer.

B Work in pairs and practise the conversations.

BBC VIDEO PODCAST

Watch people talking about the creative activities they do on ActiveBook or on the website.

Authentic BBC interviews

www.pearsonELT.com/speakout

UNIT
10

SPEAKING
> Plan your dream adventure holiday
> Talk about ambitions
> Negotiate a plan for a film festival
> Talk about your ideal job

LISTENING
> Listen to an author reading from his memoir
> Listen to a talk about stages in a negotiation
> Watch a BBC competition to become a wildlife film-maker

READING
> Read about an epic motorcycle journey
> Read an essay about celebrity culture

WRITING
> Write a 'for and against' essay
> Apply for your dream job

BBC CONTENT
▣ Video podcast: What are your goals in life?
◉ DVD: Wildest Dreams

horizons

▶ **GRAMMAR** | inversion   ▶ **VOCABULARY** | collocations   ▶ **HOW TO** | describe a memorable journey

READING AND VOCABULARY

1 Work in groups and discuss the questions.

1 Do you think travel can broaden your horizons? How?

2 Would you like to travel around the world on a motorbike?

3 What do you think would be the good/bad things about an experience like this?

2A Match 1–7 with a)–g) to make collocations.

1 an epic   a) at border crossings
2 an obsession   b) by the kindness of strangers
3 physical   c) journey
4 the depths   d) with motorbikes
5 (be) humbled   e) privations
6 (be) held up   f) mobsters
7 gun-wielding   g) of depression

B Discuss. How do you think the phrases above could relate to a story about two people travelling around the world on motorbikes?

3A Read the article to check your ideas. What were the good and bad things about the journey?

B Put sentences a)–g) in the correct places 1–6 in the article. There is one extra sentence.

a) Hearing everyone was all right freed us to get on with what we were doing.

b) The idea grew into a plan for an epic road trip, which would also highlight the global work of the children's charity UNICEF.

c) They were just curious and looking to be friendly.

d) ~~Or their both being young British actors who had each married recently, and were then the proud fathers of months-old baby girls.~~

e) I just couldn't stay on the bike!

f) In remote Mongolia, for example, one of the bikes broke down.

g) And although McGregor has owned bikes ever since he bought his first – a 100cc Honda – at nineteen while studying drama in London, he still needed a bit of help with his off-road technique.

4 Work in pairs and answer the questions.

1 What did Charley Boorman and Ewan McGregor have in common?

2 What previous biking experience did the two men have?

3 Why did their attitude towards strangers change during the trip?

4 How did the two men keep in touch with their families? Why was this important?

5 How did the Ukrainian shopkeeper surprise them?

Change your life

Take your time. Take the Long Way.

*L*ong *Way Round*, filmed for the BBC, is the gripping account of an epic round-the-world motorcycle journey undertaken by Ewan McGregor and Charley Boorman, during which they covered 20,000 miles and crossed twelve countries and nineteen time zones in just 115 days.

When Ewan McGregor and Charley Boorman first met on a film set in Ireland, it wasn't the experience of co-starring in a little-remembered costume drama that bonded them. [1] _d_ Rather, it was mutual love of – obsession with, some would say – motorbikes and bike-riding.

'It was like discovering you had another brother,' says McGregor. 'So I asked Charley to be my daughter's godfather and we and our families have been involved pretty much constantly ever since.'

The idea for *Long Way Round* all began when McGregor and Boorman first thought of taking off on their bikes together – initially (with their wives riding pillion) to Spain, and then as far as China. [2] _____ And when McGregor mentioned it to a TV producer, the proposal to film their journey soon followed.

But were the two actors ready for the challenge? One nearly wasn't. 'Charley was far better at riding off-road than me, having had much more experience,' admits McGregor. Even though he first sat astride a 50cc Honda at the tender age of six, for years, he says, he was a 'biker without a bike'. (Boorman, by contrast, had been riding bikes on the family farm since he was a boy.) [3] _____

'Two days' pre-training with BMW was supposed to bring me up to speed,' says McGregor, 'but actually began by sinking me into the depths of depression. [4] _____ Here I was, about to embark on this awesome journey, and I couldn't even master the key core skill!'

Luckily, by the end of day two, latent ability had kicked in. And that, plus their close relationship and a small technical support team, saw the pair through a journey involving more than 20,000 miles, on and off road, across three continents. 'We promised before leaving that we'd always be honest with each other,' says Boorman of the potential stress on their friendship. 'If something started to bug me about Ewan's behaviour, he knew I'd tell him. And vice versa.'

Both admit to having been humbled by the kindness so often shown to them by strangers who had no idea who they were. 'Early on,' says McGregor, 'passing through the Czech Republic and Slovakia, we became aware of just how suspicious we were. If someone approached us, our hard, city-based response would be, "Who is this guy? What does he want?" But they didn't want anything. 5_____ So, gradually, we found ourselves relaxing and looking at others in a different way.'

There were, of course, physical privations – in the more remote areas they had to camp, live on rehydrated packet foods and wash in river water, or not at all – but being apart from their families was the toughest trial. Most nights, a fifteen-minute phone call was possible. 'That call home became such a highlight,' says McGregor. '6_____ Without it, I'd have been travelling through some of the most desolate, beautiful landscapes on earth with my mind elsewhere.'

Along the way, they'd experienced the extremes of camping alongside nomads and staying in luxury with gun-wielding mobsters (a Ukrainian shopkeeper, who offered them a bedbug-free room, turned out to own a mansion complete with swimming pool and he and his mates eagerly showed off a Kalashnikov and other scary weapons). Occasionally McGregor and Boorman fumed, as they were sometimes held up at border crossings for up to fifteen hours. But it was, they agree, the adventure of a lifetime.

'Now we're back, I almost can't believe we did it,' admits McGregor. 'I went all the way around the world? On a motorbike? Surely not. But I did. We did.'

SPEAKING

5A Work in groups and read the leaflets below. Would you like to go on one of these trips? Why/Why not?

B Plan your own dream adventure. Where would you go and what would you do? Read the information below and plan a trip for your group.

There is one constraint: you can only make one journey by commercial aeroplane. For the rest, you can use any other means of travel. Think about the following questions.

- How are you going to travel?
- What countries will you visit?
- What will be the main aim of your trip?
- How long will the trip take?
- Could you use the trip to highlight any particular issues? Which ones? How?
- What problems do you think you might have? How will you deal with them?

C Tell the class about your plans. Which group has the most interesting idea for a dream adventure?

Zebra Bus Touring Company

Experience the beauty of Africa on one of our vintage tour buses. Take the ultimate trip across Africa on this classic bus.

It's a life-changing holiday.

Favela painting, Brazil

With volunteer vacations you can experience life in the heart of the favela. This community project paints the favela in bright colours to help give pride to the people living there. Work with the children's club, keeping the kids off the streets and start every day with a two-hour samba lesson!

Whale spotting, Newfoundland

Experience the world's largest gathering of humpback whales and a fabulous diversity of marine wildlife with

Sea Experience Holidays

Make your holiday truly memorable.

GRAMMAR inversion

6A Read the text. What was similar about the two journeys?

When Ewan McGregor and Charley Boorman travelled around the world on their motorbikes, it was a life-changing feat. Not only did the *Long Way Round* journey challenge their view of the world, it also tested their physical endurance. Had they known how difficult the journey would prove, they might never have started. But their shared passion for adventure and the kindness they encountered on the way kept them going. Never before had they experienced such hospitality from complete strangers. It was the trip of a lifetime but, three years later, they fixed up their bikes and embarked on a second journey together. For the *Long Way Down*, the two men travelled 15,000 miles through two continents (Europe and Africa) in eighty-five days.

B Read the sentences. What do you notice about the word order? Rewrite the sentences beginning with *If*.

1 Had the first journey not been such a success, they never would have considered the second.

2 Had he been a more experienced rider, he might not have fallen so often.

C Choose the correct alternative to complete the rule. Then find another example of inversion in a conditional clause in the text above.

Rule:

In *formal/informal* written texts, the word order in conditional clauses may be inverted.

D Look at sentences 1–4. Notice how inversion is also used after negative adverbials to add dramatic effect. Find two examples in the text in Exercise 6A.

1 **No sooner had they finished** one trip than they were planning another.

2 **Rarely/Never before/Seldom had they seen** such spectacular scenery.

3 **Not once/At no point did they stop** to question their decision.

4 **Only later/Not until the journey was finished did they appreciate** some of the places that they had visited.

→ page 146 **LANGUAGEBANK**

PRACTICE

7A Complete the second sentence so that it has the same meaning as the first.

1 He didn't think about leaving his family until they were ready to depart.
Not until …

2 I then saw the danger that we were in. Only …

3 As soon as we left the tent, it collapsed. No sooner …

4 If we had thought about it more, we would have taken extra fuel.
Had …

5 They had never ridden motorbikes for such extended distances.
Never before …

6 They did not consider giving up the expedition at any point.
At no point …

B Think about a difficult journey you have experienced. Complete the sentences for you and tell a partner.

1 Had I known … then …
2 Never before had I …
3 No sooner had I … when …
4 Not only … but also …

VOCABULARY *PLUS* synonyms

8A Look at six extracts from the article on page 116. Can you think of words/phrases with similar meanings to the words in bold?

1 *Long Way Round* is the **gripping** account …

2 … of an epic round-the-world motorcycle **journey** …

3 The trip would also **highlight** the global work of the children's charity UNICEF.

4 I was about to **embark on** this awesome journey …

5 … and I couldn't even **master** the key core skill!

6 If something started to **bug** me …

B Which word in each set has a different meaning?

1 **gripping**: thrilling, exhilarating, dull

2 **journey**: trip, tracker, expedition

3 **highlight (v)**: stress, overemphasise, accentuate

4 **embark on**: undertake, complete, set off on

5 **master(v)**: train, grasp, get the hang of

6 **bug (v)**: excite, irritate, get on (my) nerves

speakout TIP

Use a thesaurus. A good learners' dictionary will often give you a thesaurus to help you expand your vocabulary range. Look up the word *interesting* in a thesaurus. How many alternatives does it offer? Think of example sentences for each word and write them in your notebook.

9 Complete the sentences with the words in the box.

| exhilarated embarked expedition |
| mastered emphasised bugs |

1 It just _____ me that I have to work so many extra hours for no extra money.

2 Dan felt _____ after reaching the top of the mountain.

3 The Prime Minister _____ that there are no plans to raise taxes.

4 He _____ on a new career as a teacher.

5 I never quite _____ the art of walking in high heels.

6 He went on an _____ to Borneo to film the wildlife there.

10 Write down five words from the lesson. Work in pairs and think of as many synonyms as possible for each word.

→ page 157 **VOCABULARYBANK**

▶ **GRAMMAR** | comparative structures   ▶ **VOCABULARY** | ambition   ▶ **HOW TO** | talk about your ambitions

SPEAKING

1 Work in groups and discuss the questions.

1 Imagine you a) scored three goals in a World Cup final, or b) were the subject of a film. How would your life change?

2 Read about people who experienced these events. Are any of your ideas from question 1 mentioned?

When England won the World Cup final in 1966, Geoff Hurst scored three goals. The third, according to the BBC, is the most frequently shown sports footage of all time. Back in 1966, it wasn't such a big deal – Hurst spent the weekend after the World Cup washing the car and mowing the lawn. However, he now says, 'Scoring a hat-trick in the World Cup final has completely transformed my life.'

Erin Brockovich became famous when a movie, starring Julia Roberts, portrayed her fight against water contamination in California. The film completely changed her life. She went to premieres, did lots of publicity and appeared in magazines and on TV, but later said, 'I found it difficult to cope with the attention, difficult that people were judging me and making comments.'

GRAMMAR   comparative structures

2A Answer the questions about the texts above.

1 Whose life was **barely any different** immediately after the event?

2 Whose life became **significantly more** stressful after the event?

3 Who received **far more** opportunities soon after the event?

B Check what you know. Which phrases in bold in Exercise 2A mean a small difference and which mean a big difference?

3A Which words in the box can complete sentences 1 and 2 below?

much	just	far	nothing like	considerably	slightly	infinitely
a bit	a lot	nowhere near	marginally	miles	not	every bit
way	a good deal	decidedly	significantly	barely any	loads

1 My life now is _____ better than it was before I became famous.

2 My life now is _____ as good as it was before I became famous.

B Discuss the questions.

1 What type of difference do the words in Exercise 3A describe: a small difference, a big difference or no difference?

2 Which words are formal and which are informal?

C Read about two other comparative structures. Match structures 1 and 2 with rules a) and b).

1 Double comparatives

The harder you search for fame, *the more* difficult it is to find it.

2 Progressive comparatives

*She gets **more and more** beautiful every time I see her.*

Rules:

a) A _____ comparative describes how something increases or decreases by repeating the same comparative. We put *and* between the forms.

b) A _____ comparative describes how a change in one thing causes a change in another. We use two comparative forms with *the* and a comma after the first clause.

▶ page 146 **LANGUAGEBANK**

PRACTICE

4 Imagine you are the world's most famous celebrity, photographed by the paparazzi every day. What might you say about your life?

1 My life would be considerably better if …

2 Being a celebrity is nothing like as …

3 One good thing about fame is that it's far …

4 Even for a celebrity, it's every bit as …

5 I find it more and more difficult to …

6 The more famous I become, …

7 The more money I make, …

8 Life gets better and …

5A ▶ 10.1 Listen to completed sentences 1–4 from Exercise 4. Notice how we emphasise differences by stressing the modifier (*considerably, nothing like*, etc.). Read your sentences aloud, emphasising the modifier where appropriate.

B ▶ 10.2 What do you think expressions 1–3 mean? Do you have equivalents in your language? Listen to the rhythm of double comparatives and repeat.

1 The more, the merrier.

2 The sooner, the better.

3 The bigger they come, the harder they fall.

LISTENING

6A Read about a writer called Frank McCourt and discuss questions 1–3.

1 Why do you think Frank McCourt published his first book only when he was in his sixties?

2 How do you think his life changed after *Angela's Ashes* became a bestseller?

3 Who do you think he met after becoming famous?

Frank McCourt came from an extremely poor Irish-American family. His ambition was to be a writer, but the longer he waited, the more unlikely it seemed that his dream would come true. So, having spent most of his adulthood as a teacher, he was delighted when his memoir, *Angela's Ashes*, was published. By now in his sixties, he was every bit as surprised when the book became a bestseller. Life became a good deal better for him with his sudden fame. He went on to write two more books: *'Tis* (1999) and *Teacher Man* (2005), which cemented his reputation as a first-class memoirist.

B ▶ 10.3 Listen to an extract from *Teacher Man*. Were your answers to questions 1–3 correct?

7A Listen again. What is the significance of the numbers and names below?

1 thirty years	6 hundreds of times
2 a few hundred copies	7 President Clinton
3 thirty languages	8 Sarah, Duchess of York
4 1996	9 Elton John
5 five a day	10 William Butler Yeats

B Find words 1–6 in audio script 10.3 on page 174. What do you think they mean?

1 a scrap (of attention) (n)	4 clamour (n)
2 dazzled (adj)	5 geriatric (adj)
3 ascension (n)	6 a beacon (of hope) (n)

C Turn to page 163 to check your answers.

8 Read the extracts from the recording and discuss the questions.

1 'The book was my second act.' What do you think this means? What was Frank's 'first act'?

2 'A woman in a coffee shop squinted and said, I seen you on TV. You must be important.' Do you think Frank felt he had become important?

3 'I was asked for my opinion on Ireland, conjunctivitis, drinking, teeth, education, religion, adolescent angst, William Butler Yeats, literature in general.' How do you think Frank feels about his new 'expertise'? What is his tone of voice?

4 'I travelled the world being Irish, being a teacher, an authority on misery of all kinds.' From this comment, what can you guess about the book *Angela's Ashes*?

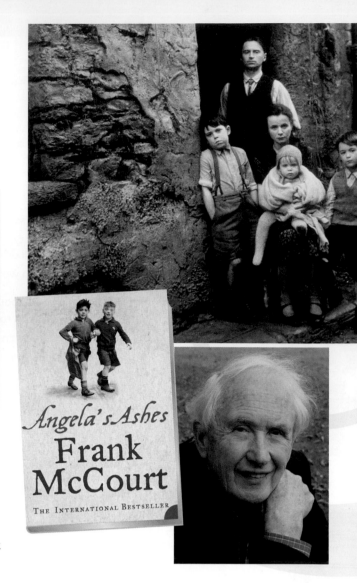

Angela's Ashes
Frank McCourt
THE INTERNATIONAL BESTSELLER

VOCABULARY ambition

9A The pairs of phrases in bold have similar meanings. Underline the correct alternative to complete sentence b). Work out what the phrases mean.

1 a) I know people who **crave** fame and fortune.
   b) Nobody I know has ever **hankered** *before / after* fame.

2 a) It must be terrible to **be in the spotlight** all the time.
   b) I like to **be the centre of** *fame / attention*.

3 a) I don't think you need to **serve an apprenticeship** to become good at something.
   b) In any artistic profession, it's important to *pay / give* your **dues** even if it takes years.

4 a) It's not important to **be held in high esteem** by your colleagues.
   b) It's important to *think / be* **renowned** for good work.

5 a) I'd hate to **become an overnight success** like Frank McCourt.
   b) It would be great to *shoot / jump* **to fame** like Frank McCourt.

6 a) I'm **set on** becoming an expert in my field.
   b) I don't *have / like* **aspirations** to become well known.

B Tick the sentences above that you agree with. Compare your ideas in pairs and ask for more information.

⫸ page 157 **VOCABULARYBANK**

SPEAKING

10 Work in groups and discuss the questions.

1 What were your ambitions when you were younger? Are they the same today?

2 Have you had any experiences that made your dreams come true? How was your life different before and after the experience?

3 Are any of these your dream come true? If not, what is?

- getting a job that you really love
- living in a magnificent house
- finding the 'perfect' partner
- winning the lottery
- speaking English perfectly
- passing an upcoming exam

WRITING   a 'for and against' essay

11A Work in groups. Read the quotes and discuss questions 1–4 below.

'If you become a star, *you* don't change; everyone else does.' (Kirk Douglas, actor)

'A celebrity is a person who works hard all their life to become well known, then wears dark glasses to avoid being recognised.' (Fred Allen, comedian)

1 Do you think the quotations are true?

2 What is 'celebrity culture'?

3 Do you read gossip columns or magazines about celebrities? Do you watch chat shows or look at websites that focus on celebrities?

4 Do you think celebrity culture is a good or a bad thing?

B Read the essay. What arguments does the writer give for and against celebrity culture?

12 'For and against' essays often follow the structure below. To what extent does the essay in Exercise 11B follow this structure?

1 Introduction to the issue

2 Points for (plus examples)

3 Points against (plus examples)

4 Conclusion

Celebrity culture – a blessing or a curse?

The world's first celebrity was Alexander the Great. Not only did he want to be the greatest man in history, but he also wanted everyone to know it. Alexander employed historians, sculptors and painters to tell his story for posterity, and they succeeded. But of course his achievements were astonishing. Today, many people become celebrities by doing little more than craving to be the centre of attention. With so many magazines, chat shows and websites needing content, such 'celebrities' fill a void, but many would argue that they fill a void with another void. The question is, does celebrity culture matter? Is it just harmless fun or does it erode our values?

On the one hand, there is the fame industry: *Hello* and *OK* magazines, gossip columns, Oprah Winfrey-style chat shows. These give us insights into the rich and famous. They show us the ups and downs of people whose lives seem far larger than our own. Most of us enjoy a bit of gossip, and what could be better than hearing about some superstar finally getting what he deserves (whether good or bad)? This view sees celebrity culture as a branch of the entertainment industry. In addition, fame has become democratised. On reality shows like *Big Brother*, the participants needn't have any talent and many see this as a good thing. Not everyone can be an Einstein or a Messi.

On the other hand, there are those who believe celebrity culture has got out of control. They argue that people now idolise mediocrity. It is no longer the greatest who win our hearts, but the loudest. A recent poll discovered that almost fifty percent of teenagers simply want to 'be famous', without specifying the profession and presumably without making any effort to learn a skill. The danger is that fame can be confused with achievement. Appearing on TV is not the same as spending years mastering an instrument or working for peace or inventing a cure.

So, is celebrity culture a blessing or a curse? Those in favour say it entertains us, sells newspapers and allows us to dream. Those against say it promotes 'fame for fame's sake' and doesn't value effort or skill. One thing we know is that the actions of most of today's celebrities will soon be forgotten, while real achievements won't. William Shakespeare, Joan of Arc, Helen Keller, Mahatma Gandhi, Nelson Mandela: their work will live on. And we're still making movies about Alexander the Great two thousand years after he died.

LEARN TO   describe pros and cons

13A Which phrases in the table were not used in the essay above?

contrasting arguments	
On the one hand … on the other hand …	
While … is true, it is also true to say …	
pros	cons
What could be better than … ?	The danger is …
One of the benefits is …	One of the drawbacks is …
Those in favour (say) …	Those against (say) …

B Add the expressions in the box to the correct column of the table.

In contrast to this, …   One advantage is …   One disadvantage is …
The arguments against … include …   The arguments for … include …
We also need to take … into consideration   On the positive side, …
On the negative side, …

14 Choose one of the topic statements below. Write down as many pros and cons as you can think of. Write a 'for and against' essay (350–450 words).

- University education should be free for everyone.
- All books should be available free on the internet.
- Fast food should be prohibited.
- Governments should pay musicians to play on the streets.

VOCABULARY negotiation

1 Think about the questions. Then discuss them in groups.

1 Why might the people in the photos need to negotiate?

2 What negotiations do you think the following people sometimes have? What experience do you have of these types of negotiations?

- parents and children
- bosses and employees
- companies and customers

3 What do you think makes a good negotiator?

2A Read seven tips for negotiating. Which three are the most important for you?

1 Approach the negotiation in the right way. Don't think of the other negotiator as your enemy. There are bound to be similar things that you both want, so try to **establish common goals**.

2 Be realistic when **haggling** or bargaining. Don't start with an insultingly low offer. This will only annoy the other party and make a successful conclusion less likely.

3 Be aware that you won't get everything you want. You will need to surrender some points. This means you need to **make compromises**.

4 Always be **tactful** and diplomatic. Never talk badly about anyone or anything. If you do, it may come back to haunt you.

5 Don't be afraid to postpone or **defer** a decision. As the negotiation progresses, you may find that the conditions aren't right. You can always come back the next day and start again.

6 Don't **bluff**. If you don't know something, say you don't know. If you say 'this is my final offer', it must be your final offer. If you are caught bluffing, you will lose your credibility as a negotiator.

7 Keep your eye on the main goal. Once the main deal is done, **make concessions** on small details. The idea is not to 'win', but to make sure both parties are happy.

B Can you think of any other tips for negotiating?

C Which words/expressions in bold in the text can be replaced by definitions a)–g)?

a) let the other person have something in order to reach an agreement

b) careful about what you say so that you don't upset or embarrass anyone

c) pretend something in order to achieve what you want

d) delay (until a later date)

e) accept less than what you originally wanted in order to reach an agreement

f) find out what you both want

g) arguing to agree on the price of something

FUNCTION negotiating

3A Put the stages of a negotiation in the correct order.

> make an offer   establish common goals   follow up the deal
> refuse or accept the deal   name your objectives

B ▶ 10.4 Listen to someone talking about negotiating and check your answers.

4A Work in pairs and answer the questions.

1 In a negotiation, what does 'exploring positions' mean?

2 What is the most important word in a negotiation?

3 What should you do if you switch off and miss something during a negotiation?

4 What is 'always delicate' during a negotiation?

5 What word should you never say in a negotiation, according to the speaker?

6 What might you need to do in a business negotiation?

7 What is the purpose of following up the deal?

B Listen again to check.

C Discuss the questions.

1 Do you think the speaker's advice is relevant to all types of negotiation or only some types, e.g. business?

2 Did the speaker say anything that you particularly agree or disagree with?

5A Read the phrases for negotiating. Which ones did the speaker use? Check your answers in audio script 10.4 on page 175.

naming your objectives	refusing an offer
We want to sort this out as soon as possible.	That would be difficult for me because of …
By the end of the day, we want to resolve this.	I'm not sure I can do that because …
exploring positions	accepting an offer
What do you have in mind?	Good. That sounds acceptable to me.
Can you go into more detail?	Great. We've got a deal.
making conditional offers	following up the deal
If you do … for me, I'll do … for you.	Let me know if you have any queries.
What if we supported your idea?	Get in touch if anything needs clarifying.

B Can you think of any other expressions that could go under the headings in Exercise 5A?

⟱ page 146 **LANGUAGEBANK**

6 There is one word missing from each sentence. Add the missing word.

1 We want to sort this as soon as possible.
2 Can you go more detail?
3 Great! We've got deal.
4 What you have in mind?
5 If you sponsor this idea for me, I make concessions for you.
6 What we supported your project from the beginning?
7 I'm not sure I do that because of what I told my friend.
8 That be difficult for me because I already agreed to something else.
9 Let me know you have any queries about the arrangements.
10 Get touch if anything needs clarifying.

LEARN TO stall for time

7A The speaker mentions 'stalling for time'. What do you think this means? Read the expressions below. Which one is not used to stall for time?

1 I'd like to think about it.
2 I'll have to ask about that.
3 I need more time to consider it.
4 I can give you an answer to that right now.
5 Can I get back to you on that?

B ▶ 10.5 Listen and repeat the expressions in Exercise 7A. Copy the intonation.

SPEAKING

8A Read some notes about a plan to hold an International Film Festival at your school. Which unresolved issues are the most important?

- Name of event: International Film Festival
- Who for: all students at the school
- Place: the school
- Films: ?
- Dates: ?
- Times: 5.30 first film
           8.00 second film
- Cost: ?
- Food and drink: ?
- Advertising the event: ?

B Work in two groups. Group A: turn to page 161. Group B: turn to page 163. Read your roles and answer the questions.

C Work with a student from the other group. Negotiate a deal. At the end, try to come up with three films from three different countries that you can show at the festival.

D Tell the class what you decided.

DVD PREVIEW

1 Read the programme information and answer the questions.

1 Where do the contestants travel to and why?

2 What do they hope to win and what happens if they are not good enough?

BBC Wildest Dreams

Wildlife film-making is one of the most difficult jobs on earth. Thousands want to do it, but few get the chance. The BBC has chosen nine people with ordinary jobs to see if one of them has what it takes to become a wildlife film-maker. Presented by Nick Knowles, *Wildest Dreams* puts them through their paces in one of the natural world's greatest arenas – Africa – with the ultimate prize for just one of them: a job at the BBC's prestigious Natural History Unit. In this episode, the hopefuls face their first challenges in the vast swamps of Botswana's Okavango Delta. If any of them aren't good enough, this will be the end of their journey and they'll be sent home.

▶ DVD VIEW

2 Watch the DVD and number the statements in the order you hear them.

a) The bees are obviously getting a bit more angry now. Please don't sting me.

b) I've never even been on a plane before, so to be going over African wilderness is just absolutely amazing.

c) We've got to throw ourselves into it. We've got to put ourselves on the line.

d) I've never been anywhere like this in my life, so this is all really, really amazing experience for me.

e) I'm feeling really under pressure and I'm gonna lose my temper in a minute.

f) It's exhilarating, but it's made my day. I can't stop smiling.

3A Complete the extracts.

1 It takes people with a very special mix of _____ and _____.

2 How will this factory worker from Rotherham cope filming thousands of _____?

3 And when _____ to the limits, how does it feel to track the most powerful _____ on earth?

4 Today, nine ordinary people are on a journey to one of the world's remotest spots, the Okavango Delta in Botswana, to start a _____ in wildlife film-making.

5 East London mum Sadia Ramzan dreams of _____ and loves animals, so this could be just the _____.

6 For one of you, this will be a _____ experience.

B Watch the DVD again to check.

4 Work in groups and discuss the questions.

1 What skills and qualities do you think are important for this job?

2 Would you enter the competition? Why/Why not?

speakout a dream job

5A ▶ 10.6 Listen to someone talking about his dream job. How does he answer the questions?

1 What is your dream job?

2 What skills/qualifications/experience do you have that would help you qualify for the job?

3 What qualities do you think are important for the job?

4 What could you do to help you on your path to your dream job?

B Listen again and choose the correct alternatives to complete the key phrases.

keyphrases

I guess my dream job *would have to be/ has to be* a (film-maker).

I'd *relish having the opportunity/love to have the opportunity* to work in an environment like that.

I'm fairly qualified in that *I'm doing a degree in …/I have a degree in …/I studied at …/I have previous experience in …*

I'd like to think that I'm a fairly *organised/motivated/creative* individual.

I'm not afraid to *try out new ideas/tell people what I think/get stuck in/put myself on the line.*

I've got a good eye for *detail/a product/things that are going to work.*

I think it's essential to be *hardworking/open-minded/flexible.*

I'm doing *some work experience/a part-time course in …*

6A Think of your own dream job. Prepare to answer the questions in Exercise 5A. Make notes.

B Work in groups and take turns to present your ideas. You each have three minutes for your presentation. At the end, decide who you would give the dream job to.

writeback a job application

7A Read about Francesca's dream job. What do you think the job is?

Get-your-dream-job.com

Do you want to apply for your dream job?

If you want to be sure of getting the job, send us a short paragraph explaining why it's your dream job and how your skills and experience qualify you.

Francesca: My absolute dream job by far would be an _____. I've always been fascinated by people who taste food and drink for their jobs, like chocolate tasters, restaurant critics, etc. I'd like to think that I have a very fine palate. I'm what you'd call a real foodie, always cooking and enjoying fine food. Perhaps that's because of my Italian background. In the summer, one of the things I most enjoy is going out in the evening with a few friends to have an ice cream. In Italy, there's an ice cream shop on nearly every street corner, selling a frightening number of different flavours of ice cream. I think I've tried them all, including some of the strangest combinations, like English trifle and pistachio. To my mind, my passion for flavour combined with my creative instinct would make me ideal for the job.

B Write a short paragraph about the dream job of your choice (150–200 words). Don't include the name of the job.

C Read other students' descriptions of their dream jobs. Can you guess the jobs?

COLLOCATIONS

1 Complete the sentences with the words/phrases in the box.

> an epic   held up   humbled by
> the depths   an obsession

1 Gambling became _____ and he lost everything.
2 On hearing the news, she sank into _____ of depression.
3 He went on _____ journey through South America.
4 I'm sorry we're late. We were _____ at the police station for hours.
5 We were _____ the generosity that was shown to us.

INVERSION

2A Put the phrases in the correct order to make sentences. Add capital letters and punctuation.

1 a knock at the door / than / no sooner / had she / there was / sat down
2 the last chocolate, / did you eat / any more / but you / not only / also didn't buy
3 called you earlier / realised / had I / would have / to happen, / I / what / was going
4 they / like it / see / would /never again / anything
5 can I / been / it / how difficult / only now / must have / appreciate
6 have overslept / might not / they gone / had / earlier, / they / to bed

B Work in pairs. Use the prompts to write a five-line story using only inversions.

1 Never before …
2 No sooner …
3 Had she known …
4 On no account would she have agreed …
5 Only now would she …

1 Never before had she seen the beautiful mountain flower.

2 No sooner had she picked it than …

C Read your stories to other students. Who has the best story?

COMPARATIVE STRUCTURES

3A Work in pairs. Student A: look at box A. Student B: look at box B. Write four comparative sentences using the phrases in your box.

Student A

> nothing like as   every bit as
> the more … , the more …
> bigger and bigger

Student B

> better and better   a good deal
> the more … , the more …
> nowhere near

B Compare your sentences.

AMBITION

4A Complete the words/phrases in bold by adding the missing letters.

1 What you would do if you suddenly **s _ _ _** to fame:
2 Someone who became an **o _ _ _ _ _ _ _ t** success:
3 Someone who always has to be the **c _ _ _ _ _** of attention:
4 One reason someone in your field might be **h _ _ _** in **h _ _ _** esteem:
5 A job for which you need to **s _ _ _ _** an **apprenticeship**:
6 Someone who is **renowned _ _ _** outstanding work:
7 Something you were **set _ _ doing** when you were younger:
8 Something you **cr_ _ _** regularly:
9 An **asp _ _ _ tion** that most people in your country have:
10 Something you used to **hanker a _ _ _ _**, but no longer care about:

B Write an example sentence for the phrases in Exercise 4A. Are your answers similar to other students'?

If I suddenly shot to fame, I would go and hide on an island!

NEGOTIATING

5A Sentences a)–g) are from a meeting about a company's annual party. Cross out the extra word in each sentence.

a) OK, so you'd like to take everybody to Sweden instead of having a party. Can you go into the more detail?
b) Get in to touch if anything needs clarifying.
c) Welcome, everybody. By the time end of the meeting, we want to have some concrete plans for our Christmas party. *1*
d) If that you can pay for some of the trip, I can ask the board to subsidise the rest.
e) Good. That sounds acceptable for to me.
f) Firstly, can you tell me a little about what you have taken in mind?
g) I'm not of sure we can do that because of the cost.

B At what stage of the meeting did the sentences occur? Put them in a logical order. The first one has been done for you.

C What do you think were the responses from the other people in the meeting?

Response to sentence c): 'Fine. That sounds good.'

BBC VIDEO PODCAST

Watch people talking about their plans and goals on ActiveBook or on the website.

Authentic BBC interviews

www.pearsonELT.com/speakout

IRREGULAR VERBS

VERB	PAST SIMPLE	PAST PARTICIPLE
be	was	been
beat	beat	beaten
become	became	become
begin	began	begun
bend	bent	bent
bet	bet	bet
bite	bit	bitten
bleed	bled	bled
blow	blew	blown
break	broke	broken
bring	brought	brought
broadcast	broadcast	broadcast
build	built	built
burn	burned/burnt	burned/burnt
burst	burst	burst
buy	bought	bought
catch	caught	caught
choose	chose	chosen
come	came	come
cost	cost	cost
cut	cut	cut
deal	dealt	dealt
dig	dug	dug
do	did	done
draw	drew	drawn
dream	dreamed/dreamt	dreamed/dreamt
drink	drank	drunk
drive	drove	driven
eat	ate	eaten
fall	fell	fallen
feel	felt	felt
feed	fed	fed
fight	fought	fought
find	found	found
fly	flew	flown
forbid	forbade	forbidden
forget	forgot	forgotten
forgive	forgave	forgiven
freeze	froze	frozen
get	got	got
give	gave	given
go	went	been/gone
grow	grew	grown
hang	hung	hung
have	had	had
hear	heard	heard
hide	hid	hidden
hit	hit	hit
hold	held	held
hurt	hurt	hurt
keep	kept	kept
know	knew	known
lay	laid	laid
lead	led	led
leap	leapt	leapt
lean	leaned/leant	leaned/leant
learn	learned/learnt	learned/learnt

VERB	PAST SIMPLE	PAST PARTICIPLE
leave	left	left
lend	lent	lent
let	let	let
lie	lay	lain
light	lit	lit
lose	lost	lost
make	made	made
mean	meant	meant
meet	met	met
mistake	mistook	mistaken
pay	paid	paid
put	put	put
read /ri:d/	read /red/	read /red/
ride	rode	ridden
ring	rang	rung
rise	rose	risen
run	ran	run
say	said	said
see	saw	seen
sell	sold	sold
send	sent	sent
set	set	set
shake	shook	shaken
shine	shone	shone
shoot	shot	shot
show	showed	shown
shrink	shrank	shrunk
shut	shut	shut
sing	sang	sung
sink	sank	sunk
sit	sat	sat
sleep	slept	slept
slide	slid	slid
smell	smelled/smelt	smelled/smelt
speak	spoke	spoken
spell	spelled/spelt	spelled/spelt
spend	spent	spent
spill	spilled/spilt	spilled/spilt
split	split	split
spread	spread	spread
stand	stood	stood
steal	stole	stolen
stick	stuck	stuck
sting	stung	stung
swim	swam	swum
take	took	taken
teach	taught	taught
tear	tore	torn
tell	told	told
think	thought	thought
throw	threw	thrown
understand	understood	understood
wake	woke	woken
wear	wore	worn
win	won	won
write	wrote	written

GRAMMAR

1.1 the continuous aspect

An aspect is a way we look at something. With verb forms, there are three aspects: simple, continuous and perfect. The simple aspect emphasises that an action is complete. The perfect aspect emphasises that an action is completed before another time.

The continuous aspect focuses on the action and its duration (how long it lasts), rather than the result. It is used to show that an activity is temporary and its duration is limited.

In contrast to the continuous aspect, we usually use simple tenses to talk about facts, permanent situations, finished actions and habits. Some verbs – called state verbs – are not usually used in the continuous, e.g. verbs that describe personal feelings (*love*, *prefer*), the senses (*hear*, *smell*) and thoughts (*believe*, *understand*).

Use the continuous aspect to talk about:

* actions that we see happening over a period of time.

They've been waiting here for an hour.

* actions in progress when another thing happens.

John was crying when I arrived.

* temporary or incomplete situations.

He's living with his parents until he can find a house.

* repeated actions (that may be annoying).

She's always playing her music loudly.

* situations in the process of changing.

The economy is getting worse.

* plans (often using the past continuous).

I was thinking of going home this weekend.

* tentative ideas (to avoid being too direct with a request).

I was wondering if I could borrow some money.

* actions in progress at a particular time.

Everyone seems to be working at the moment.

1.2 describing habits

Use *will* to describe present habits and behaviour (both good and bad).

She'll tell you everything she has done during the day, even if you're not interested.
He'll always bring me flowers.

Use present continuous + *always*, *keeps* + *-ing* and *will keep* + *-ing* in the same way. This often implies annoyance.

He's always telling me what to do.
She keeps texting me.
They will keep nagging me to go and visit them.

Use *would* to describe past habits and behaviour (both good and bad).

My parents wouldn't drive me to parties on Saturday nights.
They would make me stay at home.

Note: We can only use *will*/*would* to describe habits, not states.

He would get angry very easily. (NOT He would be angry very easily.)

Use past continuous + *always*, *kept* + *-ing* and *would keep* + *-ing* in the same way.

They were always complaining.
We kept asking for a refund, but we were ignored.
He would keep going on about his brother. It drove me mad.

Use *keep on* to emphasise that the action is repeated frequently.

Sorry, I keep on forgetting your name!

Use *tend to* to describe typical states.

She tends to shout a lot.
My parents tended to be very laid-back.

spoken grammar

Will and *would* may be stressed to emphasise the annoyance at a habit.

He will turn up late.
They wouldn't listen to me.

other expressions

I'm inclined to …/I have an inclination to …
I tend to …/I have a tendency to …
I'm prone to …
I'll spend hours …/I'd spend hours …
As a rule, I …
Nine times out of ten, I …
Andy is inclined to act first and think later.
I'm prone to falling asleep in front of the TV in the evenings.
He has a tendency to be very critical, and this makes him unpopular with colleagues.

1.3 speculating

Use the following phrases to speculate about people or situations.

speculating	
I suppose/guess/reckon he's/she's about …	There's something … about him/her.
I'd say he/she looks/doesn't look …	He/she gives the impression of being …
I wonder what he/she … ?	He/she could be/must be/might be …
I'd hazard a guess (that) …	It seems like he/she … /It seems to me … /It looks to me as if he/she …
If I had to make a guess, I'd say (that) …	It makes me think (that) maybe he/she …
I'm pretty sure he/she …	It might suggest (that) …

PRACTICE

1.1

1 Which of the underlined verbs are better in the continuous form? Change them as necessary.

1 The photocopier <u>doesn't work</u> at the moment, but the engineer will fix it this afternoon.

2 You can't go to the cinema because you <u>haven't finished</u> your homework.

3 I <u>had</u> a great time at the party when my dad arrived and dragged me home!

4 The postal worker <u>weighs</u> the package right now.

5 That's a tricky question and I <u>don't know</u> the answer.

6 I <u>looked</u> through my old papers and I found this letter from you.

7 Can you turn down the volume? I <u>talk</u> on the phone.

8 I <u>didn't hear</u> the doorbell so I carried on watching TV.

9 She <u>has studied</u> all morning.

10 I live in Krakow, but I <u>do</u> a course in Warsaw this summer.

2 Complete the questions. Use the correct continuous form of the verb in brackets where possible. Which sentences need a simple form?

1 A: _____ (cry)?
   B: Because I just fell off my bike and it hurts!

2 A: _____ (work) there before they fired him?
   B: About twenty years. He was devastated.

3 A: _____ (do) since you graduated?
   B: I've mainly been looking for jobs, but no luck so far.

4 A: _____ (live) in Madrid?
   B: Twenty-seven years. I moved here when I was twenty.

5 A: _____ (talk) to when I saw you earlier?
   B: Oh, she's an old schoolmate.

6 A: _____ (want) to be when you were a child?
   B: A fireman. I loved the uniform!

7 A: _____ (wait) long?
   B: About an hour. The hospital is always busy on a Saturday.

8 A: _____ (not finish) your degree?
   B: Because I ran out of money and couldn't pay the tuition fees.

1.2

1 Add will/won't/would/wouldn't to the sentences in the correct place.

1 On Sunday mornings, I get up early and go for a run along the river before anyone else is awake.

2 I sometimes wait for hours before a bus arrives.

3 My mother-in-law always bake a cake for us when we visit.

4 He keep bothering me for my telephone number, but I don't want to give it to him.

5 The children stop fighting. It's driving me crazy.

6 She spend the first half an hour chatting before she even starts work.

7 My parents take us on camping holidays in the rain. We hated it.

8 My grandfather shout, or tell you off. He was a very gentle man.

2 Complete the sentences using the prompts in brackets.

1 The drug _____ headaches if used for prolonged periods. (tendency/cause)

2 He _____ paintings which cost far too much money. (inclined/buy)

3 We're _____ about politics at the dinner table. (prone/argue)

4 I _____ whether or not I've been given the job. (keep/wonder)

5 She's _____ a fuss about the way I dress. (always/make)

6 They _____ at cards, so I decided not to play with them. (kept/cheat)

7 As _____, I _____ a lot of herbs and spices in my cooking. (rule/not use)

8 My father _____ me back a present from his travels. (would always/bring)

1.3

1 Complete the conversations with the words in the box.

sure	seems	wonder	guess	give	~~reckon~~
say	hazard	looks			

1 A: I _reckon_ it might rain later.
   B: Yes, it _____ as though it could.

2 A: How much do you think that painting is worth?
   B: I'd _____ a guess at about $500.
   A: Not quite. It's worth $1.2 million.

3 A: What time do you think they'll arrive?
   B: I'm pretty _____ they'll be here by six.

4 A: What do you think it's supposed to be?
   B: I _____ it could be an animal of some sort.

5 A: I _____ if she'll remember we're coming?
   B: If not, we'll surprise her.

6 A: If I had to make a guess, I'd _____ it was that way.
   B: It _____ to me that we're lost.

7 A: Have you seen that Rafael and Lina have got a smart new car?
   B: Yes, they _____ the impression of having plenty of money.

GRAMMAR

2.1 conditionals and regrets

The most common conditional sentences refer to permanent facts (zero conditional), future possibility (first conditional) or imaginary situations (second conditional).

third conditional

Use to talk about something that could have happened, but didn't, or should not have happened, but did.

*If I **hadn't eaten** that shellfish, I **would have been** fine.*

other forms with a third conditional meaning

***Supposing** you**'d** met the President, what **would** you **have said**?*

***Imagine** you**'d** missed the flight, what **would you have done**?*

In more formal contexts, it is possible to replace *if* by inverting the subject and *had*.

***Had I** known her, I **would have said** hello.*

Or replace *if* with *but for* + noun (+ gerund)

***But for** Wilkinson's heroics, they **would have lost** the match.*

mixed conditional

Use to say how, if something had been different in the past, the present or future would be different.

*If she**'d listened** to me, she **wouldn't be** in debt now.*

regrets

Use *regret* + gerund, *if only* + past perfect or *wish* + past perfect to say we want something in the past to have been different.

*I **regret going out** last night.*

*If only I **hadn't** left the oven on. He **wishes** he**'d gone** to university.*

Use *if only* + past simple or *wish* + past simple to say we want something to be different now.

*If only we **had** some matches! I **wish** you **were** here.*

Note: After *if*, *if only* and *wish*, we often use *were* instead of *was*. *Were* is considered more correct in formal English, although *was* is often used in spoken English.

Use *if only* + *would* or *wish* + *would* to show we are annoyed by something now.

*If only you**'d** be more sensible! I **wish** you **would** be quiet!*

2.2 verb patterns

verb + -ing

Many verbs can be followed by a verb in the *-ing* form.

Some of these verbs are related in meaning: *like, dislike, adore, love, detest, can't bear/stand.* Some can also be followed by the infinitive, but the meaning may change.

*We **regret to inform** you …* (We are sorry **before** we speak.)

*He **regrets telling** her …* (He is sorry **after** he speaks.)

Prepositions are followed by an *-ing* form.

*Are you still **interested in buying** the property?*

-Ing forms when they function as nouns (gerunds) are often the subject of a sentence.

***Smoking** is bad for you.*

infinitive with to

Use an infinitive with *to*:

• after certain verbs including *appear, decide, fail, need, offer, refuse, want, wish.* Verbs with a future meaning (*hope, expect, promise,* etc.) are often followed by the infinitive.

*They **hoped to negotiate** a better deal.*

• after certain verb + object combinations, e.g. *advise, allow, ask, cause, encourage, forbid.*

*The police **asked everyone to remain** calm.*

• with some nouns, often as part of semi-fixed phrases (*It's time to …*, etc.).

• after most adjectives.

*I was **happy to help**.*

passive infinitive or -ing form

Use the passive *-ing* form (*being done*) to describe actions which are done to the subject.

*I hate **being told** what **to do**.*

Use the passive infinitive (*to be done*) after some verbs (especially reporting verbs).

*He was **considered to be** the right person for the job.*

perfect infinitive or -ing form

Use the perfect *-ing* form (*having done*) or the perfect infinitive (*to have done*) to emphasise when one action happened before another.

*She mentioned **having seen** him leave.*
*They seem **to have solved** the problem.*

After verbs of preference (*would like/love/hate/prefer/rather*) we can use the perfect infinitive to talk about an action in the past.

*We **would hate to have lost** the match.*

negative infinitive or -ing form

Not + infinitive and *Not* + *-ing* are also important.

*It's quite common **not to understand** at first.*
***Not understanding** is quite common.*

Infinitives can be the subject of a sentence.

***To learn** is important. **Not to thank** her would be impolite.*

2.3 introducing opinions

Use the following phrases to introduce opinions or knowledge.

If you want my honest opinion, …	According to (the statistics), …	To my knowledge, …
Quite frankly, …	From what I can gather, …	Look at it this way.
The reality is, … /In reality, …	As far as I'm concerned, …	If you ask me, …

PRACTICE

2.1

1 Complete the sentences with the correct form of the verbs in the box. Use the negative form where necessary.

> take over   know   be   spend   find   cause   stay   pull
> die   become   tell   arrive   win   listen   call   cook

1 If you _____ to my advice, you _____ in such a terrible situation now.
2 I regret _____ a manager so young; I wish I _____ more time in the industry first.
3 We _____ your house if we _____ you on the mobile.
4 Imagine if Donner Textiles Ltd _____ the company, it _____ all kinds of problems.
5 Had they _____ us about that hotel, we _____ there now, instead of in this dump!
6 But for the emergency services _____ so quickly, many more people _____ in the fire.
7 If I _____ she didn't eat wheat, I _____ pasta.
8 It's such a shame: had she _____ a muscle, she _____ the race.

2 Rewrite the sentences using the word(s) in brackets.

1 We gambled on red. We lost.
   (If/won) _____.
2 They only asked him to the party because he's famous.
   (wouldn't) _____.
3 The boys feel bad about borrowing your car.
   (regret) _____.
4 She didn't know you were a vegetarian! She bought fish!
   (Had) _____.
5 I forgot my keys. Now we're locked out!
   (If only/wouldn't) _____.
6 I'm working in a boring, low-paid job. I shouldn't have dropped out of university.
   (If) _____.
7 Ahmed is sorry he didn't speak to you before you left.
   (wishes) _____.
8 He had an injury. We would have won otherwise.
   (But for) _____.

2.2

1 Underline the correct alternatives.

We all know how important [1]*make/making/to make* a good first impression is. We've heard the statistics: when you meet someone for the first time, only seven percent of their impression is based on what you say, thirty-eight percent on how you say it, and a massive fifty-five percent on your appearance and manner. So, it's vital not [2]*underestimate/underestimating/to underestimate* the importance of choosing your clothes carefully when you go to that key meeting or job interview. This is your opportunity [3]*impress/impressing/to impress*. On [4]*walk/walking/to walk* into the room, most people are likely [5]*to have form/to have forming/to have formed* an opinion of your character based on your appearance in less than three seconds. It's difficult [6]*say/saying/to say* why people insist on [7]*judge/judging/to judge* by appearances, even when we know that it's so unreliable [8]*do/doing/to do* this. Even in courtrooms, juries and judges appear [9]*give/giving/to give* lighter sentences to people who are well-dressed.

2 Find and correct the six mistakes in sentences 1–8.

1 I can't bear seeing people smoke in cars.
2 I don't know why you waste all your time sit in front of the computer.
3 Cooder was encouraged play the guitar by his father.
4 They hoped meet up with some of the stars after the show.
5 They were rumoured to have get married in secret.
6 I gave up the idea of go into politics when I was in my thirties.
7 We were tempted ask if we could stay the night, but we thought it might seem rude.
8 I would prefer to have seen it for myself.

2.3

1 Match the sentence halves.

1 If you want my   a) honest opinion, there isn't much evidence to support this theory.
2 The reality   b) frankly, this is the best film of the decade.
3 Look at it   c) is, we can't keep sending them money.
4 As far as   d) gather, he's very well-established in his field.
5 If you ask   e) knowledge, Yum Yums is the best brand for baby food.
6 According to   f) me, you should put aside more time for your family.
7 Quite   g) the boss, we're making a profit of €100,000 every month.
8 From what I can   h) I'm concerned, this company is living on borrowed time.
9 To my   i) this way: we must do something now or things will get worse.

GRAMMAR

3.1 noun phrases

A noun phrase is a group of words which function as a unit to describe the noun. Information can be added before or after the noun to add further information about it.

before the noun (pre-modification)

Compound nouns are formed when another noun is added to help describe the noun head. These can be written as two words, with a hyphen, or as one word.

coffee cup   build-up   fingerprint

Compound adjectives can be used for expressions of measurement. Plural expressions become singular.

A forty-five-minute journey (it takes forty-five minutes)

Adverb + adjective combinations can be used to give more information about the noun.

an amazingly simple process

Adjectives before a noun need to be in a specific order.

determiner	value	size	age	shape	colour	origin	material	compound	noun
two	lovely		old			French			vases
my	shabby				black		leather	biker	jacket
some		small		oval			silver	ear	rings

after the noun (post-modification)

Prepositional phrases can be used to help modify the noun.

*the light **from the setting sun***
*a suggestion **for how to arrange the meeting***

Participle clauses also give more description.

*people **rushing in and out of their offices***

Relative clauses can also be used to modify the noun phrase. See 3.2 below.

*the man **who I spotted in the restaurant***

Sometimes, the relative clause can be rewritten as a noun phrase.

research that has been conducted recently ⟶ *recent research*

3.2 relative clauses

defining relative clauses

Defining relative clauses give essential information about a noun. Compare:

1 My uncle, who lives in New York, is coming to Oxford.
2 My uncle who lives in New York is coming to Oxford.

In sentence 1, *who lives in New York* is a non-defining relative clause. It gives extra non-essential information about the uncle. In sentence 2, it is a defining relative clause. The speaker has more than one uncle so she identifies which uncle she is talking about.

In defining relative clauses, we can omit the relative pronoun if it is the object of the verb.

I've eaten the cake (which) I made yesterday.

non-defining relative clauses

Non-defining relative clauses give extra information about a noun. Use a comma before and after the relative clause.

*That project, **which I started years ago,** still isn't finished.*

relative pronouns

Use: *who* for people, *which* for things/groups of people, *where* for places, *whose* for possessions belonging to people and things. *That* can replace any pronoun except *whose* in defining relative clauses.

Use a relative pronoun after *some of, all of, a few of, none of*.

*She has four sisters, **none of whom** are married.*

fixed prepositional phrases and relative clauses

There are a number of fixed phrases which use a preposition in a non-defining relative clause.

*The company ran out of money, **at which point** I quit my job.*
*He may work late, **in which case** I'll get home first.*
*We watched the final, **the** result **of which** was never in doubt.*

In informal sentences, the preposition stays with the verb. In formal sentences we put the preposition before the relative pronoun. Compare:

He completed the book which he'd been working on. (informal)
He completed the book on which he'd been working. (formal)

3.3 making a proposal

introducing your proposal	justifying your idea	soliciting questions
Just to give a bit of background information, … To start with, I'm going to talk briefly about …	This solution will help us to … This idea is feasible because …	Does anyone have any questions? Is there anything that needs clarification?
stating the purpose	**listing the benefits**	
The aim of the project is to … The main goal/objective of our proposal is to …	In the first instance, this would mean … The short-term/long-term benefits include …	
describing your idea	**summarising your proposal**	
What we plan to do is … We're going to build/develop/come up with …	So, basically, what we're proposing is to … To sum up, we're proposing …	

PRACTICE

3.1

1 Make one sentence by adding the information in brackets to the noun phrase. Pay attention to word order.

1 I like coffee. (black / strong / small cups of / freshly-ground)
_____.

2 He bought the house. (by the river / little / pretty)
_____.

3 She made cakes. (with strawberries and fresh cream on top / delicious / dark chocolate / two)
_____.

4 He smokes cigars. (which Juan gives him / hugely expensive / Cuban / those / enormous)
_____.

5 They carried the bags. (ridiculously heavy / massive pile of / all the way up seven flights of stairs)
_____.

6 It was a dog. (incredibly smelly / hairy / guard / but rather friendly)
_____.

2 Rewrite the sentences to make one sentence with a complex noun phrase.

1 I went to the shop. It sold shoes. It was advertised on television.
I went _____.

2 The man was old. He was walking with a stick.
He was _____.

3 We ate the cakes. They were home-made. They were absolutely delicious. We were sitting in the sunshine.
We ate _____.

4 They rented a house. It was nice. It was near the airport. It had a swimming pool.
They rented _____.

5 We went to a restaurant. It was big. It was a pizza restaurant. It was on the outskirts of town. It was run by two Italian brothers. They were called Gino and Rino.
We went _____.

3.2

1 Complete the sentences with one word in each gap.

In my early twenties, [1] _when_ I was a student, I used to hang out in a few places, none [2] _____ which were exactly posh. There was one seedy dive called Schubert's, [3] _____ an acquaintance of mine, [4] _____ name I've forgotten, played the piano. But my favourite haunt, [5] _____ which I remember everything including the decor (a Matisse poster [6] _____ edges were peeling off the wall), was Johnny Bee's Café. The table [7] _____ I regularly sat faced a window from [8] _____ you could see the street. I must have gone to Johnny Bee's every day until I graduated, by which [9] _____ I was virtually living there. Most of the dissertation [10] _____ which I was working was conceived in Johnny Bee's. I went back last year and saw the same people, none of [11] _____ had changed except for a few grey hairs.

2 Complete the second sentence so it has a similar meaning to the first. Use the word in brackets.

1 There were lots of children there and all of them sang really well. (whom)
There were lots of children there, _____.

2 When the fire alarm went off, the lesson ended. (point)
The fire alarm went off, _____.

3 We stayed in that woman's house. (house)
That's the woman _____.

4 Clare's the person I learnt the most from. (whom)
The person _____.

5 If you get a scholarship, you won't need to pay. (case)
You may get a scholarship, in _____.

6 There are two photocopiers in the office, which are both out of order. (of)
There are two photocopiers in the office, _____.

3.3

1 Underline the correct alternatives to complete the proposal.

Just to give a bit of [1]*background information/information background*, we're computer programmers who have travelled all over the world and have contacts everywhere. To start [2]*up/with*, we're going to talk briefly about our plan for a website to organise student trips abroad.

The main goal [3]*to/of* our proposal is to get funding for this internet start-up, and the [4]*target/aim* of the project is to help students travel abroad for life-changing trips.

OK, [5]*how/what* we plan to do is create personalised trips according to the client's interests. We're going to come [6]*up with/down to* a menu of travel options linked to the client's profile.

This idea is [7]*possible/feasible* because students book everything online and they love travelling, but they also want to avoid the problems of independent travel. This [8]*opportunity/solution* will help them to realise their dreams.

Here are the benefits: in the first [9]*instance/case*, our idea would mean the client didn't have to organise anything. Secondly, there is the [10]*term-long/long-term* benefit of security. We will plan safe itineraries and we'll always know where the traveller is.

So, basically, [11]*that/what* we're proposing is to tailor holidays for the client using our contacts abroad. To [12]*sum up/the sum up*, we want to provide amazing experiences for future generations, and you can be a part of this by providing start-up funds for our site.

GRAMMAR

4.1 introductory *it*

Use *it* as an 'empty' subject to introduce or identify something later in the phrase.

'What's the problem?' '**It's** nothing. **It's** just that I'm worried about work.'

Use *it* + *be* to talk about:

*   weather.
It's a bit chilly for this time of year.
*   time/dates.
It's about half past two.
*   situations.
It's a very peaceful place.
*   distance.
It's about thirty kilometres away.

Use *it* before some phrases to describe probability.
It looks as though we're going to lose.

Use *it* before some phrases to report events.
It would appear that they have left without us.

Use *it* as an 'empty' object after certain verbs to introduce a clause.

(subject + verb + *it* + complement + infinitive/clause)
I'd appreciate it if …
I find it impossible to …

other common expressions with *it*

it + *be* + adjective
It's hard to know if …
It's easy to believe that …

it + verb phrase
It always amazes me that …
It looks/seems as if …

it in the middle of the phrase
I'll leave it to you to decide …
I find it easy to …

fixed expressions
It's no wonder/no coincidence that …
It's considered rude to …
It's pointless/no use + -ing …

4.2 the perfect aspect

The perfect aspect looks back from one time to another and emphasises that an action is completed before another time. In some cases, the exact time may be unimportant or unknown. Sometimes the event is incomplete. It started in the past and is still relevant now.

present perfect

Use the present perfect to look back from now to a time before now.

I've been here since June.

Use the present perfect continuous to focus on the length of time the action takes.

She's been waiting for hours.

past perfect

Use the past perfect to look back from a time in the past to a time before that.

I had to go back because I'd forgotten my passport.

Use the past perfect continuous to focus on the length of time the action takes.

She'd been doing the same job for fifteen years.

future perfect

Use the future perfect to look back from a time in the future to a time before that.

*By next week we **will have finished** the project.*

Note: We also use *will have* + past participle to make predictions about the present or the future.

*Don't call the house, she'**ll have left** for work by now.*

Use the future perfect continuous to focus on the length of time the action takes.

*In 2020, I'**ll have been living** here for fifty years.*

perfect infinitive

Use the perfect infinitive after verbs like *seem* and *appear* to look back to a previous time period.

*He seems **to have forgotten** us.*

It can be used with different time periods.

*It's great **to have finished** my exams.*
*He said he was sorry **to have missed** your party.*
*We hope **to have done** the work by 5.00.*

4.3 hypothetical preferences

Use the following phrases to express hypothetical preferences.

hypothetical preferences	
If it was up to me, I'd … / I'd have (+ past participle)	Far better to … than …
I'd sooner (+ infinitive without *to*)	This would be by far the best option.
I'd just as soon (+ infinitive without *to*) … as	My preference would be to …
Given the choice, I'd …	Without a shadow of a doubt, I'd …
If I ever found myself in this/that situation, I'd …	No way would I (+ infinitive without *to*).

PRACTICE

4.1

1 Add *it / it's* in the correct place(s) in sentences 1–8.

1 I can't stand when all does is rain for days on end.

2 I'd appreciate if you could give me a little more notice next time.

3 No use just standing there. You'd better get on with it.

4 I find hard to believe that the summer is here already.

5 Appears that the police have video footage of the incident.

6 Pointless arguing with her when she's in that kind of state.

7 I'll leave to the others to decide what time we should meet.

8 I've always made clear that my family has to take priority over my work.

2 Complete the second sentence so it has a similar meaning to the first. Use three to six words including the word in brackets.

1 Don't cry about the situation now. It won't help.
(pointless) It's _____ about the situation now.

2 Being trustworthy is vital in this profession.
(essential) It's _____ in this profession.

3 He appears to have misplaced his keys.
(seems) It _____ his keys.

4 We need to be hospitable to them as they were welcoming to us.
(owe) We _____ hospitable as they were welcoming to us.

5 I am not surprised by her lack of enthusiasm as she has heard the talk before.
(wonder) It's _____ when she had heard the talk before.

6 It's easy for me to keep abreast of the latest news online.
(find) I _____ of the latest news online.

4.2

1 Underline the correct alternatives.

1 UNICEF *will have provided / has been providing / is to have provided* humanitarian assistance to developing countries since 1946.

2 My family *will have lived / has lived / had been living* in that house for over 100 years by the time we were forced to move.

3 Next year, it *had been / will have been / has been* twenty years since we met.

4 They *have closed / have been closing / will have closed* that shop because it wasn't making money.

5 Judging by the state of the garden, she *will have abandoned / had been abandoning / appeared to have abandoned* her home.

6 By 2018, Tom *will have been running / has been running / is to have run* the company for twenty years.

2 Complete speaker B's responses using the prompts. Use perfect tenses.

1 A: Is the protest still going on?
   B: Yes. The workers / march / since 8.00 this morning.

2 A: Why did you shout at the students at the end of class?
   B: They / talk throughout the whole lesson.

3 A: Eliana is the most experienced person in the office, isn't she?
   B: Yes. This time next year she / work / here / for forty years.

4 A: Do you think they'll be at the airport now?
   B: Yes. It's 8.00. They / arrive / by now.

5 A: Why is he losing so badly?
   B: He / seems / forget / how to play!

6 A: I hear Mary lost her job because the company went bankrupt.
   B: That's right. She / only / work there for two months when the company closed.

4.3

1 Match the sentence halves.

1 If I found myself in
2 This would be by
3 I'd just as
4 Far better
5 Given the
6 No way would
7 My preference would
8 I'd sooner eat at home
9 Without a shadow of
10 If it was up to

a) than go to Grisky's.
b) soon listen to the radio as watch TV.
c) choice, I wouldn't take any tests.
d) that situation, I'd panic.
e) far the best option.
f) be to speak to the manager.
g) me, I'd have told her earlier.
h) to tell the truth than to make up a story.
i) a doubt I'd buy it if I had the cash.
j) I ever steal anything.

GRAMMAR

5.1 modal verbs and phrases

Use modal verbs and phrases to express degrees of obligation or whether or not something is necessary, desirable, permitted or forbidden. Modals are also used to refer to people's abilities.

have to, must, should, ought to, had better for obligation

We **ought to set** the alarm for an hour earlier.

Had better is stronger than *ought to* and implies a warning.

We**'d better leave** now. We don't want to be late.

need for talking about obligation or lack of it

We **needed to ask** for directions. (If we had done this, we wouldn't be lost.)

Notice the difference between *didn't need to* and *needn't have*.

We **didn't need to ask** for directions. (We had a map.)

We **needn't have asked** for directions. (We asked for directions, but it was unnecessary as we found a map.)

can, (be) allowed to, (be) supposed to, (be) permitted to for talking about what is permissible/possible

We **couldn't leave** the premises after 6p.m. (It wasn't allowed.)

Be supposed to implies that someone expects you to do this (maybe it's a rule). We can use this when we don't obey the rule.

We**'re supposed to leave** the key on the desk when we finish. (But we may not, we may take it with us.)

other phrases which can be used with modal meaning

(be) allowed, (be) permissible; (be) forbidden, (be) banned; (be/feel) compelled, (be) compulsory; (be) forced to, (be) obligatory; have the courage to, dare to

They **were forced to wear** army uniform. (Army uniform was compulsory.)

We **weren't allowed to contact** the teachers. (It wasn't permissible to contact them.)

5.2 the passive

Use the passive to sound objective and impersonal. The passive is particularly common in formal writing, e.g. academic writing and news reports.

Use the passive to emphasise the important information at the beginning of the sentence.

Penicillin **was discovered** *by Fleming.* (The most important point is the invention of penicillin.)

Use the passive if who performs the action is unknown or unimportant. The emphasis is on the action itself.

The museum **was built** *in the seventeenth century.* (We aren't interested in who built it.)

Use the passive to show that we are not certain.

It **is believed** *that this ancient society used aspirin.* (There is no proof. It's just a theory.)

Use the passive to distance ourselves from a statement.

*It***'s said** *that it's unlucky to walk under a ladder.* (The speaker might not believe this.)

The passive is often used in formal English to describe rules, processes or procedures.

Membership cards **must be shown** *at the door before entry.*

It is common to use the passive with an infinitive or with *to have* + past participle.

She **was thought to be** *the best swimmer in the city.*

He **is known to have been** *present during the crimes.*

We can use a causative form with a passive meaning. The form is *have/get* + object + past participle.

She **had** *her car* **broken into**.
He **got** *his teeth* **removed**.

spoken grammar

Get is more informal than *have*.

A spoken form of the causative *have* is common in the US.

I **had** *the mechanic* **fix** *my car.*

5.3 making a point

making a point	clarifying a point	challenging a point
There are several reasons why I think that …	What I'm basically saying is …	Do you think that's always the case?
The reason (why) I say that is …	The point I'm trying to make is that …	Can you be sure about that?
The facts suggest … /The evidence shows …	Actually, … /In fact, …	Is there any way/evidence to prove that?
After all, …	Let me put it this way …	But that's not the point.
The point is …	I think you'll find that …	I don't see how you can say that.
If you think about it, …		But that doesn't take account of the fact that …

PRACTICE

5.1

1 Complete the second sentence so it has a similar meaning to the first. Use the word in brackets.

1 We couldn't bring our own food to school.
(allow) We weren't _____.

2 I wish I hadn't told him that I cheated in the exam.
(should) I _____.

3 Turn your mobile phones off. They are not allowed in the cinema.
(better) You'd _____.

4 You must hand this work in first thing in the morning.
(have) You _____.

5 I didn't have the courage to tell them the truth.
(dare) I didn't _____.

6 They aren't allowed to have their lights on after 10p.m.
(supposed) They're _____.

2 Find and correct the mistakes in sentences 1–8. There is one mistake in each sentence.

1 You didn't need rush. There's another five minutes before the film starts.

2 We'd better to leave plenty of time to get to the airport in case of heavy traffic.

3 You didn't have got to buy a present. That's very kind of you.

4 You should don't drive a car if you're tired.

5 We didn't had to stop at all on the way.

6 They were supposed deliver the furniture today.

7 You ought to trying this programme – it's very good.

8 You shouldn't to talk to people like that. It's rude.

5.2

1A Complete the second sentence so it has a similar meaning to the first. Use the passive or causative and the word in brackets.

1 Police are investigating the case.
(being) The _____.

2 The university lets you borrow a car for official business.
(allowed) You _____.

3 They are delivering Mike's washing machine today.
(having) Mike _____.

4 Some people say the tradition began in the nineteenth century.
(claimed) It _____.

5 There's a possibility someone recognised Wilhelm.
(might) Wilhelm _____.

6 She instructed the players to stretch before the game.
(had) She _____.

7 Someone is checking in our luggage right now.
(being) Our _____.

8 The researchers have only tested the product on volunteers.
(been) The _____.

B Why might sentences 1–8 be better in the passive? Which might be formal written English?

2 Rewrite the underlined phrases in the passive. Omit the 'doer' of the action.

[1] They say that the world's greatest keepers of secrets are spies. While this may be true, there is another secret connected to spies that is less well known. They are a huge problem for their employers. Why? Like most workers, spies retire when they get old. However, unlike most workers, spies retain numerous high level secrets. [2] They need to keep these secrets even after the spies retire. So [3] what can the authorities do with retired ex-spies? In the 1960s, [4] they considered brainwashing. But [5] they discovered that brainwashing didn't work. They also tried hypnotism, in the hope that [6] they could erase certain memories from the mind. But it turned out to be impossible to erase some memories and not others, e.g. the names of your family members and your street address. So what did they do in the end? We don't know, of course. It's a secret.

1 _____   4 _____

2 _____   5 _____

3 _____   6 _____

5.3

1 Put the underlined words in the correct order to complete the conversations.

A: [1] saying I'm is what we need to be very careful who we give the information to. [2] suggest facts the that the more people who know about the idea, the riskier the situation.

B: I guess so. But we need to tell people about the product before we launch to get people excited about it.

A: That's true, but [3] the is point if the competition find out about it, they will probably steal the idea.

B: [4] think always you is that case the do?

A: Yes. [5] All after, what have they got to lose?

C: [6] are several think reasons there why I this is the right thing to do and [7] about think it if you, we don't have any other options.

D: [8] say you don't can how see I that. I just don't think the idea will work in practice.

C: Well, [9] way put this me it let, we don't have any more time to consider options. We need to decide.

D: I know there are time pressures, but [10] that trying make is I'm point to the we need to think about the costs as well.

GRAMMAR

6.1 future forms

be going to

Use *be going to* + infinitive to:

• express personal intention. The action has been considered in advance and some plans have already been made.

We '***re going to stay*** with John next summer.

• make a prediction based on present evidence.

I think she '***s going to fall***! (She is off balance.)

will

Use *will* to:

• make predictions. *We '**ll** win the Cup this year.*

• talk about future facts. *He '**ll** start school next year.*

We often use *will* with adverbs of probability.

I '***ll probably*** see you tomorrow.

We also use *will* for decisions made at the moment of speaking.

I think I '***ll*** have a nap.

present continuous

Use the present continuous to talk about a pre-arranged action in the future. *Be going to* is for intentions, while the present continuous is for planned events or arrangements for a specific time.

I '***m visiting*** Sheila **on Sunday**.

present simple

Use the present simple to talk about fixed future events in timetables or programmes.

My train ***arrives*** at 5.00.

future continuous

Use the future continuous to:

• talk about an action that will be in progress at some time in the future.

This time next week I '***ll be lying*** on a beach.

• make a deduction about the future based on normal practice.

I expect the Smiths ***will be having*** their annual party soon.

• talk about something that will happen as part of the normal course of events, not because you planned it.

I '***ll be seeing*** Jackie at college, so I'll give her the note.

future perfect and future perfect continuous

Use the future perfect to talk about a future event which will be finished at a certain point in the future. Use the future perfect continuous to talk about the length of an action as seen from a moment in the future.

The builders ***will have finished*** our house **by January**.

By 2018, I '***ll have been studying*** French **for twenty years**.

modal verbs

Could, *might* and *may* are also used to make predictions. They have similar meanings, but *may* is more formal.

be to

Use *be* + *to* + infinitive to describe official plans and arrangements.

The company ***is to provide*** insurance for all of its workers.

be due to

Use *be due to* + infinitive to describe a formal arrangement.

The plane ***is due to land*** at 6.00.

6.2 concession clauses

Use concession clauses to give information that contrasts with the information in the main clause.

The clauses can be introduced with conjunctions such as *although, however, even though,* etc.

Although he was a good linguist, he took five years to learn Mandarin.

We can also use *while* and *whilst* (formal) to replace *although.*

While/Whilst I'd like to be with you, I have to attend a meeting.

Use *much as* to replace *although* with verbs for like and hate to talk about strong feelings.

Much as we appreciate your efforts, sadly we won't be able to use the report.

Use adjective/adverb + *as/though* + subject + verb clause for emphatic sentences.

Hard as we tried, we failed to get hold of anybody.

Difficult though it was, we eventually secured the premises.

Use *however/whatever/wherever,* etc. to express the idea of 'no matter what/who/where', etc.

Whatever he says, I'm going anyway.

Use *in spite of* and *despite* + noun phrase/*-ing* form to express contrast.

In spite of the fact that we had no ID on us, the porter let us in.

Despite feeling awful, we stayed until the end.

Note: Sentences using *in spite of/despite* are not concession clauses, as the linker is not followed by a verb clause, but is followed by a noun/*-ing* form.

We can use adverbs and adverbial phrases to introduce contrast.

We were exhausted but we carried on ***all the same***.

We were exhausted. ***Nevertheless***, we carried on.

6.3 describing cause and effect

Cause		Effect	
informal and neutral	formal	informal and neutral	formal
It all started …	It has its origins/roots in …	It led to …	It resulted in …
It originated in/from …	It can be traced back/attributed to …	It has caused …	It gave rise to …
It's because of …	It stems from …	Because of this, …	It brought about …

PRACTICE

6.1

1 There are ten words missing from the speech. Complete it by adding the missing words.

'Yesterday we announced that we are merge with Jonas Inc. We are due do this in May, so today I'm going speak about the company's history and the decision to merge. This time next year, the company will have building houses for twenty-five years. By January, we will built more than 100,000 homes, and I hope that we'll still be houses in 2050. Although we be discussing the new situation with you individually, we are sure your jobs will secure. Through this merger, we be expanding and so we will be moving into unknown markets. By February, we will sent you a document about the company's plans. For now, I promise there will be opportunities for all.'

2 Complete the second sentence so it has the same meaning as the first. Use the words in brackets and a future form.

1 It's our twentieth wedding anniversary tomorrow.
   (married) By tomorrow, we will _____.
2 The arrival time for the London-Brussels flight is 2.00.
   (at) The London-Brussels flight _____.
3 The government will pass a law prohibiting guns.
   (is) The government _____.
4 I work in the same office as John, so I can speak to him.
   (seeing) I'll _____.
5 We arrived here in July five years ago.
   (living) By July, we'll _____.
6 The committee has scheduled a meeting with the owners.
   (due) The committee is _____.
7 Roger always puts up his Christmas decorations in November.
   (putting) I imagine Roger will _____.
8 My son celebrates his eighteenth birthday next March.
   (old) My son _____.

6.2

1 Complete the sentences with the words in the box.

| however despite although as whenever |
| whereas matter spite |

1 American cars are generally too large for the Japanese market, _____ Japanese cars are popular in the USA.
2 Hard _____ she tried, she couldn't get the door to open.
3 No _____ how difficult it is, I'm determined to do my best.
4 They explained that we could leave _____ we wanted to.
5 She went to Spain _____ the fact that her doctor had told her to rest.
6 We went out in _____ of the rain.
7 I really want the car, _____ much it costs.
8 We decided to take the room, _____ we knew we couldn't really afford the rent.

2 Rewrite the sentences using the words in brackets. Write one or two sentences.

1 I spend much too much time on the internet. I know that it's bad for me.
   (Despite) _____.
2 My grandmother is still fully independent. She is nearly ninety-six years old.
   (Even though) _____.
3 He's an excellent manager. He can be a bit scary to work for.
   (… although …) _____.
4 They tried hard. They couldn't persuade him to give up his work.
   (Hard as) _____.
5 I understand how difficult the situation is. I'm afraid I can't help.
   (Whilst) _____.
6 He's very charming. I wouldn't trust him at all.
   (… However, …) _____.

6.3

1 Underline the correct alternatives.

The Second World War gave [1]*rights/arise/rise* to the term 'The First World War'. Impossible? No. It's all because of 'retronymy'. A 'retronym' is a word invented for an object/concept whose original name has gone out of date. Retronyms are invented because new developments change the way we perceive the world. The term 'The First World War' can be traced [2]*up/on/back* to 1939. Before that date, nobody knew there would be a World War II, and World War I had, until then, been called 'The Great War'.

Another example is the guitar. All guitars used to be acoustic. The invention of the electric guitar [3]*caused/led/moved* to the term 'acoustic guitar'. Similarly, nobody said 'black and white TV' before the invention of colour TV [4]*developed/resulted/traced* in the need for the term. Many retronyms [5]*affect/stem/rise* from modern technology. The invention of laptops brought [6]*with/for/about* the term 'desktop computer' and the proliferation of mobile phones resulted [7]*on/in/to* the word 'landline'. The word 'retronym' is [8]*attributed/given/caused* to Frank Mankiewicz, an American journalist.

GRAMMAR

7.1 cleft sentences

Cleft means 'divided'. In cleft sentences, one sentence is divided into two parts, each with its own verb. This adds emphasis to part of the sentence.

John loves Mary. (one verb)
It's Mary that John loves. (two verbs, emphasises *Mary*)

The following structures are commonly used to begin cleft sentences.

It + …	What + …
It was a … who …	What I like about … is
It was in … that …	What they didn't realise was …

other structures
The person who …
The place that …
The thing that … is/was …
Something that … is/was …
The reason why … is/was …
The only thing that … is/was …
All that I would … is/was …

We can use *Wh-* words with cleft sentences. To emphasise the action, we use a form of *do*.
Jane invested well. ⟶ *What Jane **did was** invest well.*

emphasising with *what*, *all* and *it*

To emphasise an action or series of actions, we can use sentences beginning with *What*.

He dropped the vase. ⟶ ***What happened was** (that) he dropped the vase.*

We can use *Wh-* clauses as introductory phrases.
***What I would like to know is** where the money went.*

We can use *all* instead of *what*.
***All I'd like to say is that** the company appreciates your work.*

Use *It + be + that/who* to emphasise parts of a sentence.
Karin left her bag on the train. ⟶
*It was **Karin** who left her bag on the train.* (Karin – not Fatima)
*It was **her bag** that Karin left on the train.* (not her umbrella)
*It's **because you have such a good sense of humour** that I enjoy your company.* (emphasising reason)
*It was **only yesterday** that I discovered the documents were missing.* (emphasising time)
*It was **by chance** that they met in Paris.* (emphasising prepositional phrase)

7.2 participle clauses

Participle clauses are used to make our writing and speaking more economical, efficient and, sometimes, more elegant. They can also be used to add information about reason, condition and result.

past participles
Past participle clauses have a passive meaning. Use past participles to add extra information. They sometimes serve the same purpose as adjectives (describing a noun).
***Loved** by everyone, Don was a wonderful character.* (describes Don)
***Exhausted** from her efforts, she struggled on.* (describes 'she')

present participles
Present participle clauses have an active meaning. Use present participles (-*ing* form):
• as reduced relative clauses. Here the present participle serves the same purpose as an adjective.
*The **woman who is smiling** in the photo is my grandmother.* ⟶
*The **woman smiling** in the photo is my grandmother.*
*I smelt the **bread that was burning**.* ⟶ *I smelt the **burning bread**.*

• as adverbial clauses (like adverbs): expressing manner, conditions, cause, result, etc. This is especially common in formal or literary texts. To make the negative, use *not* before the present participle.
***Moving silently**, the lion follows its prey.*
***Lying face down in the sand**, he looked like some strange sea beast.*
***Not being qualified**, she couldn't work there.*
*There was a fire, **resulting in serious damage**.*

having + past participle

Having + past participle is used:
• to show the cause of a second action.
***Having won** every competition, he decided to retire.*
• to show a sequence of actions.
***Having made** breakfast, she sat down and read the paper.*

7.3 exchanging opinions

agreeing
That's absolutely right.
I couldn't agree more.
Absolutely! I'm with you 100% on that.

agreeing in part
I agree with you up to a point.
I suppose you've got a point, but …

questioning someone's opinion
Oh come on, you must be joking.
Surely you don't think that …
That goes against my better judgement because …
How can you say that?
Where's the logic in that?
You can't honestly think that …

strongly disagreeing
It just doesn't make sense to me.
Oh that's ridiculous!

PRACTICE

7.1

1 Complete the second sentence so it has a similar meaning to the first. Use the word in brackets.

1 He lost his job because he kept breaking the rules.
(reason) The _____ kept breaking the rules.

2 He only realised who she was when he left the theatre.
(recognised) It was only _____ her.

3 I want to persuade them to come with us. (do)
What I _____ to come with us.

4 The thing that concerns me is whether she will have enough money.
(worry) All _____ whether she will have enough money.

5 They have such a fantastic range of spices.
(amazing) What is _____ such a fantastic range of spices.

2 Rewrite the sentences in three different ways using the prompts. You may need to change some words.

1 Elections have given these people their first real opportunity to decide who will govern them.

a) What elections have done is _____.

b) The thing that _____.

c) It's the elections _____.

2 Heavy snow and severe weather caused widespread disruption to the country's airports, roads and rail systems.

a) It was the airports _____.

b) It was heavy snow _____.

c) What caused disruption _____.

3 Hundreds of students marched through the city centre to protest against the new laws.

a) What caused students _____.

b) The reason hundreds of _____.

c) What happened was _____.

7.2

1 Complete the pairs of sentences using the same verb, once as a present participle and once as a past participle.

1 a) _____ as much noise as she could, Lola attracted the attention of the rescuers.

   b) _____ in China, this new gadget will be cheap and efficient.

2 a) _____ he had six months to live, he shocked everyone by living another twenty years.

   b) _____ his staff he was visiting a client, Jones disappeared with all the company's money.

3 a) _____ for her ticket, she suddenly realised she had never been to a theatre before.

   b) _____ by the hour, the employees rarely worked at the weekend.

4 a) Many of the clothes _____ by famous people are kept in the museum.

   b) All participants _____ a badge will receive a free meal.

5 a) In my opinion, it's one of the best books ever _____.

   b) _____ on his blog today, Mick Davies says the economic crisis is over.

2 Find and correct five mistakes in the text.

Arming with nothing but a donated caravan, a solar laptop and toothpaste made from crushed cuttlefish bones, Mark Boyle lives without cash. Having graduate in economics, he was a food company manager. One afternoon while to discuss the world's problems with a friend, he decided to act on Gandhi's words: 'Be the change you want to see in the world.' Giving a caravan by a stranger, he moved out of his home. A friend donated a bike and he got himself a stove and began his new life. He now lives off the land, cycles everywhere and writes a blog. Is it true freedom? Asking what he misses about his old life, he says stress, traffic, bank statements and utility bills. He's joking.

7.3

1 Complete the conversations with the words in the box.

| honestly | suppose | where | more | sense | 100% |

1 A: The sales department have asked us to talk through the material with them.

   B: Why do they want to do that? It just doesn't make _____ to me.

2 A: No one would ever want to actually wear something like that. It's too uncomfortable.

   B: I _____ you've got a point.

3 A: I think we've done more than enough for today.

   B: Absolutely! I'm with you _____ on that.

4 A: When we finish the tour, we need to go back to the beginning and start again.

   B: _____'s the logic in that?

5 A: Brilliant. I think that's an excellent idea.

   B: I'm sorry, but you can't _____ tell me you think that is a good idea.

6 A: We'll have trouble finishing everything in time.

   B: I couldn't agree _____.

GRAMMAR

8.1 future in the past

Sometimes when we're talking about the past, we want to mention something that was in the future at that time. To do this, use future structures but make the verb forms past, e.g.

is going to ⟶ *was going to*

*I **was going to** help you, but I didn't have time.*

present continuous ⟶ past continuous

*They **were hoping to** have a picnic, but it rained all weekend.*

will ⟶ *would**

*I arrived in Recife, where I **would spend** ten years of my life.**

*This is a different use from *would* for repeated actions in the past. Compare:

*At sixteen, I got a job at Limo Company, where I **would** later **become** CEO.* (future in the past)

*For years, I **would go running** at 5.00a.m. every morning.* (repeated actions in the past)

We can also use *was/were to* + infinitive and *was/were to have* + past participle. These are quite literary and more commonly found in writing than speech. The expression *was to have* is usually used when the plan did not become a reality.

*They told me I **was to give** a speech the following day.*

*I **was to have taken** a job with my father's company, but it went bankrupt.*

other expressions to talk about the future in the past

To describe a plan that did not become reality, use:
- *was/were supposed to.*

*I **was supposed to go** to Nick's house, but my car broke down.*

- *meant to.*

*I **meant to mention** the cost of tickets, but I forgot.* (active)
*We **were meant to check in** an hour ago!* (passive)

For events that very nearly happened, use:
- *was/were on the verge of* + gerund.

*She **was on the verge of giving up** her dream when she received a letter from an agent.*

- *was/were on the point of* + gerund.

*They were **on the point of leaving** when the boss arrived.*

- *was/were about to* + infinitive.

*Hi! I **was about to text** you!*

8.2 ellipsis and substitution

ellipsis

Sometimes words which we might expect to be present from a grammatical point of view are left out because we can understand the meaning from the context (the preceding or following text). Often the words which are left out are auxiliary verbs, modal verbs or subjects.

She immediately got up and (she) left the room. (subject)

Should we wait for a while or (should we) phone him straightaway? (modal verb)

They have finished lunch and (they have) gone for a coffee. (subject + auxiliary verb)

It is possible to leave out repeated verb phrases or adjectives and just repeat the auxiliary or modal verb.

Marisa has never tried Asian cooking, but I have (tried Asian cooking).

Harry always thinks he's right about things, but he isn't (always right about things).

I thought we'd be able to finish this before Monday, but we can't (finish this before Monday).

spoken grammar

Ellipsis is very common in spoken English as the situational context is usually very clear between the speakers.

Didn't know you were going. (*I didn't know …*)

Sounds good to me. (***That/What you've just suggested** sounds good.*)

This means that some common phrases are often shortened.

Did you have a nice weekend? ⟶ *Nice weekend?*

I suppose so. ⟶ *Suppose so.*

It's nice to meet you. ⟶ *Nice to meet you.*

substitution

Instead of repeating a word/phrase, they are sometimes replaced with a substitute word/phrase. Determiners (*many, a little, some,* etc.), *so, do* and *not* are all used for this.

A: *Do you know a lot of the people coming tonight?*
B: *Not **many**.*

A: *What do you think of this dress?*
B: *Actually, I prefer the other **one**.*

A: *Do you think they'll be here soon?*
B: *I expect **so**.* (*so = them to be here soon*)

A: *Who ate all the chocolate biscuits – you?*
B: *No, Max **did**.* (*did = ate all the chocolate biscuits*)

A: *Will you have to pay a fine?*
B: *I hope **not**.* (*not = I won't have to pay a fine*)

8.3 discussing ideas

acknowledging an idea	
Absolutely.	I'm with you there.
Definitely.	That's interesting.
That's a good idea.	Right, OK.
(That) makes sense.	Yes and no.
That's (very) true.	I know what you mean.
Good one!	I never thought of that.
Sure.	

introducing an alternative
Mind you, …
I also think …
Actually, …
But looking at it another way, …
(Although) having said that, …
Alternatively, …
On the other hand, …

PRACTICE

8.1

1 Match the sentence halves.

1 I was supposed to
2 The three musicians were going
3 At the time, I didn't know that
4 Paul was on the verge of
5 Honestly, I was
6 You were about to

a) I would never see her again.
b) planning to help you in the garden, but I got backache.
c) giving up when he saw the top of the mountain.
d) to be the greatest band in history.
e) make the biggest mistake of your life.
f) call home, but I forgot.

2 Find and correct the seven mistakes in sentences 1–10.

1 We are about to ascend the mountain when snow started to fall.
2 Just as Clancy was on the point of escaping, a guard entered the hallway.
3 Melissa meant tell you about the dinner invitation, but she forgot.
4 We were to had taken the 6.02 train to Manchester, but it was cancelled.
5 She got sick when she was on a verge of becoming a superstar.
6 He was going to stay with his brothers for a while before emigrating.
7 Thompson then travelled to Bali, where he will later meet his sixth wife.
8 I was but hoping to work with Donna again, but she left the company.
9 It was to have been a surprise party, but she found out about it.
10 I was to meeting Daley and his gang in the subway at midnight.

8.2

1 Complete the sentences with words in the box.

mine	so	one	there	do	some
ones	not				

1 This jacket is in a terrible state. I need to buy a new _____.
2 Louise loves Italian food, and I _____ too.
3 A: Is it safe to come out?
   B: I think _____.
4 They'll probably lose the match, but I hope _____.
5 These batteries are too small. I need those _____ over there.
6 I've been to the Seychelles. We went on holiday _____.
7 A: Is that your car?
   B: No, _____ is parked across the road.
8 A: Do you know where all the tools are?
   B: There are _____ in the garage.

2 Decide which words can be omitted in sentences 1–8.

1 I'm not sure if they've finished, but I think they have finished.
2 We could have met them later, but I didn't want to meet them later.
3 Do you want a coffee? I've just made some coffee.
4 I'd be happy to help if you need me to help.
5 A: What time were we supposed to arrive?
   B: We were supposed to arrive at six.
6 Erica had ice cream for dessert and Bill had chocolate cake.
7 They'll be here soon, but I don't know exactly when they'll be here.
8 A: Have you got the time?
   B: The time is half past two.

8.3

1 Put the underlined phrases in the correct order to complete the conversation. Capitalise letters where necessary.

A: Teachers, my idea is that from now on students set their own homework.

B: That's interesting, [1] of I that thought never.

A: If they set the homework, there's more chance they will do it.

B: [2] with there you I'm. [3] sense makes that.

C: [4] way another at but it looking, won't they set very small amounts of homework?

A: [5] mean you what know I, but I don't think it will happen. Students know what is good for them.

C: Yes and no. Many of them want to learn, but [6] hand the on other, my students hate homework. They prefer going to parties in the evenings!

A: Mine too.

C: [7] that said having, maybe they can write about their parties for homework.

B: Nice idea!

GRAMMAR

9.1 verb tenses for unreal situations

After some expressions, we use past tenses to describe unreal or imaginary situations. These ideas may refer to the past, present or future.

it's time

Use *it's time* + past simple to say that something is not happening but it should be.
It's time you **went** home.

We can also use *it's high time* + past simple or *it's about time* + past simple. These are more emphatic than *it's time*.
It's high time she **left** her boyfriend!
It's about time you **found** a job!

what if/ suppose/ supposing

Use *what if/ suppose/ supposing* + past simple to ask about imaginary situations and their consequences in the present or future. These are similar to second conditional questions.
What if you **missed** the plane?
Suppose you **got** injured, what **would** the coach **say**?
Supposing they **gave** you the prize, how **would** you **feel**?

We can also use these expressions with the past perfect. This is similar to the third conditional.
What if you'**d failed** your exam last week, what **would** you **have done**?

would rather/ would sooner

Use *would rather/ would* sooner + past simple to describe preferences.
I'**d rather** you **didn't play** football inside.
I'**d sooner** they **gave** me a cheque than a watch when I retire.

If the person expressing the preference is also the subject of the preference, use the infinitive (not the past tense).
I'**d rather go** to Madagascar than Hawaii.
I'**d sooner eat** bread than cake.

as if/ as though

Use *as if/ as though* + past simple to say that appearance is different from reality.
She treats me **as if** I **had** a disease. (The speaker knows he doesn't have a disease.)
They use this place **as though** it **was** a playground. (It isn't a playground.)

Use the present simple/ present perfect with these expressions when the situation may be true.
He acts **as if** he **knows** what he's doing. (Maybe he knows what he's doing.)
You look **as though** you **haven't slept** for days. (Maybe she hasn't slept for days.)

9.2 adverbials

Adverbs or adverbial phrases give us information or detail about how, when, why, how often, where, etc., something happens. They can be single words or groups of words.

adverbials of manner
These describe how something happens.
He left the room **quietly**.
She spoke **in a soft voice**.

adverbials of time
These describe when something happened.
In 2008, the government was overthrown.
We saw him **yesterday**.

adverbials of frequency
These describe how often something happened.
We must have gone there **pretty much every day** for fifteen years.
I **often** blog about this topic.

adverbials of probability
These describe how probable or improbable something is.
He is right, **without a doubt**.
She is **undoubtedly** right.

adverbials of purpose
These describe the reason behind/for an action.
They play chess **to work on their strategic thinking skills**.
She apologised **for being so insensitive**.

comment adverbials
These describe someone's viewpoint.
The clothes in that shop are **ridiculously** expensive.

For more examples, see page 111.

Adverbs and adverbial phrases usually go at the end of a sentence in the following order: how, where, when. Adverbials of purpose generally come last.
They wandered **aimlessly** (how) **around the park** (where) **at the end of the concert** (when) **in search of the keys** (purpose).

Some adverbials can go at the start of the sentence for emphasis.
On the radio, they played his music all day long.

Adverbs/Adverbials of frequency usually go before the main verb (or after the verb *to be*/auxiliary verb).

Our paths have **frequently** crossed.

9.3 ranting/raving

raving
It was the most wonderful/amazing/awesome …
It was absolutely fantastic/incredible.
It's really the best (show) ever.
There's (absolutely) nothing better than …
(It was) one of the most spectacular (sunsets) I've ever seen.
I couldn't believe my luck when …
It was idyllic.
It's an all-time classic.

ranting
If there's one thing I can't stand, it's …
It drives me up the wall.
It was absolutely horrendous.
It was a total waste of money.
It's not my style/kind of thing/cup of tea at all.

PRACTICE

9.1

1 Cross out the incorrect alternative.

1 I'd *prefer/sooner/rather* we went somewhere picturesque than stay here.

2 He scores goals *as if/as were/as though* it was the easiest thing in the world.

3 *What if/Suppose/How about* that half-baked idea became a reality?

4 It's *the/high/about* time she started living up to her name.

5 She'd *rather/want that/sooner* they came up with some ideas than just criticise.

6 *Supposing/Rather/Suppose* your career went downhill, what would you do?

7 Isn't it *one time/time/about time* you took her feelings into consideration, too?

8 In meetings, I'm treated *as if/as though/as* I was an idiot.

2 Rewrite the sentences using the words in brackets and the past simple.

1 You really should speak to your mother.
(high time) _____.

2 What would happen if I pressed this button?
(Suppose) _____.

3 The way they treat that girl, you'd think she was a princess.
(as though) _____.

4 Given the choice, I would learn Chinese instead of German.
(sooner) _____.

5 Imagine a volcanic eruption in a densely populated area.
(What if) _____.

6 She ought to stop smoking now.
(about time) _____.

7 Anyone would think they own the place, the way they behave.
(as if) _____.

8 I don't want you to go there.
(rather) _____.

9.2

1 Choose the correct option, a), b) or c), to complete the text.

The £40 Art Collection

Tom Alexander, began ¹_____ collecting British Modern art after moving to the Isle of Arran, UK in 1947. Having ²_____ established a shop ³_____ with his brother in the village of Brodick, he joined the Officers Emergency Army Reserve in order to do something 'public spirited'. ⁴_____, the Officers Emergency Army Reserve paid him an ⁵_____ sum of money – around £40. With the encouragement of his wife Catherine, he decided to use this money to buy one work of art per year. Alexander had acquired an interest in avant-garde British art after purchasing his first piece in 1943 and visited the Tate and National Gallery ⁶_____. In a fashion that would be impossible today, Alexander wrote ⁷_____ to artists whose work he liked and asked them to send him a piece of their own choosing. Many famous artists ⁸_____ responded to Tom Alexander's direct and eloquent approach, often enjoying the idea of having works on Arran. The exhibition includes examples of correspondence Alexander had ⁹_____.

1 a) often	b) clearly	c) regularly
2 a) obviously	b) successfully	c) frequently
3 a) here	b) there	c) everywhere
4 a) To his surprise	b) Surprised	c) For a surprise
5 a) per year	b) per month	c) annual
6 a) always	b) whenever possible	c) impossibly
7 a) straight	b) immediately	c) directly
8 a) generously	b) often	c) used to
9 a) obviously	b) usually	c) with the artists

2 Put the phrases in the correct order to make sentences. There may be more than one possible order.

1 I / just grab / if / at lunchtime / I'm in a hurry / quickly / a sandwich / to eat

2 generally / sit / too tired to talk / in front of the television / in the evenings / my husband and I

3 to reduce the number / carefully plan / in English / I / always / of mistakes / anything I write

4 in front of / too much time / I / the computer / consistently / spend / unfortunately

5 enjoyed each other's company / online / for a while / they met / and

6 about six months ago / painting / I / took up / to help me relax

7 when I left this morning / my things / I left / on the kitchen table

8 have more time / probably / I'll / when my exams are finished / to see my friends

9.3

1 Find and correct the six mistakes in the conversations below.

1 A: Did you enjoy the concert?
B: It was awesome – really, the best concert never!

2 A: How was the exhibition?
B: I didn't really like it. I wasn't my mug of tea.

3 A: Did you enjoy the film last night?
B: No, it was a horror film and if there's one thing I can't stand for it's violence. I walked out halfway through.

4 A: Did you like the book?
B: Yes, it's an all classic.

5 A: What did you think of the acting?
B: Oh, I thought it was absolute incredible.

6 A: Was the restaurant good?
B: No, the food and the service were terrible. It was total waste of money.

GRAMMAR

10.1 inversion

Inversion is when we put an auxiliary verb before the subject of a clause.

I never saw such a wonderful sight again.

auxiliary + subject + clause
*Never again **did I see** such a wonderful sight.*

Inversion is common in written formal texts, but it is also used in informal spoken English to add dramatic effect or emphasis.
*No way **would I** ever **go** on a trip like that!* (There is no way/chance that I would ever go on a trip like that.)
*Not in a million years **would I agree** to cross Africa on a motorbike!*

negative adverbials

In formal English, it is common to use inversion after negative adverbial expressions and restrictive words such as *only*, *never*, *hardly* and *little*.
***At no time** did they stop to think about the consequences.*
***Not until** the ambulance arrived did we realise how serious it was.*
***Hardly** had the film begun when she fell sound asleep in her chair.*
***Never before/Rarely/Seldom** had I seen such landscapes.*
***Little** did they realise how stupid they had been.*
***No sooner** had they opened the packet than the biscuits were finished.*
***No longer** will we accept these poor conditions.*
***Only then** did they see what a fantastic chance they'd been offered.*

***Only now** that I am pregnant has he finally agreed to stop riding his motorbike.*
***Not only** did they leave their families for more than two months, **but** they **also** travelled to some of the most dangerous places on the planet.*
***Under no circumstances/On no account** should you leave the bike unattended.*
***Scarcely** had they left the room than people started talking about them.*

conditional clauses

In formal English, inversion can be used with conditional sentences.

If we had known how much it was going to cost, we would never have chosen it.
***Had we known** how much it was going to cost, we would never have chosen it.*

If you were to have approached from the other direction, you might have seen the signs.
***Were you** to have approached from the other direction, you might have seen the signs.*

10.2 comparative structures
modifiers

	big difference	small difference
formal	considerably, infinitely, decidedly, significantly	marginally, fractionally
neutral	much, far, a lot, a good deal	slightly, a bit, a little, barely any
informal	miles, way, loads	

*Their technology was **considerably more** advanced **than** ours.*
*We're **way** better **than** you at football!* (spoken English)
modifiers with as + as
We also use modifiers to give more detail about *as + adjective + as* statements.
To show a big difference, use *nothing like*, or *nowhere near*.
*He's **nothing like as** obstinate **as** his brother.*
*She's **nowhere near as** good **as** me at chess.*

To show a small difference use *almost* or *nearly*.
*He's **almost as** neurotic **as** me.*

To emphasise no difference use *just* or *every bit*.
*I'm **just as** clever **as** you.*
*We're **every bit as** good **as** our competitors.*
double comparatives
Use double comparatives with *the* to say that one situation leads to another.
***The bigger** the lie, **the more** people believe it.*
***The more** you read, **the more** you'll learn.*
progressive comparatives
Use the progressive comparative form to say something is escalating. Use the comparative word twice (separated by *and*) to emphasise the adjective.
*House prices are getting **lower and lower**.*

10.3 negotiating

naming your objectives
We want to sort this out as soon as possible. By the end of the day, we want to resolve this.

exploring positions
What do you have in mind? Can you go into more detail?

making conditional offers
If you do … for me, I'll do … for you. What if we supported your idea?

refusing an offer
That would be difficult for me because of … I'm not sure I can do that because …

accepting an offer
Good. That sounds acceptable to me. Great. We've got a deal.

following up the deal
Let me know if you have any queries. Get in touch if anything needs clarifying.

PRACTICE

10.1

1 Match the sentence halves.

1 No sooner had I reached the door
2 Little did I know what
3 At no time did she
4 Only after the film had started
5 Scarcely had I walked in through the door
6 Had I suspected that he was untrustworthy,

a) admit that it was her own mistake.
b) I obviously wouldn't have given him the package.
c) than I realised I had left my keys inside.
d) did I realise that I'd seen it before.
e) surprises they had in store for me.
f) when the phone rang.

2 Find and correct the five mistakes in sentences 1–8.

1 Seldom I have seen him looking so miserable.
2 Not only have they decided to move cities, but they are leaving the US altogether.
3 Under no circumstances you should leave the office.
4 We had known there would be a water shortage, we would have been more prepared.
5 Only later she realised her mistake.
6 Had he invited us, we would have been delighted to accept.
7 At no time did she consider giving up her campaign.
8 Were they to apologised more quickly, I might have forgiven them.

10.2

1 Complete the sentences with a suitable word.

1 She's nothing _____ as intelligent as her father.
2 We are _____ lot stronger than them.
3 I'm _____ any bigger now than I was aged twelve.
4 This tastes a good _____ better than it did yesterday.
5 He's _____ bit as famous as his mother.
6 Some sprinters just get faster and _____ as they get older.
7 The closer you come, _____ more dangerous it'll be.
8 I'm nowhere _____ as ambitious as my brother.

2 Put the underlined words in the correct order to complete the text.

For footballer Tiago Manuel Dias Correia, better known as *Bébé*, life [1] <u>better better just and gets</u>. He is [2] <u>as near as nowhere famous</u> Cristiano Ronaldo, but his story [3] <u>bit remarkable every as is</u>. In [4] <u>than little year a more</u>, from living in a shelter for young people in Lisbon, Bébé is on the brink of stardom. He was playing for the CAIS Association in the 2009 European Street Football Festival in Bosnia when he joked with his team-mates that one day he [5] <u>greater far would than be</u> Ronaldo. While he still has a long way to go before he achieves that, he has just [6] <u>deal closer a good come</u>. During the tournament in Bosnia, Bébé was the best player, but according to the director of Bébé's team, he was [7] <u>like nothing hero flamboyant his as as</u>, Ronaldo. 'He was a very simple sort of guy who did not have much. But … in terms of ability, he was the team. But he did not try to keep the ball. He involved the others.' After the tournament, he was signed by Estrela Amadora, a Portuguese club. Then he moved on to a club called Vitoria. After he had impressed in a pre-season game, suddenly Manchester United came calling. In August 2010, the British club signed him for a reported £7.4 million, [8] <u>more than money considerably</u> he would have expected to see in his lifetime. 'I had the dream of playing for a major club,' said Bébé, 'and that dream has come true.'

1 _____
2 _____
3 _____
4 _____
5 _____
6 _____
7 _____
8 _____

10.3

1 Two words in each sentence are in the wrong order. Correct them.

1 A: We want to sort out this as soon as possible.
   B: So do we. Can you go into detail more about your proposal?
2 A: By end the of the meeting, we want to have a concrete plan.
   B: What do you have mind in?
3 A: If you do for this me, I'll help you with the project.
   B: I'm sure not we can do that because of our contract.
4 A: Good, that sounds to acceptable me.
   B: Let know me if you have any queries.
5 A: Great! We've a got deal.
   B: Get in touch if anything clarifying needs.
6 A: What if supported we your idea for the pension scheme?
   B: OK, but the rest of the proposal would difficult be for us as it still means cutting jobs.

VOCABULARY BANK

PERSONALITY

1A Find pairs of opposite adjectives in the box.

considerate   circumspect   conservative   temperamental   impetuous
easygoing   gregarious   selfish   liberal   introverted

B Match the adjectives in the box with statements 1–10.

1 She expects everyone to help her, but she never does anything for anyone else!

2 My boss is happy one minute and screaming the next.

3 The manager doesn't like new ideas; he wants to do everything the old way.

4 That child talks to few people; he prefers to sit quietly and read or just think.

5 That girl is so relaxed that she never seems to worry about anything.

6 She's very cautious; she thinks carefully before she decides to do something.

7 She's tolerant and she wants her employees to be free to do what they want.

8 That man makes too many instant decisions without thinking about the consequences.

9 When he sees me, he always brings a gift and asks about my family.

10 She loves socialising; she goes to parties every night.

C Can you think of people (friends, famous people, fictional characters) who match the adjectives above?

IDIOMS FOR PEOPLE

2A Read sentences 1–6 and look at the pictures. How could you complete the idioms?

1 She has a lot of power. In that organisation she's a …

2 He must be the laziest person I've ever met. He's a total …

3 She sometimes gets out of control. She's a bit of a …

4 He ruined the company's reputation. He was a …

5 She broke her arm and still refused to give up. She's a …

6 He complains whenever we try to have fun. He's a bit of a …

B Check your ideas. Match idioms a)–f) in bold with sentences 1–6 above.

a) **rotten apple**: one bad person who has a bad effect on all others in the group

b) **loose cannon**: an unpredictable person who may cause damage if he/she is not controlled

c) **couch potato**: a person who lives a sedentary lifestyle, never doing any exercise

d) **wet blanket**: a negative person who ruins other people's good times

e) **big cheese**: an important, influential person

f) **tough cookie**: someone who is strong enough to deal with difficult or violent situations

METAPHORS

1 Underline the metaphors in sentences 1–12. Match the metaphors with the meanings in the boxes.

Intelligence as light

a clever idea that comes suddenly	intelligent
was especially good at something	not very intelligent

1 The solution came to me in a flash of inspiration.
2 Nico shone at maths from an early age.
3 As a small child, Akiko was obviously bright.
4 Everyone thought I was dim, but I eventually passed all my exams.

Theories as buildings

help prove   developed   basis   fails because of a particular reason

5 We analysed the findings and then constructed a theory.
6 Do you have any statistics to support this theory?
7 Your evidence is very weak; that's where your idea falls down.
8 The foundations of the argument aren't very strong.

Business as war

began an intense series of actions   aimed at merge together   a big profit

9 He made a killing from his latest investment.
10 The marketing department launched an aggressive campaign to promote the product.
11 Our new adverts are targeting eighteen-year-olds.
12 The two companies decided to join forces in 2009.

OPINIONS

2A Choose the correct alternatives to complete the phrases in bold.

1 If an opinion is one that is commonly agreed on it is the *general/ usual* opinion.
2 Sometimes it can be diplomatic to *keep/ hold* your opinions to yourself.
3 If you have an idea about something which doesn't represent your company's view, it is your *individual/ personal* opinion.
4 If someone has strong opinions and lets them be known, they might be considered *opinionated/ idealistic*.
5 If you disagree with someone you might have a *split/ difference* of opinion.
6 If there are two sides to the argument, and equal numbers of people on both sides, then we can say **opinion is** *divided/ half*.
7 If there is no right or wrong answer then it is just a *matter/ case* of opinion.
8 People have a right to make their own decisions about things. In other words, they are *entitled/ open* to their own opinion.

B Complete the sentences with the correct answers from Exercise 2A.

1 Sandie suggested splitting the work between us, but if you want my _____ opinion, I think it's a bad idea.
2 I honestly couldn't stand him. I found him both _____ and arrogant.
3 I'm afraid I don't agree. We seem to have a _____ of opinion on this one.
4 We asked over a thousand people and found that opinion was _____, with nearly forty percent against the decision.
5 I don't see how you can say that. It's a _____ of opinion.
6 You can't tell him what to believe in. He's _____ to his own opinion.
7 I think in this instance it might be better to _____ our opinions to ourselves.
8 The _____ opinion seems to be that it would be a good idea to start now.

VOCABULARY BANK

ADJECTIVES

1A Match sentences 1–4 with photos A–D.

1 It's a vast, overpopulated metropolis.

2 It's a quaint, secluded village far from any big cities.

3 It's a scenic town with awe-inspiring mountain views.

4 It's a sprawling, ramshackle slum.

B Match meanings a)–h) with adjectives in sentences 1–4 above.

a) extremely large

b) extremely impressive in a way that makes you feel great respect

c) surrounded by views of beautiful countryside

d) spreading over a wide area in an untidy or unattractive way

e) unusual and attractive, especially in an old-fashioned way

f) in bad condition and in need of repair

g) very private and quiet

h) there are too many people in a place

PREFIXES

2A Underline two prefixes in each sentence.

1 She was a supermodel when miniskirts first became fashionable.

2 Camping in sub-zero temperatures, the team soon learnt to cooperate.

3 I became bilingual by interacting with French speakers from an early age.

4 I'm semi-retired now, but I outlasted many younger men in this business.

B Complete the second column of the table with the words in the box.

> below   small   half   more/more powerful/larger
> between/among   bigger/greater than something else

C Which words are described in definitions 1–8 below? Use prefixes from the table in Exercise 2B.

1 twice every month   *bimonthly*

2 a hero who has amazing powers

3 grow too big for some of your clothes

4 a secondary plot that isn't the main story

5 between or among nations

6 a circle cut in half

7 two people who founded a business together

8 a small bar, or drinks in a small fridge, in your hotel room

D Add more examples to the third column of the table.

prefix	meaning	example words
bi	two	**bi**monthly, **bi**centenary
co	joint	**co**-author, **co**-pilot
inter		**inter**changeable, **inter**continental
mini		**mini**cab, **mini**mise,
out		**out**sell, **out**play
semi		**semi**-skimmed, **semi**colon
sub		**sub**title, **sub**way
super		**super**natural, **super**power

CRIME COLLOCATIONS

1A Complete the sentences with a preposition.

1 The men were released from prison and put _____ probation.

2 Hundreds of young fans went _____ the rampage through the city centre.

3 A new law, introduced to reduce vandalism, comes _____ force next month.

4 He was given points on his licence _____ speeding.

5 We agreed to help the police _____ their inquiries.

6 An investigation is being held _____ the causes of the accident.

7 The gang were arrested and held _____ custody.

8 Two teenagers were identified and charged _____ assault.

9 The man was described as a hardened criminal who posed a serious threat _____ the public.

10 Police fired tear-gas _____ the protesters in an attempt to disperse the crowd.

B Underline phrases in Exercise 1A which match meanings a)–j) below.

a) comes into effect

b) asked to report to a probation officer at regular intervals rather than being sent to prison

c) may cause a risk to others

d) received a penalty which involves putting numbers on your driving licence – when you reach a certain number, your licence is taken away from you for a period of time

e) took part in a course of violent, frenzied behaviour

f) assist in a police investigation

g) officially accused by a court of deliberately causing harm to another person

h) legally confined by the police

i) released CS gas in a crowd (often used during riots)

j) the police are trying to discover what caused something

SOCIAL ISSUES

2A Match the social issues with pictures A–H.

1 white-collar crime

2 illiteracy

3 poverty

4 gender inequality

5 censorship

6 ageism

7 organised crime

8 antisocial behaviour

B Complete the sentences using the words/ phrases above.

a) A definition of _____ is when people don't have enough money for their basic needs.

b) Due to _____, women often get paid less than men for doing the same job.

c) _____ is harmful to other people and shows that you do not care about other people.

d) _____ is a term for illegal activities, such as scams and fraud, carried out by businesspeople.

e) Because of _____, people are often prevented from speaking and writing the truth.

f) _____ means people cannot read or write, often because they could not get an education.

g) _____ refers to a coordinated group of criminals who engage in illegal activities to make money and gain power.

h) _____ comes from negative stereotypes about older people.

A

B

C

D

E

F

G

H

VOCABULARY BANK

IDIOMS: SECRETS

1A Match the phrases in bold in sentences 1–5 with similar phrases in a)–e) below.

1 This is **classified information**. *c*
2 She **divulged** a secret.
3 What I said is **between you and me**.
4 It's a **covert** operation.
5 She's behaving as if she **has something to hide**.

a) She **looks furtive**.
b) It's **hush-hush**, so don't tell anyone.
c) ~~These documents are **confidential**.~~
d) She **blurted out** the secret.
e) This action is **top secret**.

B Match the phrases from Exercise 1A with pictures A–E.

C Which phrases in Exercise 1A are usually used in formal situations, e.g. government and business discussions/documents?

MULTI-WORD VERBS

2A Complete the sentences using the particles in the box.

on	back	over	away	around	off	up	down

1 If you have a problem with your husband you should talk it _____.
2 Things are looking _____: sales have improved and we've got some excellent new products.
3 Even though he was exhausted, he soldiered _____ and reached the top of the hill.
4 They killed _____ my proposal because it was too expensive.
5 Those children are too excited – they need to calm _____.
6 Please tidy _____ your stuff – it's all over the floor!
7 She was well-behaved for a few days but now she's slipped _____ to her old ways.
8 Those boys are always lounging _____ doing nothing!

B Think of ways to rephrase the ideas in the multi-word verbs above.

1 We can use 'discuss it' instead of 'talk it over'.

PREPOSITIONAL PHRASES

1A Match the prepositional phrases in bold with phrases a), b) or c).

1 The ship was hit by the typhoon and blown **off course**. Now it's lost.

2 I started the race OK, but soon realised I was **off the pace** and had to give up.

3 You can't get power into a golf shot if you're **off balance**.

a) too slow to keep up
b) away from a scheduled path
c) in an unsteady position

4 We are not investigating the President. He's **above suspicion**.

5 We never do anything illegal. Everything is **above board**.

6 The planes are fast and comfortable, but **above all** they're safe.

a) the most important thing is
b) assumed to be innocent
c) legal

7 The manager said that, aged sixty-five, I was **over the hill** so he fired me.

8 When I won first prize I was **over the moon**. I celebrated a lot.

9 Her celebrations were excessive. They were **over the top**.

a) too much
b) past my best (too old now)
c) extremely happy

10 I didn't go to work because I was feeling **under the weather**.

11 Oh, do I have to cook dinner? I was **under the impression** you'd do it!

12 When you testify in court, remember you are **under oath** and cannot lie.

a) thinking (probably wrongly)
b) obliged by the law to tell the truth in court
c) a little bit sick

B How could speaker B respond to what speaker A says? Write down your ideas.

1 A: I was feeling under the weather yesterday.
   B: _____

2 A: I'm absolutely over the moon!
   B: _____

3 A: I was under the impression you were happy at work.
   B: _____

4 A: Do you think I'm over the hill? I'm only thirty-five.
   B: _____

5 A: I hear you resigned. Isn't that a bit over the top?
   B: _____

6 A: I'm above suspicion in this investigation, aren't I?
   B: _____

SPEAKING IDIOMS

2A Complete the idioms in bold with the words in the box.

| good | get | least | catch | cross | tail | run | stick | word | shop |

1 Marisa was talking so fast I just **couldn't get a _____ in edgeways**.

2 Come on! Try to **_____ to the point**.

3 After ten minutes we realised that we were **talking at _____ purposes**.

4 I'm sorry. I **didn't _____ what you said**.

5 That kind of behaviour is not acceptable. It sounds to me like she **needs a _____ talking to**.

6 I'm sorry. We've been **talking _____** all evening. Let's stop talking about work now.

7 Could you **_____ that by me one more time**?

8 I **couldn't make head or _____** of what she was saying.

9 That's **an understatement to say the _____**.

10 Unfortunately, I think he **got the wrong end of the _____**.

B Which idioms in Exercise 2A would you use in situations a)–j)?

a) Someone has completely misunderstood what you have said (so they do something different).
b) You can't understand anything that someone is trying to say.
c) You can't hear what the other person is saying.
d) Someone is talking so much it's hard for you to say anything.
e) Somebody needs to be reprimanded for something.
f) You need someone to repeat what they said.
g) There has been a misunderstanding on both sides.
h) Someone should say what they want to say (instead of talking around the subject).
i) You think a situation is more serious than someone else suggested.
j) Someone talks about their work.

VOCABULARY BANK

SUFFIXES

1A Put the words in the box in the correct column of the table according to their suffix.
One word can be used in two columns.

> censor**ship**   exorbi**tant**   national**ist**   gover**nor**   respons**ive**   senil**ity**   fabric**ate**
> likeli**hood**   person**able**   kindli**ness**   ident**ical**   repet**ition**   sar**casm**   glor**ify**
> trouble**some**   clas**sy**   exper**tise**   remi**ssion**   anx**ious**   hero**ic**

verb	noun	adjective

B Complete the sentences using the words in brackets and a suitable suffix.

1 I _____, but I really don't know how to help. (sympathy)

2 Heat therapy has been proven to be highly _____ in cases of this kind. (effect)

3 I know it's an _____, but could I possibly use your bathroom? (impose)

4 I'm not sure that such _____ helps the company's image much. (frivolous)

5 He was in the _____ position of not having to work for a living. (envy)

6 Gemma felt so nervous during the interview that her answers were a little _____. (hesitate)

7 A delay of two hours failed to dampen their _____. (enthusiastic)

8 I found his attitude really _____. (chauvinist)

WORK AND LEISURE IDIOMS

2A Match the idioms in bold with pictures A–F.

1 I'm exhausted: I've been **burning the candle at both ends**.

2 I'm going to **while away** my old age reading and swimming.

3 I'm **taking time out** from work to finish writing my book.

4 I'm going to **chill out** for a few weeks.

5 I've been **working all hours** to finish my castle.

6 We were **burning the midnight oil** to finish it on time.

B Answer the questions.

a) Which idiom means you've been doing too much late at night and early in the morning?

b) Which idiom means to change your usual routine to do something else?

c) Which two idioms refer to relaxing?

d) What do you think the other two idioms mean? Do they have a negative or positive connotation?

C Write short answers to questions 1–6.

1 What would you like to take time out to do at the moment?

2 How do you plan to while away your old age?

3 When did you last chill out?

4 As a student, do/did you ever burn the candle at both ends?

5 When might you need to work all hours to get a job or task done?

6 When is the last time you burned the midnight oil? What were you doing?

PROVERBS

1A Match the phrases in bold in sentences 1–10 with meanings a)–j) below.

1 We were so poor that we accepted the offer to live there. **Beggars can't be choosers!**

2 Ah, here's the report – two weeks late! **Better late than never**, I suppose.

3 It looks as if our team is going to win, but **don't count your chickens**.

4 He wasn't sure about starting up the business, but I told him to **strike while the iron's hot**.

5 Do what the teachers tell you, son, and **keep your nose clean**.

6 Working late again? **No rest for the wicked**.

7 It doesn't matter if you aren't top of the class, but always **put your best foot forward**.

8 Give your little brother some of your drink! **Share and share alike**.

9 I start working at 5.00a.m. My mother always told me that **the early bird catches the worm**.

10 The government was brought down by journalists and writers, not soldiers. **The pen is mightier than the sword**.

a) Do everything you can to be successful.

b) If you start (work) early, you will have more opportunities.

c) Take decisive action while the conditions are right.

d) Don't get too confident of something until you're absolutely sure it's going to happen.

e) Bad people have to work constantly and aren't allowed to stop and rest. (We say this as a joke to a busy/overworked person.)

f) If you don't have much (money, opportunity, etc.), be grateful for anything you're offered.

g) Be generous to other people with your things (food, possessions, etc.).

h) Good writing is more effective than violence. (It's better to use your intelligence rather than violence to beat an opponent.)

i) Be good and don't get into trouble.

j) Even if you can't do something on time, do it anyway. This is better than not doing it at all.

B Which of the proverbs and sayings have equivalents in your language?

C Think of situations in which you might use the proverbs and sayings above.

You might say 'share and share alike' to a young child if he/she isn't sharing.

You might say 'strike while the iron's hot' to a business associate if you see a good opportunity.

MEMORIES

2A Underline expressions in the conversations below which relate to memory or memories.

1 A: Is there anything else you can think of that would help?
  B: No, nothing springs to mind.

2 A: I travelled across South America on horseback.
  B: Wow, that's a once-in-a-lifetime experience.

3 A: I've had such a wonderful day.
  B: Yes, it's been a real day to remember.

4 A: Can you remember that woman's name?
  B: No, but it's on the tip of my tongue.

5 A: Where's your bag?
  B: I've left it somewhere, and I can't for the life of me remember where.

6 A: There you are! Why didn't you call me like I asked you to?
  B: I'm so sorry. I clean forgot.

7 A: Do you remember when we studied history together?
  B: That's going back.

8 A: Do you remember when we used to study together during the holidays?
  B: Of course. I remember it like it was yesterday.

9 A: Sorry, I've had a complete memory lapse and I can't remember your name.
  B: It's Lisbeth. Elisabeth Alexander.

10 A: Can you remember her phone number?
  B: Yes, it's etched on my memory.

B Which expressions refer to remembering or forgetting? Which refer to past experiences?

C Find expressions in conversations 1–10 which relate to meanings a)–e) below. There may be more than one possible answer.

a) I remember it very well.

b) It was an experience worth remembering.

c) I can't quite remember at the moment.

d) I completely forgot.

e) It was a long time ago.

VOCABULARY BANK

THREE-PART MULTI-WORD VERBS

1A Find the three-part multi-word verbs in headlines 1–10. Use them to complete definitions a)–j).

1 President goes back on his word, says conditions have changed

2 What did superstar Megan Kleist get up to on her last holiday?

3 Doctors say cut down on fatty foods and quit TV meals

4 People asked to look in on elderly neighbours during winter freeze

5 Experts warn public to watch out for new computer virus

6 USA will struggle to keep up with new superpowers, says economist

7 10,000 lose jobs as HRG Company goes through with plans to downsize

8 Prince goes down with flu before his big day

9 Company does away with face-to-face business, everything now online

10 Snobbish actress Lara Richards looks down on UK awards

a) _____ _____ _____ **something:** reduce the amount or number of something that you take/eat/drink, etc.

b) _____ _____ _____ **an idea/plan/scheme:** do something you had promised or planned to do

c) _____ _____ _____ **what you said/your word:** not do what you said you would do

d) _____ _____ _____ **an illness, e.g. chicken pox, a virus:** become ill

e) _____ _____ _____ **something:** get rid of something or stop using it

f) _____ _____ _____ **someone/something:** think that you are better than someone else or that something is not very good

g) _____ _____ _____ **someone/something:** move as fast as someone or something else

h) _____ _____ _____ **something/someone:** be ready for someone or something that might hurt or cause problems for you

i) _____ _____ _____ **someone:** make a short visit to someone, especially if they are sick or need help

j) _____ _____ _____: do, especially enjoyable activities (We use this multi-word verb on its own especially in questions. We don't name the activity.)

B Complete the sentences in any way you choose.

1 To be healthier I suppose I could cut down on …

2 While in my city/town you need to watch out for …

3 I would never look down on …

4 In the future I think society will do away with …

5 I sometimes find it hard to keep up with …

6 Someone who got up to something interesting recently is …

COLLOCATIONS WITH *IDEAS*

2 Look at the phrases and definitions below. Use phrases a)–f) to complete sentences 1–6.

a) **get the wrong idea about something:** misunderstand a situation

b) **(not) have the faintest idea about something:** have no understanding of something

c) **(be) full of bright ideas:** have a lot of good ideas

d) **(be) someone's idea of a joke:** someone thinks this is funny

e) **have an idea of/about something:** be fairly certain about something, but not completely certain

f) **have a clear idea about something:** have a good understanding of what you want

1 I think I _____ who took the money, but I can't prove it.

2 You mustn't _____ about Dan and Helen – they're just friends.

3 Is this _____? Because I don't think it's very funny!

4 They seem a bit confused. They don't seem to have _____ of what they want.

5 The children were _____ for how they could spend the afternoon.

6 I'm sorry but I _____ what you're talking about.

SYNONYMS

1A Circle the word in each list that is not a possible synonym.

1 impure / unadulterated / natural / genuine
2 shun / ignore / ostracise / welcome
3 guess / estimate / assume / hypothetical
4 argue / squabble / admit / dispute
5 run / stroll / meander / crawl
6 lightweight / cumbersome / awkward / heavy
7 considerable / extensive / minimal / substantial
8 sincere / dishonest / straightforward / unambiguous

B Choose the correct alternatives.

1 I have to *admit/ dispute* I was very surprised by the results.
2 We took a *stroll/ meander* through the deserted streets of the old town.
3 The porter carried my bags, which were rather *cumbersome/ awkward*.
4 I trusted him immediately. His manner was very *straightforward/ dishonest* .
5 We decided that the best policy would be to *ostracise/ ignore* what was happening altogether.
6 We have to *estimate/ assume* that they reviewed all the information available.

AMBITION

2A Look at the cartoon story. Use the words in the box to complete the captions.

lifetime	big	off	heart	stroke	desire	hogging	wonder

1 Jodie **had a burning** _____ to be famous.

2 From a very young age, she **set her** _____ **on** becoming a singer.

3 At school she was constantly _____ **the limelight**.

4 She practised every day, and everyone knew she would eventually **hit the** _____ **time**.

5 One day she had **a** _____ **of luck**: a talent agent came to her town and saw her perform.

6 When he signed her up, it looked as if all her hard work had **paid** _____.

7 She was an instant success but, not wanting to be **a one-hit** _____, she kept developing.

8 Now she's **a legend in her** _____, but she still goes home to visit her friends and family.

B Cover the captions and re-tell the story. Try to use the completed phrases in bold.

1.2

7B Check your profile. Do you agree with the description?

MBTI Profiles

ESTJ – The Overseer – responsible, logical, norm-following hard workers. You enjoy being the person in charge and often make good supervisors.

ESTP – The Persuader – action-loving, 'here and now' realists with excellent people skills. You don't always agree with rules and regulations, but are good at solving problems.

ESFJ – The Supporter – social butterflies that value relationships, supporting and nurturing others. You are dutiful and have a deep concern for others. You often end up as caretakers.

ESFP – The Entertainer – cooperative, 'here and now' people-persons that enjoy excitement and love new adventures. You like to be the centre of attention and hate being alone.

ENTJ – The Chief – strategic, organised natural leaders. You are able to understand complicated organisational situations and are quick to develop intelligent solutions.

ENTP – The Originator – logical, innovative, curious and inventive. You can always find ways to improve things and are good fun to be with.

ENFJ – The Mentor – warm, supportive and encouraging. You tend to focus on others and have excellent people skills. Good at language skills, you do well in leadership roles.

ENFP – The Advocate – introspective, values-oriented, inspiring, social and extremely expressive. You are natural advocates for things you feel to be important.

ISTJ – The Examiner – responsible, loyal and hard working. You have an acute sense of right and wrong and work hard at preserving established norms and traditions.

ISTP – The Craftsman – adventurous and independent. You like to figure out how things work and have great mechanical and technical skills. You are adaptable and spontaneous, and thrive on new and exciting situations.

INTJ – The Strategist – introspective, analytical, determined people with natural leadership ability. You are a perfectionist, expecting a lot from both yourself and others.

INFJ – The Confidant – introspective, caring, sensitive, gentle and complex people that strive for peace and derive satisfaction from helping others.

ISFJ – The Defender – traditional, loyal, quiet and kind. You are sensitive to other people's needs because you are very observant and pay attention to detail. You do not seek positions of authority.

ISFP – The Artist – artistic, creative, loyal, independent and sensitive. You have a keen appreciation for beauty, and are easy to get along with.

INTP – The Engineer – logical, individualistic, reserved and very curious individuals. You focus on ideas, theories and the explanation of how things work.

INFP – The Dreamer – introspective, private, creative and highly idealistic individuals that want to do good in the world. You often have a talent for language and writing.

1.3

7A Work in pairs. Describe and discuss the portraits below. Use the following questions to help you.
- What can you say about the person's job or character from the picture?
- How do you think he/she is feeling? Why do you think this might be?

2.1

Student B

9A Read the paragraph below and underline four metaphors related to time and money. Match them with meanings 1–4.

Stuck in a stressful job, I was living on borrowed time. I ate badly and was constantly sick. Whenever I tried to relax, I found myself thinking about work. Even at the weekends, I felt as if my boss was tapping me on the shoulder, saying, 'You're wasting precious time!' One Sunday, I visited my grandfather. I said, 'I know I should put aside some time for myself, but I just can't afford to spend time relaxing. I'll lose my job.' He said, 'No. You can't afford <u>not</u> to. If you go on like this, you'll lose your mind. Which is worse?'

1 keep time free
2 using time badly (not doing anything with your time)
3 don't have time to do something
4 survive after you would expect to be dead

B Read your paragraph to your partner twice. Which metaphors did he/she notice? Teach the four metaphors to your partner.

4.4

7A Student A: prepare to argue that the will is fair and should be upheld. Here is your case.

- James Holdicott was 'of sound mind' when he wrote the will. He was still making business decisions while in hospital.
- He understood the contents of the will and changed a previous will because he was not happy with it.
- He wanted to reward Chris for his loyal work. He believed Nicholas had no interest in the company and did not need the money.

2.3

7C Read the text to find out what really happened. Do you think the bosses did the right thing?

CASE 1

The boss decided not to fire this worker. The employee had been there a long time and in all other respects was excellent. Instead, the boss sent an email around the office saying, 'Someone is stealing supplies from us. I will offer a €100 reward to whoever catches this person.' The stealing stopped immediately.

CASE 2

The boss immediately fired the employee. The employee challenged his boss, saying, 'How do you know I wasn't sick and recuperating on the beach?' She replied, 'I'm not firing you because you took a day off to mess around on the beach. I'm firing you for stupidity. No smart person would put a picture on Facebook of himself partying on a beach when he's supposed to be at work.'

CASE 3

The boss wrote a memo to all employees, saying exactly what was and was not allowed to be charged as expenses. Without naming the woman, he included many of the items that she had been charging the company for (clothes, tickets to the theatre, etc.). He knew the employee would recognise that she had been caught. The boss also explained that any corporate entertaining needed to be cleared with him *before* it happened.

6.2

7A Student B

The English Village

At the Happy English Village in Taoyuan, Taiwan, children arrive at the end of their normal school day to spend time speaking English and having fun. The village has themed rooms (a shop, restaurant, airport, coffee shop, cookery room and dance studio). Children work in groups of twelve with volunteer foreign teachers.

7.1

7A Read the rules of the game.

THE RULES

Where are you?

You're on one of the Admiralty Islands, a group of small islands off the north coast of Papua New Guinea in the Pacific Ocean. You were able to swim there, with a few belongings, after your plane crashed en route to a conference in Australia.

What do you have with you?

A penknife, a pen and some paper, a small mirror, a bottle of alcohol and water-resistant tape. Plus, up to five items of your own choice. None of them would, in themselves, allow you to escape (so no inflatable boats, sadly). But used together, and perhaps with a few items from the island, you can hatch an escape plan.

What have you tried so far?

Building a raft, but you quickly realised it would not get you to safety on Papua New Guinea 300 km away before you ran out of the fruit you'd stashed for the journey. Shining a mirror towards the boats that pass on the horizon has failed, too.

5.2

1B Read the myths below and answer the questions.

1 What is the myth?

2 Which myths were disproved by experiments?

3 What is the truth about the myth?

5 Sugar makes kids hyperactive

Not one study has conclusively shown that children with a sugar-laden diet behave differently from those with a sugar-free diet. Most of the studies come from the US with titles such as 'Hyperactivity: is candy causal?' but time after time, no link has been found. Despite the evidence, parents simply can't believe this is a myth. In an experiment where they were told their children had been given a sugar-loaded drink, parents rated the children as 'significantly more hyperactive' than parents whose children had received a sugar-free drink. In reality, the children had been given the same sugar-free drink. The difference in behaviour was all in the parents' minds.

6 Get cold and you get ill

One professor uncovered the truth by studying volunteers who were asked to dunk their feet in cold water. He discovered that being chilled does make a cold more likely. But it's not quite as simple as that. The crucial requirement is that your body is harbouring a cold virus in the first place. No virus, no cold.

7 Turning your PC off without shutting it down damages it

According to tests in the US, as long as your PC isn't in the middle of an epic video editing project or full of unsaved documents, bypassing the full shutdown rigmarole shouldn't cause any major harm. After you've hit the power button, Word and Excel easily recover your previous spreadsheets and musings. Just take care not to power off when you've got stuff up and running – you could lose precious data.

8 Your email is private

Have you seen ads that correspond to your chat about sausages or that next gen smartphone? That's because Google scans your email for key words in order to let its advertisers target you. In other words, your emails are far from private; they are being used by big companies who want to sell you things. The scans are by robots, not people, but it's had privacy campaigners up in arms for years.

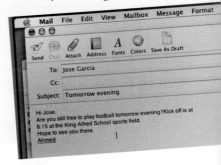

6A You are going to debunk a myth of your choice. It can be about a person, a profession, a country or a belief. Here are three ideas. Complete the title and notes on page 61.

1 We only use ten percent of our brains

This myth is often cited by people who want us to believe that we can learn to master paranormal activities such as telepathy. Brain imaging techniques, e.g. PET scans, disprove this myth. They clearly show us using the whole brain on a daily basis.

2 Sushi means raw fish

It does not mean raw fish. The name refers to the rice used in the dish. Sushi is rice made with rice vinegar, salt and sugar dressing. Traditionally, it's topped with fish, fish eggs, or a variety of vegetables

3 Bulls are angered by the colour red

Bulls do not get angry because of the colour red. Professional matadors traditionally use a red cape, but it wouldn't make any difference if the cape was a different colour because cattle are colour-blind. It is the movement of the cape that angers the bull, not the colour.

7.1

1C Read part two of the story and check your answers to Exercise 1B on page 80.

An investigation was immediately launched into his disappearance. Five days later, John Darwin was arrested on suspicion of fraud and deception. A photograph, published in a tabloid newspaper, revealed that Mr and Mrs Darwin had been seen together in Panama and had bought a house there together.

It turned out that Mr Darwin had planned the whole disappearance from the beginning after finding himself in financial difficulty. On the day of the 'disappearance', Mr Darwin had in fact pushed his kayak out to sea and later returned home to his wife. What he did then was spend the next few years hiding inside the house and rarely leaving. When visitors came, Mr Darwin supposedly hid in the neighbouring house, escaping though a hole he had made in the wall of an upstairs bedroom. He changed his appearance, spent a lot of time on the internet and applied for a passport under a false name.

Mr and Mrs Darwin travelled to Greece and then to Panama, looking for opportunities to start a new life together, while Mrs Darwin kept up the pretence that her husband was dead to her friends, colleagues and two sons. When Mrs Darwin received the life insurance money taken out in her husband's name, Mr Darwin moved to Panama, where he bought an apartment and waited for his wife to join him. When she finally managed to emigrate, they bought a £200,000 tropical estate and planned to start a hotel business selling canoe holidays. John Darwin finally returned to the UK, claiming that he was missing his sons and was fed up with living the deception.

In the meantime, in the UK, several people had become suspicious. It was a colleague of Anne Darwin's who eventually put the pieces of the puzzle together. She had overheard a conversation which Anne Darwin had had with her husband on the telephone before leaving for Panama. She then typed the names 'Anne+John+Darwin+Panama' into Google images and found the photograph, which she later sent to the media and to the police.

John and Anne Darwin were both sentenced and served time in prison for fraud and deception. Their ill-gained assets (money and property) were taken from them and their sons refused to talk to either of them, claiming that they had been victims of the scam and they no longer wished to have any contact with their parents.

John Darwin was released from prison in January 2011 and Anne Darwin in March 2011. It is thought that they still have some assets hidden in Panama.

5.1

9A This is how the story continued.

It was a small wooden box, which her mother had kept hidden in the back of her wardrobe. Madge lifted the lid gently and peered inside. The moment she saw them, she recognised his handwriting. At the bottom of the box, lying unopened after all those years, were dozens of letters from the man she had wanted to marry.

8.2

7A Student A: look at your sentences. Delete any words you can leave out due to ellipsis. Read your sentences to Student B. Student B will choose a response.

1 Have you ever been to China?
2 I don't know why I can't get this camera to work.
3 I love olives.
4 Have they nearly finished?
5 What's that? It looks wonderful.

B Listen to Student B's sentences and choose the correct responses a)–e).

a) Yes, she said she'd be at the airport at 2p.m.
b) No, I wanted to but I fell asleep!
c) No, I haven't. I've only just started.
d) Did they? Do you know who it was?
e) No thanks. I've just had one.

10.3

8B Read your role. Think about your answers to questions 1–3 below.

Group A

You are the school administrators.

- Your budget is €800 (for renting films, buying food and paying staff for overtime).
- You think students should pay €5 per evening (two films).
- You want to serve snacks only.
- You think the festival should last three days.
- You think the school administrators should choose the films because you need to make sure they are appropriate.
- You want the student Film Festival Committee to develop a web page about the festival to go on the school's website. You think this will attract students to the school.
- You want the festival to take place next term so there is time to arrange it properly.

1 What is your main objective in this negotiation?
2 What do you think the other team's objective is?
3 What are your other objectives? Which of these are quite important? Which are not so important?

8.1

9A When would you use the proverbs below? Match proverbs 7–12 with situations g)–l). Do you have equivalents in your language?

7 There's no place like home.

8 Nothing ventured, nothing gained.

9 Don't judge a book by its cover.

10 Actions speak louder than words.

11 Practice makes perfect.

12 Absence makes the heart grow fonder.

g) I love to travel but I always feel happier when I return.

h) I haven't seen Miroslav for six months and I really miss him!

i) He looks ordinary but when you talk to him, he's a genius!

j) She's a great tennis player because she works at it six hours a day.

k) He doesn't talk much but he always gets the job done.

l) If you don't take any risks, you'll never know what you can achieve.

9.1

9A You are an art dealer. Read about your clients on page 106. Look at the sculptures below and on page 106. Decide which sculpture to recommend to each company.

8.2

7A Student B: listen to Student A's sentences and choose the correct responses a)–e).

a) It's a Cajun dish with shrimps. Try some!

b) Yes, I have. I went there to see my brother who was living in Beijing.

c) Neither do I. Why don't you let Johnnie have a look? He's good with technology.

d) Do you? I can't stand them.

e) I think so. They've just got one more thing to do.

B Look at your sentences. Delete any words you can leave out due to ellipsis. Read your sentences to Student A. Student A will choose a response.

1 Have you been in the job for long?

2 Are you sure she's coming today?

3 Someone called you earlier and left a message.

4 Do you want a tea or coffee?

5 Did you see the film last night?

3.2

1B

Answers:
1C – Jack Vettriano, painter
2B – Zandra Rhodes, fashion designer
3A – James Caan, businessman

4.4

5 Read what happened to Captain Blackadder.

Captain Blackadder is about to be shot when a telegram arrives. It is from the Minister of War, who is George's uncle (George is the defence lawyer). The telegram says that Captain Blackadder's life is to be spared.

4.4

7A Student B: prepare to argue that the will was rewritten illegally and should be changed. Here is your case.

• In the months before his death, James Holdicott was not 'of sound mind' because he was taking strong medication that affected his mental capabilities.

• He was pressurised into changing the will by business associates who feared that Nicholas would make changes to the business.

• An earlier draft of the will split James Holdicott's money and assets between the brothers. This will should be upheld.

6.2

7A Student C

Mobile English

With the Millee Language Program, children in rural areas in India are learning English on their mobile phones. In remote villages, good English teachers are hard to come by, but mobile phones are reasonably cheap. The children learn vocabulary by playing games on their phones. They can then take the phones wherever they go, so that even the fields where they work can become a classroom.

10.3

8B Read your role. Think about your answers to questions 1–3 below.

Group B

You are the student Film Festival Committee.

- You think the event will cost €1500 (for renting films and buying food).
- You think students should pay €10 and be allowed to attend all films (two per day).
- You want to serve international food to match the films (e.g. during a Brazilian film, you will serve Brazilian food).
- You think the festival should last five days (Monday–Friday).
- You think the student Film Festival Committee should choose the films because you know what students like.
- You want to create a promotional leaflet to hand out to all students.
- You want the festival to take place this term because everyone is enthusiastic about it.

1 What is your main objective in this negotiation?

2 What do you think the other team's objective is?

3 What are your other objectives? Which of these are quite important? Which are not so important?

9.2

11 Read the notes about an exhibition. Write a review based on the notes (200–250 words).

First impression – nice ideas, but not very dramatic visually.

Simple layout – fifteen recent British inventions laid around the gallery with short information boards on each.

Some of the ideas are interesting – e.g. a hypersonic alarm which only teenagers can hear (called a mosquito) – used to stop teenagers loitering where they aren't wanted.

Some not so interesting or original – e.g. electric bicycle, baby bottle with automatic warmer.

Information about the story behind the invention – OK – interesting to note that some ideas have been inspired by young people (one child was just eight when he suggested the idea to his father).

Overall – disappointed – it only takes about ten minutes to go round the whole exhibition – left feeling a little flat, rather than inspired.

Highlight – section where people have written their own ideas of problems which could be solved with new ideas/solutions – some really funny, new ideas.

10.2

7C Check your answers for Exercise 7B on page 120.

1 a scrap (of attention) (n) ⟶ a very small amount

2 dazzled (adj) ⟶ amazed

3 ascension (n) ⟶ rise

4 clamour (n) ⟶ continuous loud noise

5 geriatric (adj) ⟶ old (person)

6 a beacon (of hope) (n) ⟶ a shining light

AUDIO SCRIPTS

UNIT 1 Recording 1

1 She kept on making mistakes.
2 He'll spend hours studying grammar.
3 They would complain all the time.

UNIT 1 Recording 3

M = Mariella J = John

M: For any of you who work surrounded by other people, you'll know that one of the biggest stressors in the world of work is not the work itself, it's the people we work with. There are the people who need to be noisy when you're trying to be quiet, there are the ones who 'shush' you when you're telling a really good story, there are the sweeping generalisers, and the detail-obsessed nit-pickers, the obsessive planners, and the last-minute deadline junkies. You, of course, are perfect. These days there are tests for just about everything, and personality is no exception. If you've ever been intrigued to define your type, or sat down and completed a questionnaire at work, then it's likely you'll have come across the Myers-Briggs Type Indicator, known to its fans as the MBTI. Myers-Briggs is the world's most widely used personality questionnaire. From Beijing to Boston to Bournemouth, office workers, college students, and people who are simply curious to find out more about themselves, answer a series of questions to determine which of sixteen different personality types they fall into.

J: How did you find completing the questionnaire that you completed just yesterday I think?

M: Em, I found it not particularly challenging. Maybe I didn't think about it as much as one ought to.

M: The preferences are split into four sections, so prepare yourself for the psychological bit. The first category determines whether you are an extrovert or an introvert. The second tells you whether you prefer to sense or intuit information. The third deals with decision-making: thinking or feeling. And the fourth, our approach to actions: judging and perceiving. Ultimately, you end up with a four-letter acronym like ENFP, or ISFJ, which describes your personality type.

J: How do you prefer to, if you like, recharge your batteries at the end of a tiring day?

M: Well, most of the time, I prefer to go home and be quiet and read, or slow down ... put my children to bed and so on,

J: Typically when we ask people this sort of question. Typically, introverts are more likely to talk about spending quiet time, time on their own, reading, etc. Extroverts are more likely to talk about spending time with people. ... I don't know if you ever had the opportunity to put together any flat-pack furniture, or anything like that. How did you go about doing it?

M: Well, you know, I'd lose the screws, and then the directions would be underneath the box, and then I'd lose another part of it, and it would take quite a long time, and be quite an infuriating process.

J: OK. Typically when we ask that question, people with a preference for sensing will like to follow the instructions. People who have a preference for intuition, it's not that they disregard instructions, but they're a little bit more of a guide ...

If you imagine perhaps a friend of yours gives you a call, and says, 'I've just been burgled.' What would you, what would your reaction be, what would you do?

M: Do you know, it's so difficult, because I think it depends on the person, you know ...

J: OK. In some ... matter ... to me it's a matter of what you do first, because both people with a preference for thinking, (and both people with a preference for feeling) ... will do both things. They'll do the practical things. 'Have you called the police?' 'Is the person still there?' 'Have you, you know, called the insurance?', etc., etc. And they'll then go on to, 'And how are you?'

M: Well, in that instance I would definitely fall into the thinking category, I think.

J: How do you go about doing the food shopping?

M: Em I, I'm in love with internet food ordering, um so I do that, and then all the things that I've forgotten, cos I don't do it with any great system, I spend the rest of the week running out and picking up.

J: OK. Typically, people with a preference for judging will be quite organised about those sorts of things. People with a preference for perceiving may also make lists, but those lists have a more aspirational quality.

M: Random feel, shall we say?

J: Yeah, they are things that they might buy, or they might not buy. If they see something more interesting when they get to the supermarket, they'll get that instead.

M: At the end of my conversation with John, I got my personality type, which I'll illuminate you on later.

UNIT 1 Recording 4

W1 = Woman 1 M1 = Man 1 M2 = Man 2

Portrait A

W1: I think this woman looks very intelligent.

M1: Mmm – she's got, she's got an in ... a kind of intensity to her her face, hasn't she?

M2: She looks a bit puzzled to me.

W1: I think she looks thoughtful.

M1: Yeah, pensive.

M2: Yes, maybe.

M1: But the way she's sitting ... it's unusual isn't it ...

W1: It's very unusual ... she's ...

M2: It seems like she's trying to say something – do you know what I mean?

M1: Oh, by the way she's ...

M2: Trying to make a statement by ... 'this is the sort of person I am. That I ... am relaxed ... and ... confident with ... myself,' I suppose.

M1: Yeah, she gives the impression of being very at ease with herself – doesn't she?

W1: I think she's ... it it looks to me as if she's listening ...

M1: Mmm

W1: ... to someone else talking ... that we can't see.

M1: Yeah ... off off frame yeah.

W1: I wonder what she ... does for a living?

M1: Mmm ... possibly ...

W1: D'you think she's a teacher?

M1: I was gonna say academia, I wonder if she's a ...

M2: But something that's not ... within the system, if you know what I mean ... some ... she looks ... there's something rebellious about ...

W1: Yes ... she could be a writer.

M2: The way she's ... just the way she's holding herself there, it's just very confident, and very 'I'm gonna do it my way'.

M1: Yeah yeah. I I ...

W1: Do you think she works ah ... on television ... something like that?

M1: Possibly ... she could be a presenter, or a broadcaster?

W1: Yes.

M2: That kind of stuff.

M1: Umm ... I wouldn't wanna get into an argument with her though.

W1: No.

Portrait B

M2: This guy looks kind of I'd say intellectual. You've got all the books behind him, he looks quite, umm studious – wouldn't you say?

M1: Mmm

W1: Yes ... he he looks very thoughtful.

M1: But don't you think that it's the glasses that are making us think that? Put a pair of glasses on someone and they suddenly look intelligent.

M2: Hmm, maybe.

W1: I'd ...

M2: But it's also ...

W1: ... hazard a guess that he was a writer.

M2: It's a – yeah, something like that. It's also the hand on the chair that I'm I'm ...

M1: It's quite posed isn't it?

M2: Yes.

W1: He ... he doesn't look British I don't think.

M2: Ahh!

M1: Yes!

M2: Interesting.

M1: Yeah. I'd say he looks mm ... maybe Eastern European?

W1: He could be American.

M2: Hard to say isn't it?

M1: Ahh, yeah.

W1: Do you think that's his room?

M2: I wonder if it's his study – yes.

M1: Like a study or a library? Again, it makes me think maybe he's in academia.

W1: Yes, it could be … university.

M1: But again he's dressed … he's dressed quite comfortable … comfortably, isn't he?

W1: Very casually.

M1: It's not formal, is it?

M2: So you'd think that might suggest it's his home or something.

M1: How … how d'you think he comes across though, personality wise?

M2: Um

W1: I think he looks kind.

M2: Hmm, I think there's something guarded there. I think there's …

M1: He knows something. There's something knowing in his eyes … as if he's got a secret.

M2: Yes and not necessarily going to tell us.

Portrait C

M1: Now this chap looks like he's in a world of his own … like his thoughts have just drifted off somewhere far away.

W1: I can't make out where this is.

M1: Difficult, isn't it?

M2: It looks quite set up, doesn't it?

W1: Yes it does.

M2: They look like props in front of him.

M1: Theatre … the colours in the background remind me of theatres – the colour of theatre seats.

W1: Yes – there is a mug, there's … is this a plug?

M1: Oh yes.

M2: I wondered that, with the … look … with the wire there …

W1: I can see … and a bag.

M2: And that looks like a paper bag with his lunch in or something.

M1: Brown paper bag … so maybe he's trying to tell us that he's … he's got no pretensions. He he's not a … he's not posh. He's he's brought his lunch in a … in a grocers' bag.

W1: I think it looks …

M2: I don't get the plug if it is a plug. I don't understand that.

W1: …quite funny.

M1: Yeah – incongruous.

W1: It's quite amusing.

M1: Yeah – as if he's trying to make a point about how ridiculous or absurd er his life is or life in general is.

W1: Yes.

M1: What d'you reckon his job might be?

W1: I don't know.

M2: When you said you thought somebody with glasses looked intellectual – do you think he's intellectual?

M1: No, this time not.

M2: What is it then, what …

W1: He could be an artist.

M1: Mmmhmm

W1: Possibly.

M2: 'Cos he's dressed very, sort of formally.

M1: Yes.

M2: But there's something otherworldly about the … where he's sitting, if you know what I mean.

M1: Mmm

W1: Yes.

M2: It's all that red behind him.

M1: Like he's bridging different worlds.

M2: Exactly.

M1: So he he could be a creative; he could be a novelist or a playwright, or something like that. Somebody who fuses fiction and reality.

UNIT 1 Recording 5

1 I'll be there soon. I just have a couple of things to do.

2 Why don't we meet at about eight-ish?

3 I left a lot of stuff at the hotel, but I can pick it up later.

4 Don't worry. We've got plenty of time.

5 We've sort of finished the accounts.

6 There'll be about forty or so people attending.

UNIT 1 Recording 7

My treasured possession is a very old carpet that has been in my family for four generations. My great grandfather was a salesman. He sold carpets in Calcutta. During the nineteen-fifties he went bankrupt and went to South Africa to find his fortune. Legend has it that he took nothing but the clothes he was wearing and this carpet. I'm not sure this is true, but that's the story. Anyway, he made his fortune in South Africa and the carpet remained in the family. When he died, my grandmother inherited it and instead of putting it on the floor of her house in Durban, she hung it on the wall. Even as a young child I remember it. It's brightly coloured: reds, white, green and gold, with these beautiful patterns that look like leaves, and I just remember it hanging on the wall of the dining room and always wondering why a carpet was on the wall. Anyway, eventually it was bequeathed to me and um it's now on my wall. It's a little bit old and frayed now. I suppose I should repair it. Some of the weaving is falling apart, but it still looks OK. When I die, my children will have it, and then their children, so it will always be in the family.

UNIT 2 Recording 1

1 I wish I'd been born a rich man.

2 I wish I was the sun instead of a rich man.

3 Had I known this, I'd have asked to become a cloud.

4 If I'd been stronger, I could've stopped the wind.

5 But for my weakness, I would've blown that mountain down.

6 If only I'd been transformed into a mountain, I'd be the strongest of all.

7 If only I'd known this, I would've remained a stonecutter.

8 I regret making all these wishes, and I want to be a stonecutter again.

UNIT 2 Recording 2

The book – Alex

Now, you might think of a library as a dusty old place full of books that nobody uses anymore. After all, when we need to research something, we tend to do it on the net nowadays. But in a 'living library' the books are real people. People who can share a significant personal experience, or a particular perspective on life. I volunteered to be a book at a living library event in Sheffield. The event was organised by the university and was meant to tackle prejudices. Arriving in a bit of a hurry, I looked through the catalogue of available books to sign myself in as 'a student'. Against each 'book' are a few of the typical prejudices and preconceptions people might associate with your 'title'. Next to 'student' were written things like lazy, politically apathetic, do useless degrees. And also wastes tax payers' money, can't cook and spends all his money on beer. Thinking back to the previous night, I wasn't sure how I was going to tackle any of these accusations. Sitting in the waiting room was rather surreal, with 'books' asking each other 'Who are you?' and already I was beginning to have second thoughts. When the public started coming in, it was like sitting on a shelf, waiting and hoping that someone would choose you, and hoping that you would be able to find something to say when they did. Luckily, I didn't have to wait long. An older man, grey hair and a suit, came to collect me. As we walked over to our designated corner, I planned my responses to the rail of expected accusations. In fact, as we talked over coffee, we compared experiences – student life in the 1960s, with the riots and protests, wild music, and the ambitions they had of changing the world. And student life now. Interestingly, we found that we shared a lot of the same ideologies, that many things haven't really changed. I think the directness of the experience was eye-opening really. The candid discussion forces people to keep an open mind about things, and that has to be good.

AUDIO SCRIPTS

The reader – Saba

If, like me, you're the kind of person that is curious about other types of people that you don't know personally, then I think you'd enjoy the 'living book' experience. I went to a three-hour session in Norwich, and was surprised at how much I learned. It gives you a chance to really talk to people, who may be from a different religion, or culture – people who you don't normally get to talk to in your everyday life. I met all kinds of people, some wonderful people. One of them was Karrie, a blind woman. Karrie is visually impaired, having lost her sight due to illness when she was a child. The first thing that struck me about Karrie is that she's fiercely independent. She doesn't like other people doing things for her, so you can imagine that can be a bit difficult. Her mission was to tackle the stigma that people attach to blind people, that they're helpless. She wants to challenge the stereotype that just because a person can't see, they can't do anything for themselves. Karrie lives a perfectly normal life, gets dressed by herself, goes to work, goes out socially – and does all the things that the rest of us do. Well, she can't drive, but that was really one of her few limitations. She told me about successful blind people around the world who have had a great impact on society – people who've been successfully employed, er taken advanced degrees, published books, written music and participated in athletic and even Olympic events. These are the people that have been Karrie's inspiration. She also talked about how many blind people use their other senses, which happen to be quite developed. So, Karrie feels that she's quite a good judge of character, because she is able to 'see' people for who they really are, on the inside, rather than just how they want to present themselves, or how you may judge them because of the clothes they're wearing, or the scar they may have. As she put it, she's able to 'see with her heart' rather than her eyes. My conversation with Karrie gave me a whole new perspective. It taught me not to be narrow-minded about disability, and I thank her for that.

UNIT 2 Recording 3

M1 = Man 1 M2 = Man 2 W1 = Woman 1
W2 = Woman 2

M1: As far as I'm concerned, we cannot trust the news we read these days.

W1: Mmm

M2: Why not?

M1: Because journalists have an axe to grind.

M2: What? That's debatable.

M1: I think it's very rare to get a truly impartial journalist. I don't think it's within human nature to be impartial. You side on one side or the other.

M2: Why why would a journalist want to be partial? Why would a journalist not want to be impartial? Surely that's the job of a journalist.

W2: Oooh, I don't know about that.

M1: It it is … why?

W2: No I I'm agreeing with you. I'm just saying I think there are some journalists who cannot be trusted. They have an agenda … they, they aren't there to tell the truth, they're there to sell newspapers … or they have an axe to grind.

M1: Yeah, it's a job, they're being paid and er effectively they're the mouthpiece for whoever is paying them.

M2: But isn't the job of a journalist to be, to be rigorous. I mean if somebody comes up with a piece of nonsense, or just whatever er you know a piece of received information that they're spouting, isn't the job of a journalist to get to the bottom of that and say: what do you really mean by that, have you got proof of it, who, you know, what are your sources? That's their job, surely?

W1: Exactly, you know they're going in there asking where's the evidence for what you're saying? They're not just going to say, you know – oh you tell me every sheep in Wales is blue and they're not going to go ooh right I'll just write down every sheep in Wales is blue. They're going to say right, well show me photographs, take me and show me these sheep.

M1: But but the bigger issue here if you ask me is that they're there to sell newspapers and newspaper owners have political agendas.

W2: Quite frankly, it's a business as well isn't it?

M1: It's a political business.

M2: From what I can gather about the nature of … of the dispassionate idea of being a journalist, what a journalist is after is the truth. If that journalist then goes to work for a particular paper that's got a particular angle … a particular axe to grind then, certainly that journalist may err towards one side of the political spectrum or the other. But only a bit, I would say. I would say they are still after truth at its heart.

W1: Exactly. Surely any journalist worth his or her salt is going to make the case for both sides? Anybody just arguing one side in a totally biased way is not going to be taken seriously.

M1: Why? Why are there so many libel trials then if we can trust everything journalists write?

W2: And from what I can gather, people and journalists included don't even know that they're biased and they'll write, you know, something trying to be impartial and they, they won't realise that actually they have a slant on it, you can't help it.

W1: I find that highly unlikely. I mean, they're not stupid people, are they?

M1: Some of them are, for some newspapers, the way they write, incredibly stupid.

W2: But surely the people being libelled are just people who didn't like what was said about them?

M2: Could we … do you think we could agree that the basic honesty of journalists is probably not to be questioned but that there are a few bad apples in the cart?

W2: Yeah.

M2: And that there are journalists who give other, you know, who are bad journalists, who are partisan and who are arguing a particular political slant who give other journalists a bad name.

M1: Well, I'd say that there are a few bad carts rather than a few bad apples!

UNIT 2 Recording 4

Extract 1

A: Journalists have an axe to grind.

B: What? That's debatable.

Extract 2

A: Why would a journalist not want to be impartial?

B: Oooh … I don't know about that.

Extract 3

A: Journalists don't even know that they're biased.

B: I find that highly unlikely.

UNIT 2 Recording 5

1 I really don't know about that.
2 I'm really not sure about that.
3 That's highly debatable.
4 I find that highly unlikely.

UNIT 2 Recording 6

C = Chairperson Q = Questioner
S = Speaker

S: OK, I'm going to talk about the influence of nature versus nurture. And I'd like to begin by stating that, as I see it, by far the strongest influence has to be 'nurture'. The reason I think this is that I believe the way we're brought up will have a much stronger influence on how we behave than anything that's in our genes. I mean, some people will argue that our abilities are determined pretty much exclusively by our genes, so if your father was a great scientist with a natural ability for mathematics, then there's a pretty good chance that you might inherit that same ability. Personally, I think it's ridiculous to suggest this. I think that when a parent has a particular strength, or interest, or achieves something wonderful in a particular field, then the chances are that when they have children, they will try to instil in the children the same kind of interest, they will pass on their knowledge, their passion for the subject, they are quite likely to engage the child in activities related to that field, perhaps for quite a lot of the child's time. And it's as a result of this that the child may also develop strengths or abilities in the same field. I absolutely reject the idea that nature endows us with these inborn abilities. I mean, you can be born with the best natural musical ability in the universe, but if you don't practise the piano, then nothing will come of it. On the other hand,

I think you can teach people to do just about anything, so long as you dedicate time and give the child the right kind of encouragement, or put them in the right situation. So, to conclude I would have to argue that nurture plays a much stronger role in the development of who you are and the talents that you develop than nature does.

C: OK. Thank you. And now, let's open the discussion up and take questions from the floor. Does anyone have a question for one of the speakers?

Q: Yes, I'd like to ask a question to the last speaker. I think it is quite obvious if you look around you, that people often very much resemble their parents in terms of their physical appearance, and even their characters. Why then, do you not think that it is equally possible that a child will inherit its parents' ability, or intelligence?

S: That's a good question, because yes, we can see that we do inherit physical characteristics from our parents. However, the point I'm trying to make is that we cannot rely on something we are assumed to be born with. For me, the influence of nurture is far stronger. I believe that everyone has the same potential, they just need to be given the right conditions to nurture and develop that potential. Thank you for the question.

C: Thank you. Are there any other questions?

UNIT 3 Recording 2

M = Man W = Woman

Conversation 1

M: I work in a call centre which is a … huge open plan, um well, there's tables everywhere people at little sort of boxed areas where they have to just make call after call after call.

W: Oh right.

M: Um, it's weird because it's a huge airy space, the actual the big room but everything feels quite pokey because it's, you're all crammed up next to each other …

W: Oh dear.

M: … all making your separate calls and it's very noisy, you just hear chat all the … time. You'd love to be able to get away and have a little bit of quiet, a bit of peace and quiet and somewhere nice to hang out but this isn't it!

W: No.

M: Um basically everybody's talking and depending on, it varies, depending on what what we're trying to sell and if it is a hard sell …

W: Right.

M: If it's something we're trying to sell as many units of as possible then it gets quite chaotic there but it's, the one benefit is it's within walking distance of home so at least I can get home quickly.

W: Yes.

Conversation 2

W: I'm very lucky because I work at home on a very very big dining table in the conservatory so it's very light, very airy, roomy.

M: Right.

W: There is one drawback and that is it's very cold, very chilly in the winter.

M: Oh.

W: I have a fire on, but because there's so much glass it's very cold.

M: Mmm

W: But it's lovely being at home. It's a stone's throw away from all the shops. It's near my neighbours. When I have a coffee break I can meet a neighbour, have a cup of coffee, catch up on all the local chit-chat …

M: Mmhmm

W: … and then go back to work. And at lunchtime, I'm right next to my kitchen, my fridge, make myself a lovely meal, go back to work – no time spent travelling …

M: Mmm … sounds good.

W: … which is wonderful, and it's a very lovely place to work, a little haven of tranquillity … because it looks out on to my garden with all the birds.

UNIT 3 Recording 3

Just to give you a bit of background information, Harrogate council has announced the creation of cycle hubs er, as part of its cycling strategy for the next five years. Now, the aim of this project is to set up cycle hubs. What are hubs? Hubs are areas where innovative ideas for cycling can be piloted and where resources can be targeted to increase er cycling. So what we plan to do is to introduce these new hubs in the centre of Harrogate, located in areas with a high concentration of cyclists. Er, this solution will help us er, to create a more safe environment for the cyclist. Cycling is an incredibly efficient mode of transport. It's fast, it's environmentally friendly and it's cheap – with of course the added bonus of keeping you fit. So basically, what we're proposing to do is to get everybody around the table to discuss the merits and demerits of whether or not the idea of a cycling hub in the centre of Harrogate is a good or a bad idea basically. So um, does anyone have any questions?

UNIT 3 Recording 4

W1 = Woman 1 W2 = Woman 2

W1: Er Canada has one of the highest standards of living in the world and, you know, long life expectancy … um and it's one of the world's wealthiest nations so it's really quite a nice – nice place to live. Um and on the downside I suppose there's um – in a lot of areas you have to deal with bad winter weather, so um not – not in all places but in a lot of places we get a lot of snow and um really cold temperatures in the winter um and that can be quite difficult to deal with, although you do get used to it.

I would describe Canada as er geographically massive. Um I think it's kind of difficult to explain how – just how big the country is. It's the second largest country in the world apart from Russia, or next to Russia, um and yeah, so it's just really, really, really big and very, very diverse.

Every province is different um and, you know, to visit Canada you really have to go far and go for a long time to – to really appreciate the the vastness of the country. Um what um if I was making a documentary I'd probably focus on things like, you know, we're very, very lucky in Canada to have a huge range of fresh water, um great lakes, rivers everywhere, literally. Um we have three coasts: the Pacific coast, the Atlantic and the Arctic, and we actually have the longest coastline in the world. So you get incredible um diversity, um everything from wildlife to bird life um and also diversity in climate so, you know, we have temperate rain forests and we have deserts, we have um arctic er prairies, we have volcanoes, mountains, um you know, almost half of Canada is covered in forests.

Er some similarities um between the United States and Canada um that I can think of is that um we both have a strong history and a long standing history of aboriginal peoples um and we share the longest border in the world.

W2: Well undoubtedly one of the best things about Argentina is um the values, um people and and their values, how they view life and they – we tend to attribute quite a lot of um um sort of value to our our family. We care a lot about our families and and our gatherings and we kind of gather on Sundays and we have a big barbecue and everybody comes and we all talk about our weeks and what we've been up to and it's a good chance to catch up.

Um we also care a great deal about our friends, um we celebrate Friend's Day, which is a big celebration and we have a lot of fun and we give each other cards and thank each other for our friendship. Um so I think that's kind of the best thing about Argentina: people are very warm, very caring and there's a – we've got a great sense of solidarity.

Um I guess if you – a lot of people think that Latin America is just Latin America and that all the countries are the same and, you know, like Brazil and Argentina are the same thing but we're very different um with our – we we've got like I I guess if you could put it in into words, Brazilians are very upbeat and very happy and Argentinians we're … we've got a sense of longing for for the old world and this er melancholic view of the of the world and so we … the outlooks are very different and hence the culture is is very different.

An interesting way of seeing Argentina would be um if you were to film a documentary, it would be through following one person like through a day or through a couple of days because then you start getting a sense for all the things that um go on in the country and like, you know, for instance when I used to teach, it it was like I used to start my day not knowing what my day would be about because there's always a strike, there's always a picket line, there's always

AUDIO SCRIPTS

all these difficulties you have to overcome through throughout a day and … but at the same time you can see how resourceful people are when dealing with difficulties and how er relaxed and and laid back they are about them, in a way. So it's it's an interesting way of living. Um it's a constant struggle but at the same time keeping your smile.

UNIT 4 Recording 3

Speaker 1

I really admire Annie Lennox, the singer. Not not just a singer, um I don't know what you'd call her. I suppose a humanitarian, in a way, because of the work she does er raising awareness of the impact of HIV and AIDS on women and children in particular, especially in South Africa. Um in 2009 she won the Woman of Peace award er for that work and er and it all started when um she went to take part in a concert for er a campaign, an HIV campaign that Nelson Mandela had organised er in South Africa. And from then on – I think she's raised over two million dollars now um to help with treatment, testing, HIV education and prevention programmes. And um, you know, like from a personal point of view, er I've got nearly all of her albums and there are certain of her songs that just take me back to very particular times in my life, like sad times and happy times, and so, you know, she kind of cuts straight through to the heart. But I particularly admire the fact that she's dedicated time to helping other people. I mean, when you find great success like that and you actually have the time and resources to enjoy your wealth and success and money er and you take out huge swathe of … swathes of time um to help other people around the world and be of service to others, I think that's very admirable and er and a role model for us all.

Speaker 2

Al Gore was vice president of the USA um in the nineties and at the turn of the century um and I think it's fair to say that he didn't get um that much attention because he was serving under Bill Clinton at the time, who was um generally taking the headlines and the plaudits. Um but he sort of became better known when he tried to become president himself. Um but anyway, soon after that he sort of dedicated himself um, well at least more in the public consciousness, um he became known as a kind of environmental activist. He he helped um he helped with a documentary called *An Inconvenient Truth*, which was based on his own book. Um and it had a huge effect on raising awareness of global warming and environmental issues. A lot of these things are are spoken about now and it seems um it's much more commonly in the news but at that stage really it was … it was not a very common subject and it made a massive difference and I really admired him for that. I actually got to meet him at um Notre Dame University in in America and I found him really … there was something … there's a real integrity about the man that I really admired. The only thing I wonder about is of course

he's always flying around here and there, um giving these talks, and you sort of wonder how much fuel he's burning in doing that. But I think um he's offset that by by his message and um the number of people he's managed to help create an awareness for.

Speaker 3

I'm going to talk about Sting because he's first of all gorgeous, also a fantastic singer, amazing songwriter, wonderful actor and, of course, really respected humanitarian. But personally for me um I've always been interested in him because I know that my dad years ago wrote a book on how to write a hit song, cos he had a few hits as a songwriter, and apparently um Sting er read the book and started … and embarked on his amazing career. So that um, for me, was what sparked my interest and er he started, as far as I know, in the 1980s after um he was a teacher, that was his background, so obviously he's a really clever man and knowledgeable as well, um and that was when I was growing up in the 1980s, so I remember him touring and singing in concerts for Amnesty International. And some of his songs um also deal with social justice, um like *Driven to Tears*, which I think was around the same time, um which was about world hunger. Um he also co-founded The Rainforest Foundation to help save rainforests in South America and to protect the indigenous tribes living there, which affected me um so much that I decided I'll embark on a campaign myself to help stop the destruction of rainforests.

UNIT 4 Recording 4

1 civil liberties
2 human rights
3 free trade
4 freedom of speech
5 religious freedom
6 illegal immigration
7 intellectual property
8 gun control
9 environmental awareness
10 capital punishment
11 economic development
12 child labour

UNIT 4 Recording 5

M = Man W = Woman

M: So did you see that thing on the news about that er seventy-year-old grandmother who um who stopped the jewel thieves?

W: Oh the the one yeah, who knocked one of them off their bike, off their motorbike?

M: Yeah.

W: That was amazing.

M: Wasn't it extraordinary? And they were robbing this jewel store and smashing the windows.

W: Yeah yeah yeah, and she just came up and completely …

M: And nobody was doing anything about it.

W: … hit them straight over the head with her massive great handbag.

M: With her shopping bag.

W: Shopping bag or something.

M: Full of, I don't know, beans or something.

W: Cans of beans, yeah!

M: But I mean would you do that in that situation?

W: Oh I I, if it was up to me I think I would probably be too cowardly and I'd end up just calling the police, I'm afraid to say.

M: I know, it's interesting, isn't it? I mean, you know, if if I ever found myself in that situation I would like to think that I would be, you know, a have-a-go-hero as well but come, you know, push come to shove, whether or not you actually do it or not is another question, isn't it?

W: Yeah, yeah, I mean.

M: I mean the fact is that it's dangerous.

W: How many … were there six of them she took on?

M: Something like that, yeah.

W: That really is …

M: And she knocked one of them off their scooter and then … and it was only then that all the other passersby came and, you know, landed on him yeah.

W: Oh yeah, jumped on the bandwagon, yes.

M: But she'd done done the whole thing.

W: No you have to … I completely take my my hat off … hat off to her for that because that is truly heroic to just charge in there, but no way would I do that. I just can't see my er yes I I own up to cowardice. I would be ringing someone.

M: Well a friend of mine said that he thought it was absolutely, you know, completely stupid, totally wrong thing to do. I said no, I thought that if more people, you know, were like that you'd have a better society.

W: Yeah. The thing is, as you said before, I don't know, I think it has to be one of those instantaneous reactions. You either don't think about the consequences and you you pile in and you you do what you can, or it's, I mean as soon as you hesitate I think you're lost really.

M: Yeah.

W: And er …

M: I think to be absolutely honest, if it was up to me, in the same situation, I'd probably leg it.

W: Really? Yes, well I I think I'd probably do my bit by calling the police.

UNIT 4 Recording 7

M = Man W = Woman

W: This kind of thing seems to be quite common. Families are always being torn apart by money.

M: By arguments about money, it's true. But what do you think should happen in this case?

W: Well, my first point is that it's quite rare to have a will overturned in court so you need really solid evidence.

M: Right.

W: And it seems as if the younger brother …

M: Nicholas.

W: Nicholas. He doesn't have any proof that …

M: Um, any proof that the father was pressurised.

W: ... that the father was pressurised into changing his will.

M: And without proof you have no case.

W: Exactly.

M: But having said that, there's also the issue of whether the father was 'of sound mind'. He was taking a lot of medication apparently so maybe he wasn't thinking straight.

W: Again, the question is can you prove that? It's very difficult to do in retrospect, especially if there's no evidence to suggest he'd lost his mental capabilities.

M: Right.

UNIT 5 Recording 1

J = Jenni Murray A = Ailish Kavanagh
E = Eva Price G = Girl W1 = Woman 1
W2 = Woman 2

J: Now, if I'd ever told anybody how much my dad earned, he'd have been absolutely furious. I'm not sure that I ever really knew. We were raised in an atmosphere where families kept themselves to themselves and you told nobody your business. And then it all changed as we became more knowledgeable about the kind of dangerous secrets that might be held behind closed doors, and the damage they could do. We were encouraged as a society to tell these tales and let it all hang out. So, can we still keep a secret?

G: One of my friends told me to keep a secret about how she was going out with this other girl's boyfriend. And I kind of went up to the girl and told her by accident, it just fell out. She got really, really annoyed and it was – oh, it was horrible. It was like I thought she was actually going to slap me. It was so bad. Oh my god. We made up like two hours later but it was just the initial, you know, ... I should never have told her secret though. So, it was my fault.

A: Have you ever given away anyone's secret by accident?

W1: Probably, just Christmas presents maybe accidentally telling someone what their Christmas present was. My husband nearly did that yesterday actually. He took an afternoon off work to go and er go and get something for my ... for Christmas for me. He wouldn't tell me for days where he was going, and almost let it slip where he was. I really wish he had given it away.

A: What's the hardest secret that you've ever had to keep?

W2: I revealed a secret of a of a romance that I had with an older man ... that I revealed to my husband because I decided that I had to tell him ... er so that ... because I couldn't live with this secret. If I had to live in honesty with my husband, I had to reveal to him this secret and face the consequences. And, as you can see this is the consequence – we've grown closer together as a result of that.

A: So the consequences were quite good then, it seems?

W2: They were. Here he is, still at my side, and I'm at his side. So that was a very big secret that I kept, but I did reveal it.

J: Ailish Kavanagh talking to people in Croydon. So when do you spill the beans and be honest, and when is it better to stay schtum? Well, Christine Northam is a counsellor with Relate. Eva Rice is the author of a novel called *The Lost Art of Keeping a Secret*. Do you really think we have lost the art of keeping a secret?

E: I, I certainly do. I think that nowadays everyone's so encouraged to say everything at all times, and express the way they feel, umm, at the drop of a hat. And I think that the point of my book was to get across the fact that sometimes keeping a secret isn't always a bad thing. It can be something that um ... can bring a more positive outcome than always, always telling everyone how you feel.

J: So what kind of secret would you keep?

E: I think well, like the characters in my book, if you're keeping a secret that is, in some way, going to protect somebody from something. Obviously I don't want to give away too much of the plot. But if you're protecting somebody in a way that isn't going to damage them when they do ultimately find out um I think that in that case a secret is a very good thing to keep. But nowadays, it's something that is frowned upon, and something that is considered wrong. And you're supposed to tell everyone the way you feel twenty-four hours a day, and so it's something that you shouldn't do is keep a secret.

UNIT 5 Recording 4

M = Man MA = Marc W = Woman

W: What do you think about organisations like WikiLeaks?

M: Well, to be honest, I think they should be stopped. And the reason why I say that is because they are responsible for leaking all kinds of confidential information, some of which is highly sensitive information about people who work in government, or military strategy, and they release this kind of information in a way which is, which is quite honestly ... completely reckless. They seem to have no regard for the ethics of what they're doing, and um I think they should be stopped. They've exposed people who they say are informants, and now the lives of those people and their families are now in danger.

W: Hold on a minute. Can you be sure about that? Is there any evidence to prove that?

M: Well, no, probably not, not absolute proof. But that's not the point. The only way to prove it'll be if something terrible happens to those people as a result of the information which has been disclosed. The the point is that governments and you know certain organisations simply have to be able to keep some information private. It doesn't make sense for everybody to have access to all the information that they want. Let me put it this way. It's like saying you need to give everybody your bank details, because we all have the right to know, but you don't. You don't have that right, and it's simply ridiculous to think that you

do. If you think about it, it's just irresponsible and it's dangerous.

W: I don't see how you can say that. Don't you think that there are cases when it's right for the public to know what's happening? Marc, where do you stand on this?

MA: Well, yeah, absolutely. I agree. It's not something I've thought much about before, but in fact I think that WikiLeaks is one of the best things to happen in the last few years. It's opened up access to information and it means that big companies and governments will need to be much more careful about how they deal with things in the future, because they can no longer hide behind secrets. And that's how it should be. After all, if you think about it, you can't give people the protection to do whatever they want without fear of being discovered. Whether it's companies using spies to find out what rival companies are planning, or governments holding people illegally, or using illegal practices to get information. I think freedom of information can only be a good thing, and it's like a wake-up call to all those who previously thought that they could get away with wrongdoing by just keeping it quiet. That just doesn't work anymore.

M: But that doesn't take account of the fact that some information, like um military information is highly sensitive, and shouldn't be allowed to spread around the internet where simply anybody can get hold of it and use it for whatever purposes they wish.

MA: I think you'll find that actually information has always been leaked. It's just the medium that has changed now, so that with the internet it's that bit easier, but there've always been whistleblowers, and there will continue to be. It's no different. The point I'm trying to make is that if the chances of you being discovered are increased, the likelihood of you being exposed, then it'll make you think twice about the actions you're taking, whether you're in government or in a big corporation. I think you'll find that people will be more careful in the future, and in my opinion that can only be a good thing.

UNIT 5 Recording 5

OK, well, to start off with, I have a tattoo on my back. It's a sea horse and I had it done when I was eighteen. Second on my list is my birthday. I was born on Christmas Day. It's a bit of a disadvantage really because no one ever gives you two sets of presents and people tend to forget your birthday because they're so busy celebrating Christmas. Third, it's not what you'd call a big secret but I sing in a local choir. We practise once a week and do occasional concerts. Number four. My favourite film is *The Usual Suspects*. I've seen it about twenty times. Number five. If I didn't work in an office, I'd like to be a dancer. I used to dance every day when I was a child and I really loved it. I might have taken it further but as a teenager I had back trouble for a couple of years and had to stop. My next one: a few close friends know this. I like gardening. I have an allotment where I grow vegetables like tomatoes and leeks, and I'm quite good at it. I like to potter around there on Sundays. It's sort of like therapy – very relaxing. And last but not least, at the age of thirty I still don't drive. I'm planning on getting round to it some time, but I've been saying that for years.

UNIT 6 Recording 2

S = Stephen Fry   D = David Crystal

S: Professor David Crystal says that the migratory patterns of our language as it continues to move across the globe, gives us a whole range of Englishes, and that process is becoming ever more intense.

D: So just as once upon a time there was British English and American English, and then there came Australian English and South African English, and then Indian English and then Caribbean English. Now, it's down to the level of Nigerian English, Ghanaian English, Singaporian English and so on. And these are the new Englishes of the world. What happens is this: that when a country adopts English as its language, it then immediately adapts it to suit its own circumstances. I mean why have a language? You have to express what you want to say which is your culture, your people, your identity. And when you think of everything that makes up an identity – all the plants and animals that you have, the food and drink, the myths, the legends, the history of your culture, the politics of it, the folk tales, the music, everything has to be talked about in language. And that means your local language, local words to do with the way you are, and different from the way everybody else is. And so the result has been, as English has been taken up by, well over seventy countries in the world as an important medium of their local communication. But they have developed their own local brand of English.

S: How many people spoke the language we are now conversing in say six hundred years ago?

D: Ahh, well, certainly we know around about 1500, 1600, there were four million speakers of English in England.

S: And now in the early part of the twenty-first century, how many … ?

D: Well, if you distinguish between, sort of first language speakers and foreign language speakers there's about 400 million or so first language speakers, English as a mother tongue – or father tongue, depending on your point of view – around the world, and about five times as many who speak English as a second or a foreign language, so we're talking about two billion people, you know, a third of the world's population really. The important point to notice is that for every one native speaker of English, there are now four or five non-native speakers of English, so the centre of gravity of the language has shifted with interesting consequences.

UNIT 6 Recording 3

Speaker 1

It's a trend that started in the States and spread certainly in Europe. And it's when guys wear their jeans halfway down their hips so you can see their underwear. Apparently it all started in the prison system in the States. What happened was that prisoners aren't allowed to wear belts cos these can be used as a weapon. And the prison uniforms were often too big for the inmates. So you'd have a little guy wearing a huge baggy pair of prison issue trousers and so the prisoners ended up with these trousers halfway down their legs. So the trend has its roots in the prison system but somehow it spread beyond those walls so rappers like Ice T started wearing their trousers like this and it led to widespread adoption of the style. It's known in some parts as a kind of gangster look because obviously it originated in prison, but actually it's pretty common now amongst young people, so basically it's crossed over into the mainstream. And I guess this is how fashions start and spread cos they kind of come from nowhere, out of the blue, and then early adopters, I think they're called, help to make them fashionable and suddenly you've got a trend.

Speaker 2

As a TV producer, I've obviously looked at the trend of reality TV. It all started to take off In the nineties with the emergence of programmes like *Big Brother* and *Pop Idol*. But actually I'd say it originated from earlier programmes, stuff that was done in the seventies and eighties. I think the popularity of these shows has caused a big shift in how programmes are made. Production values are quite low and the emphasis is now on making something cheap and quick. Because of this, TV companies make bigger profits and it's this that resulted in these shows spreading around the world. So what I'm really saying is we'll keep making these programmes now until the, erm, the public tires of them. And it's because of the public's taste for knowing about real people and real lives.

UNIT 6 Recording 4

1 People now expect to download music for free and CD sales are at their lowest ebb. Basically, the music industry has had to completely change its business model.

2 We saw some great presentations at the conference. The hotel was wonderful and we loved the food! So overall, it was really worth it.

3 Bloggers take news from real reporters and write comments. They do hardly any reporting themselves. So what I'm really saying is that without real reporters, there's no news.

4 Sales of the game soared in May, jumped again in July and rose dramatically at the end of the year. To sum up, we've had an incredible year.

5 This report says young people believe in openness. They share details of their private lives enthusiastically online. In conclusion, young people don't value their privacy as much as older generations.

6 We had developed a great product, so logically it should have been a success. However, we had technical problems. Then we ran out of money and a competitor stole the idea. All in all, it was a complete disaster.

UNIT 6 Recording 6

The nineties feels like such a long time ago now, but lots of important things happened in that decade. There were obviously some major historical events, like umm … well, Mandela was released from prison, and became President in 1990. There was Mad Cow disease throughout quite a lot of the nineties, which although it was a UK problem, caused a lot of panic – certainly in the rest of Europe. I remember that really well. And then when Mother Teresa died. That was in '97, I think, and I remember it had quite an effect on me. The nineties was when the internet first took off as well, and we started to hear about companies like eBay and Yahoo. I remember getting my first email in the nineties! And I got my first mobile phone then too. It had a changeable face, so that you could change the colour to suit your mood. I had a yellow face, and one with a strawberry on it. I'm not sure what that really says about me. Generally though, the nineties was quite a prosperous time, you know, lots of people were earning good money. So, I think the atmosphere was about enjoying yourself, and having a good time. I think one of the most memorable things about the 1990s has to be the music. Big bands like *Take That* and *The Spice Girls* were around. I remember going to the *Take That* concert in '93 – it was amazing, it was the best night of my life, definitely. And clubbing was generally really big too. There were loads of big clubs. Dance music really took off during the nineties. Thinking about fashion back then makes me cringe, to be honest. Shell suits were all the rage at that time, and I had a purple one. I wore it all the time. It was my favourite, I absolutely loved it. Other fashion items I remember were light-up trainers, you know, when you walked the lights started flashing. Everyone thought they were really cool. It's funny to look back on it all really, but the nineties was a great decade to be a teenager in, definitely.

UNIT 7 Recording 2

Speaker 1

The best way for me to switch off from my day-to-day routine is a series of very relaxing and healing movements called Qigong. Qigong it means literally moving the energy and I find that it's the only way to ease my mind after a stressful day. I've been doing it for a few years now and the more I practise it the more effective it is for me. Um those movements, very slow movements with the hands and arms just pull the focus inwards rather than outwards towards the distractions and worries of the day. And um you're not thinking about what's happened or what will happen, your thoughts are truly in the present and my mind is totally freed up.

Speaker 2

I'm a teacher and my week is usually very busy and very stressful. When I come home from school I don't stop, I still have a lot of marking and preparation so it's not until the weekend that I'm able to begin to switch off. On a Saturday morning I drive to … Trowlock Island, a little island on the Thames – takes me about ten minutes by car to get there. I then go across on the ferry to the island. There's a little five-minute walk to the end of the island, no cars, beautiful flowers, spring flowers at the moment, trees, it's very peaceful, lovely, the sound of birds and then I get onto my boat, turn on the engine and chug away. And instantly I am in another world and completely relaxed with the water, the swans around, the ducks, the sky. It is instant relaxation. It's very peaceful at night sleeping on board, getting up early and I just completely forget about all the worries and stresses of the school and the pupils there and it's a, it's a very very quick, very instant way of relaxing.

Speaker 3

Um I think the only thing I find really relaxing on a day-to-day basis is gardening. Um I try and get out in the garden most days, mainly because if I don't I'll probably start shouting at, at people. Um I think one of the disadvantages of being a mum is that you never, you're never on your own, someone always walks in when you're in the middle of just thinking about something, you can't finish a thought. So if I go out and garden I can finish a thought. Plus, being a very impatient person um you can't be impatient in the garden, you have to wait and you have to watch and you have to, you can just be in the moment planting things and, and watching things happen and, and I find it incredibly peaceful and relaxing and … almost meditative. The thing is it can't be hurried and there's nothing else to do except watching, waiting and, and as a result my mind is free. Um yes I have a great sense of freedom in the garden um both physically and mentally um and I think it's that sense of freedom, I think, that sense of getting away from everything. Uh and the sense of peace that comes with uh with the activity and the slow, gradual process of things growing and changing and um blossoming. It's, it's a very joyful and very freeing activity.

UNIT 7 Recording 3

M = Man W = Woman

M: Did you read that article recently about um, uh I can't remember her name, a New York journalist who …

W: Oh the one about the nine-year-old child?

M: Yeah who left her son uh in central New York and left him to come back on his own, to make his own way back at the age of nine.

W: Brilliant!

M: Brilliant?

W: Yes!

M: Oh come on, you must be joking.

W: I'm absolutely serious.

M: Well in what way brilliant? I mean he could have got lost, he could have been attacked, he could have been mugged, he could have …

W: That's absolutely right and we have …

M: What and that's good?

W: Look we have to, as parents, now take a stand against all this mollycoddling, cotton wool rubbish. I was allowed to do a lot at a very young age and it helped me make the right decisions about how to protect myself and learn to be streetwise. These kids don't know anything these days.

M: Well I agree with you up to a point, but I mean you can't think that a nine-year-old should be left alone to kind of grow up in the course of two hours.

W: Surely you don't think that he should never make his own way home then and never learn?

M: Of course not, but not at the age of nine!

W: Right, well that goes against my better judgement because I actually think it's, it's more responsible as a parent to show them by chucking them in at the deep end.

M: Right so its, you think it's more responsible to abandon your child, you can't think that surely?

W: She didn't abandon the child.

M: Well effectively she did.

W: The, you know he lives in New York and anyway …

M: What, so who, well that's one of the most dangerous places in the world!

W: How can you say that? There are far worse places in the world. It's all relative.

M: Of course it's all relative, but if you look at the muggings and the crime rate in New York it's horrendous and a nine-year-old wouldn't have a clue how to deal with all of that. It's, it just doesn't make sense to me.

W: It wasn't from what I know at two o'clock in the morning so, you know, you have to take it with a pinch of salt a bit.

M: Right.

W: Right, so …

M: Because all crime happens at two o'clock in the morning?

W: Surely you don't think then that it's terribly dangerous to leave a child in a, in a city in the middle of the morning, that they know and they're not four …

M: I do at the age of nine, he didn't even have a mobile phone!

W: He's probably a nine-year-old that's really got a lot going on you know, that's the whole point I think to take the child as an individual.

M: I understand the wanting the empowerment, I just think we're in a hurry to, to push our kids to grow, grow up too soon …

W: Oh come on.

M: … these days, I don't understand it.

W: Oh please!

M: What's the hurry?

W: You know everybody feels that, if everybody feels like that we're never going to get anybody that stands up for themselves.

M: Oh that's ridiculous! We're talking about a nine-year-old!

W: Well that's absolutely right.

UNIT 7 Recording 5

After twenty long years he was finally free. He breathed deeply. The air smelled good. He thought to himself he would spend the rest of his days outside, by the ocean, at the foot of a mountain, in a valley, in a field, under the stars, it didn't matter as long as he could breathe the air and never be confined again. But before all that, he knew there was something else he had to do. He walked to the nearest town. He had some savings and the first thing he bought was a shovel. This is the best thing I'll ever spend my money on, he said to himself. After this, he walked a while until he came to a car rental office. Using his old ID card, he rented an old blue Chevrolet. No sooner had he got in it than he realised he barely remembered how to turn on the ignition. He fiddled around for a while, but once he'd got the engine going, he drove long into the night. He was sure he would remember the tree. How could he forget? It was burnt into his memory like a scar. Even in the darkness he would remember the rise of the hill, the curve in the road, the thick branches hanging over a rusting iron gate. He'd been looking forward to this moment for twenty years. Having waited so patiently, he knew his moment was close.

UNIT 8 Recording 2

G = Geoff Watts M1 = Man 1 M2 = Man 2
C = Claudia Hammond S = Simon Chu
L = Louise J = John Aggleton

G: Hello. We're looking back quite a bit in this week's programme, back to childhood for a start. Now, ever had that feeling of being suddenly carried back in time by a particular odour? You probably have because it's a common experience. The smell of coal does it for me, and even more specifically mint sauce. One whiff of that, and it's back to Sunday lunch in the house where I was born. There is, it seems, something special about smells when it comes to evoking memories. Now, as Claudia Hammond reports, psychologists think they may be getting to the root of it.

AUDIO SCRIPTS

M1: The smell that always really takes me back in time is the smell of disinfectant, and kind of cedary wood. And for some bizarre reason it reminds me of being at school when I was about seven.

M2: Whenever I smell privet, walk past a hedge or something, it takes me instantly back to my kindergarten, to the rather smelly passage through from the garden to the school restaurant, where we had our lunches. It takes me straight back there.

C: For some reason, the memories evoked by smells seem to be stronger than memories that come back to you, say from looking at a photo. In the field of psychology, they call it the Proust phenomenon, after the famous incident with the madeleines in *Remembrance Of Things Past*. One of the people studying the Proust Effect is Doctor Simon Chu, a lecturer in psychology at Liverpool University. The link between smell and memory has hardly been touched by researchers, because until recently, it's been very difficult to prove in the lab. Using familiar smells, like vinegar and talcum powder, Simon Chu tries to trigger autobiographical memories.

C: So, what have you got here? You've got about eight little plastic boxes.

S: Here we've got things like raw mixed herbs, we've got um some cigarette ash, some vinegar, ketchup, got some paint. What I'm going to do is I'm going to give you a word, and I'm going to ask you to tell me as much as you can about a particular experience that the word reminds you of.

C: First, he gives his volunteer Louise a word, like cigarette. And she has to come up with an event from her past linked to the word. Once she's remembered everything she can, he lets her sniff the real thing from one of his special boxes.

S: I'd like you to sniff gently at this and tell me anything else you can remember about that particular experience.

L: Oooh um stale cigarette smoke …that's a horrible smell. I can still smell it from here. I just remember … just the smell of it and the fact that it, you can still smell it on yourself ages later. And then when you go home, you suddenly realise that your parents are probably going to be able to smell it on you as well. And then you get that fear inside you that they're going to know that you were smoking, and you know there were the polos, and the perfume and that kind of thing – desperately trying to cover up the smell, so that your parents don't know what you've been up to.

C: Confronted by the actual smell of cigarettes, Louise remembers far more about the event than she did when she was simply given the word 'cigarette'. In particular, she remembered the fear that her parents would find out she'd been having a sneaky cigarette. It seems that smell is very good at bringing back the emotional details like this.

S: There is something quite unusual and special about the relationship between smells and memory.

J: For me, the most evocative smell is that smell you get when candles have just been snuffed out. And it takes me back to my childhood when I was a chorister in a church choir, in a village in Berkshire. And towards the end of the service, one of the servers used to come out and extinguish the big candles up by the altar. And if I just smell that smell, of candles being snuffed out, I'm instantly back at that time and the memories are of the music of my boyhood, the church music of the time.

G: Odours that prompt the memories of times past.

UNIT 8 Recording 3
Conversation 1
A: You coming to the party?

B: Yes, I think so.

Conversation 2
A: Did you just delete the file?

B: Hope not.

Conversation 3
A: Want to try this perfume?

B: No, but I'll try that one.

Conversation 4
A: You think we'll have enough time to discuss this later?

B: We'll have a little.

Conversation 5
A: You going away on holiday this year?

B: No. Ann Marie doesn't have enough money, and nor do I.

Conversation 6
A: You sure you've got enough copies for everyone?

B: Yes, lots.

UNIT 8 Recording 4
M1 = Man 1   Man 2 = Man 2
W1 = Woman 1   W2 = Woman 2

M1: OK so uh what ideas do we have for saving time?

M2: Well like for example at university, if we've got a lot to read, there's like a massive reading list um, I'll like take a report or an analysis that someone else has written, and I just simply haven't got time to read the whole thing, so I just often just skip to the conclusion and just like make bullet point notes of what I read there.

M1: Right OK.

M2: Well it's not ideal obviously but it does save time.

W1: Yeah, yeah.

M1: Sure, sure.

W2: And I find when I'm really busy and I just have to um have a very, very quick lunch to save time, I just bring something in, in a tupperware, put it in the microwave on a plate.

M1: Ah that's a good idea.

W1: Yeah and certainly …

W2: Five minutes, my lunch is over in ten.

W1: … I mean with the kids like, you know I'll try and make something at the beginning of the week um. You know if everyone's eating at different times, going out in different things, microwave, I don't really like them but they, they really save a lot of time. You can just put a small portion in the microwave, heat it up, a couple of minutes, they can eat it and go.

M2: Yeah makes sense.

W2: Yeah, it's a real short cut.

M1: Does anyone else make lists? Cos I find that really helps if I, I have lists … that help me divide up the day and know what I'm doing when.

W2: Yes I …

M2: Cos you can focus on particular tasks then, assign particular times.

M1: Exactly.

W2: Yes, yes, yes. To do all your phone calls in one go …

M1: Exactly, I know I've got that amount of time and that's it.

W2: … all your emails in, in one after the other.

W1: Yeah it's nice to be able to tick things off and know …

M2: Mind you, if the list becomes too long then I'll procrastinate for so long about which to do first, that it actually wastes time.

M1: Yeah … it has to be realistic.

W2: I also think when, I don't know if any of you have had to make up um furniture from a flat pack.

M2: Oh yes.

W2: I think … I often don't read the instructions properly. I glance at them and then I really wish that I had taken some time and really studied it before I embarked.

M1: Yes, cos in the long run that would've helped.

M2: I am with you there.

M1: Absolutely.

M2: I've been caught out like that many times.

W1: Yeah, but I mean when it comes to something like … I mean I found one of the most time-consuming things is trying to sort out a computer problem myself, when I don't really know what I'm doing. And I have had to conclude that paying someone for an hour of their time is gonna save about three hours of mine.

M1: Absolutely.

W1: Ultimately.

M1: That's true.

W2: Absolutely, yeah I, I certainly believe in bringing in the expert. There's a wonderful organisation called Tech Friend, that you ring up, you pay a yearly fee and you can ring them at any time with your computer problems.

M1: Oh that's interesting.

W1: Brilliant – a very good idea.

M1: OK well anything to add? I mean to sum up we, we've talked about the idea that you use the microwave, you make lists, you read the instructions first properly and divide up your day so you have things sort of more organised um. Can you think of anything else? Any other suggestions?

M2: Actually yes recently, for my birthday, I knew of this restaurant in town that I'd been to on like a Friday or Saturday night one time. And I was gonna have a Sunday lunch there, so I got everybody to meet there and it was closed. I did not realise it would be closed on a Sunday so …

M1: Ah.

M2: You know the telephone was invented many years ago, why do we not use it? Phone first.

W1: Yes, yeah, yeah.

M1: That's true. Yeah good idea.

W1: Good one.

UNIT 8 Recording 6

When I was about nine or ten and everybody uh from primary school was moving up to secondary school, my parents gave me the option to go to a specialised theatrical school or a regular comprehensive. And um it was very important, cos I remember being sat down and shown brochures of everything and there was no pressure either way. And at that young age I made the decision to go to a theatre school. And luckily for me I, I, it's panned out and I've had a career in that um, that line of work. But I then found myself faced with another decision, because we were moving house and uh we had to leave school, and did we want to continue with theatre school or did we want to go to a normal school? And at that point I was about fourteen, and I decided actually I want to get an education and leave the theatrical world at that point, still very, very young to make those decisions. And I did, I left and went to a regular comprehensive and got some uh you know qualifications behind me and everything, and my sister didn't she carried on at theatre school and she went straight into work, very early, and was really successful. I've always wondered if perhaps I should have chosen the other option, cos it was a longer road for me, and I'm still very much on it. And um, and I suppose that the next major decision, the final decision was whether to have children or not or take this huge job that was offered to me, and I chose my children, in that case. So I'm very grateful I've got two lovely boys um, and I've still got my career but I just um, kind of wonder what would have happened if …

UNIT 9 Recording 2
Speaker 1

People always ask me that, and it's a very difficult question to answer. One thing is that it's no good just sitting around waiting for an idea to come. If I'm stuck for an idea, I have to switch off and do something else for a while. If I'm stuck with the plot, or I need to work out how a particular character should behave, then I'll go off and do something else for a bit. Doing the washing-up is quite good, doing something mundane, that you don't have to think too hard about. So, I like to invite lots of people round to dinner, so that in the morning there are lots of plates to wash, and that gets me thinking. When you free the mind it helps spark creative connections. So you're doing the washing-up, or having a shower, and suddenly an idea might come to you. You actually have to take your mind off the writing, off the task in hand. And that's when you think of something creative. It's funny how our brains work. Sometimes, I'll go out into the garden, or go for a run to clear my head. When I get back to my desk, the ideas flow a lot more easily.

Speaker 2

I use a lot of mixed media, so I get my ideas from all over the place. But one place I often start is with a photograph. I really like old black and white photographs, so I might start with a photo of someone, and then I'll gradually build up a story around the photo, using a collage of different ideas and colours. Sometimes I read poems, or write them, and I put quotes on the pictures to help tell the story. But it usually starts with the photo. Sometimes when I'm out with a group of people, I get very inspired just watching what's happening. I look at the colours, the clothes people are wearing, how the colours change in the candlelight, things like that. I might take a photo, or I just try to keep the image in my head – take a mental picture of what it looks like, and the feeling I have, and then I'll use that in a painting that I'm working on.

Speaker 3

Um books mainly, old recipe books … like Margaret Costa, a classic. I'll look through old recipes and then try to recreate the same idea but with a modern, more contemporary twist. Yes, old tomes. Larousse is another one, with plenty of ideas, or sometimes I'll go to the Michelin guides, you know the restaurants with stars – they have books, so I look there too. Unfortunately, I rarely eat out myself, so I don't get ideas that way, but books are a great inspiration. And there's something about having big, heavy books in the kitchen that have been with you a long time. They inherit your character a little, and hold in them so many memories of enjoyable meals.

Speaker 4

I sometimes go to museums or exhibitions, and I'll go and look at some Picasso, or Van Gogh, someone who used big bold colours, and I'll just sit in the gallery with my notebook, and do a few sketches, or try out some colours. Or if I don't have time, I'll buy some postcards, and then when I get home I'll choose from the various patterns and shades. I have an inspiration board at home – a wall in my studio where I put images, photos, things I like the look of. If I go into a shop and see a design I like, then I'll try to take a picture of it (or do a quick sketch) and that will go onto the board. I won't copy it exactly, but it might feed into something I'm working on. There are all sorts of things there, quotes I read, cards that people send me. The idea is that I can use the board as a starting point for a new design. It's important that I can see and touch lots of different textures, and materials. These are very important in fashion. Sometimes just looking at something aesthetically pleasing helps to get the creative juices flowing, and gives you a few ideas to reflect on.

UNIT 9 Recording 3
Speaker 1

If there's one thing I cannot stand it's getting off a tube train on the London underground and lots of people on the platform try to get on the carriage before I have gotten off. Honestly, it drives me up the wall! Don't they understand that if I can't get off then they can't get on, so they need to let me off. And I have in the past actually raised my voice at tourists.

Speaker 2

The last time we went to Cornwall we went to the lovely little town of Fowey, and I discovered what I could describe for me as paradise, it's a tearoom which somebody could describe in a book and it still wouldn't be as good as, as the actual experience when you go in – beautifully decorated. It's got those little um cake plates with, piled up with the most beautiful sumptuous cupcakes. And then in the back part they've got a lovely Rayburn, and if you decided you wanted sardines on toast or scrambled egg or something they'll just whip it up for you. Every single thing you could imagine on your dream menu. I could have sat there for a week and worked my way through the menu. It was the most wonderful, delicious and, and, the people were so friendly. And they'd gone to such sort of trouble to make this gorgeous place to eat. And um I'd definitely go back there again.

Speaker 3

The other night I saw the best show ever, it was a show called *Dirty Dancing*, it's on in the West End, absolutely fantastic. The acting was brilliant, the dancing was brilliant, the songs were terrific! I mean uniformly they were absolutely terrific. And I don't know who played the mother, but she was especially good, honestly, really the best show ever, you must see it!

AUDIO SCRIPTS

Speaker 4

I cannot recommend highly enough a trip to one of the beautiful islands of Thailand. I went there last year and there is absolutely nothing better than finding yourself on a private beach with a cool drink in hand and having a dip in tropical warm waters. And I saw one of the most spectacular sunsets I've ever seen. And honestly, I couldn't believe my luck when I saw turtles in the water, I've always wanted to see turtles. It was idyllic.

Speaker 5

The worst meal I ever had was quite recently. It was absolutely horrendous. The restaurant was grossly overpriced, honestly it was a total waste of money. But it's also you know minutes of my life that I won't get back. Um the service was appalling, and the waiter just seemed like he'd rather be doing anything else. Clearly it's hard to cook for a lot of people, I understand that, at the same time. But you know meals were coming out at all different times. We had appetisers arriving and then the main course and then nothing for about an hour. It was horrendous.

Speaker 6

I bought the 'one touch can opener' and it has changed my life, seriously, and I'm not even overstating how amazing it is. It's an all-time classic of products, you have to get one, and I couldn't believe my luck when it arrived in the post, just for me, and it does exactly what it says it will. You touch it once and you leave it alone. It's incredible! It's the most incredible thing. You don't have to, you can do something else if you want. It's one of the most spectacular life-changing products you can buy, because all of that mess and effort taken away um. So if you're ever thinking about it, just do it, it's awesome, seriously, the best product.

UNIT 9 Recording 6

I live in Sydney, Australia and I'd recommend the Sydney Opera House. I'd say it's one of the world's most recognisable landmarks, certainly for anyone interested in modern architecture. The most striking thing about it is the shape of the roof, which looks like … well, like a group of open shells, or maybe sails unfurling, just like a ship. Its size is quite dramatic as well – it's a lot bigger than it looks in pictures. I think the best time to go is either really early in the morning when there's no one there or in the evening. If you go in the evening, you can watch the sun setting over the Sydney Harbour Bridge and you'll see the birds overhead circling the roof, which is just an amazing sight. And as it gets dark, there are the city lights reflected off the water and you can stroll along the harbour and pop into any of the great restaurants or bars there. The building itself is obviously admired all over the world, but it's also been very influential in modern architecture. It was one of the first buildings to use computer-aided design – back in the 1960s when it was being built, and a lot of the techniques involved in its construction have been copied by other architects. For example the use of reinforced concrete was very …

UNIT 10 Recording 1

1 My life would be considerably better if I had a normal job.

2 Being a celebrity is nothing like as glamorous as it seems.

3 One good thing about fame is that it's far easier to book a table in a restaurant.

4 Even for a celebrity, it's every bit as difficult to enjoy life.

UNIT 10 Recording 3

When I taught in New York City high schools for thirty years no one but my students paid me a scrap of attention. In the world outside the school I was invisible. Then I wrote a book about my childhood and became mick of the moment. I hoped the book would explain family history to McCourt children and grandchildren. I hoped it might sell a few hundred copies and I might be invited to have discussions with book clubs. Instead it jumped on the best-seller list and was translated into thirty languages and I was dazzled. The book was my second act. In the world of books I am a late bloomer, a johnny-come-lately, new kid on the block. My first book, *Angela's Ashes*, was published in 1996 when I was sixty-six, the second, *'Tis*, in 1999 when I was sixty-nine. At that age it's a wonder I was able to lift the pen at all. New friends of mine (recently acquired because of my ascension to the best-seller lists) had published books in their twenties. Striplings. So, what took you so long? I was teaching, that's what took me so long. Not in college or university, where you have all the time in the world for writing and other diversions, but in four different New York City public high schools. (I have read novels about the lives of university professors where they seemed to be so busy with adultery and academic in-fighting you wonder where they found time to squeeze in a little teaching.) When you teach five high school classes a day, five days a week, you're not inclined to go home to clear your head and fashion deathless prose. After a day of five classes your head is filled with the clamour of the classroom. I never expected *Angela's Ashes* to attract any attention, but when it hit the best-seller lists I became a media darling. I had my picture taken hundreds of times. I was a geriatric novelty with an Irish accent. I was interviewed for dozens of publications. I met governors, mayors, actors. I met the first President Bush and his son, the governor of Texas. I met President Clinton and Hillary Rodham Clinton. I met Gregory Peck. I met the Pope and kissed his ring. Sarah, Duchess of York, interviewed me. She said I was her first Pulitzer Prize winner. I said she was my first duchess. She said, Ooh, and asked the cameraman, Did you get that? Did you get that? I was nominated for a Grammy for the spoken word and nearly met Elton John. People looked at me in a different way. They said, Oh, you wrote that book, This way, please, Mr McCourt, or Is there anything you'd like, anything? A woman in a coffee shop squinted and said, I seen you on TV. You must be important. Who are you? Could I have your autograph? I was listened to. I was asked for my opinion on Ireland, conjunctivitis, drinking, teeth, education, religion, adolescent angst, William Butler Yeats, literature in general. What books are you reading this summer? What books have you read this year? Catholicism, writing, hunger. I spoke to gatherings of dentists, lawyers, ophthalmologists and, of course, teachers. I travelled the world being Irish, being a teacher, an authority on misery of all kinds, a beacon of hope to senior citizens everywhere who always wanted to tell their stories. They made a movie of *Angela's Ashes*. No matter what you write in America there is always talk of The Movie. You could write the Manhattan telephone directory, and they'd say, So, when is the movie?

UNIT 10 Recording 4

Much of negotiating is in body language and gesture, but it's also vital that you use the right words. So you're at the beginning of some kind of negotiation. The first thing you want to do is name your objectives. So you can use a phrase such as 'we want to sort this out as soon as possible'. This makes it clear to everybody what you want from the discussion. Another thing you need to do is explore positions. What does that mean? Well, it means asking questions like 'Can you tell me more about this?' 'What do you have in mind?' Exploring positions is all about asking what the other guy wants and then really listening. In this way you can establish common goals. Um, so then you need to make an offer. And this is where the real negotiating starts, and the 'if' word becomes so important because your offer is going to be conditional on certain terms being met, concessions and compromises being made. So you might say, 'If you do this for me, I'll do this for you.' 'We'd be prepared to help you if you help us.' And, as for questions, again we can use 'if'. 'What if'? 'What if we gave you access to this?' 'What if we gave you a helping hand?' 'What if we supported your idea?' In negotiating, the word 'if' is the biggest word in the language. OK. Check that you understand. Negotiations can be long and tiring, but you cannot switch off for a moment. If you missed something, don't bluff. You have to ask about it. Go over the points more than once. Be sure. Ask 'Have I got this right?' 'Are you saying this or that?' 'If I understand you correctly, you mean this.' OK, so then you get towards the endgame. The haggling is over. It's decision time and you need to refuse or accept the deal. Refusing is always delicate. You really don't want to close off all further discussion, so you need to be tactful and phrase the refusal carefully. You never just say no. 'No' is a word that closes doors. Instead, you give reasons and explanations. For example, you might say, 'That's more than I can offer'. 'That would be difficult for me because of my situation'. 'I'm not sure I can do that because I promised something else'. In other words, you refuse without saying no. It's at this stage you might want to stall for time, or defer the decision, or if you're in business, consult a more senior colleague. The next stage is when you've reached agreement. You say something like, 'Good. That sounds acceptable to me.' Or 'Great. We've got a deal.' But that's not it. It isn't over. You need to follow up the deal. Be polite and civil. Say something like, 'We can talk about it again and review the situation in a few months'. If it's a more formal deal, we can say 'Let me know if you have any queries.' 'If there are any other points, I'll email you.' The thing is to follow up the deal. Always keep the conversation open.

UNIT 10 Recording 6

I guess my dream job would have to be a film-maker. Making short films, well, making full-length films too – that would be wonderful. The kind of films I'm interested in are those realistic animation films. What appeals to me is that it's wonderfully creative. There's so much you can do. You can do anything. I'd relish having the opportunity to work in an environment like that.   I'm fairly qualified in that, well I'm doing a degree in time-based art and digital film at university so we do a lot of work on film, image, sound and performance. I've made a series of short films, using various different techniques, so I've got a bit of experience behind me. And I'd like to think that I'm a fairly creative individual. I have lots of ideas about how to do things, and I'm not afraid to try out new ideas, to experiment. I'd say I've got quite a good eye for things that are going to work. Like an instinct. I can sense if something is working or not visually, or if we need to change it. I think it's essential to be open-minded and forward-thinking. There are a lot of people now doing fantastically creative things, and making films, so it's quite hard to be able to stand out from the crowd. So you need good business sense too, to make sure your film is successful. It's not just about having the ideas. You need to be a good organiser, so you can manage a project. And you have to be flexible. As for moving towards getting my dream job, as I said, I'm still studying at the moment, but I try to do as much creative work as I can in my spare time. I'm also doing some work experience with an advertising company, looking at how we can use short films in advertising. I'm hoping that this experience will help me to find a job when I graduate.

Pearson Education Limited
Edinburgh Gate
Harlow
Essex CM20 2JE
England
and Associated Companies throughout the world.

www. pearsonelt.com

© Pearson Education Limited 2012

The right of Antonia Clare and JJ Wilson to be identified as authors of this Work has been asserted by them in accordance with the Copyright, Designs and Patents Act 1988.

First published 2012
Sixth impression 2015

ISBN: 978-1-4082-6749-3

Set in Gill Sans Book 9.75/11.5

Printed in China(GCC/06)

Acknowledgements
The publishers and authors would like to thank the following people and institutions for their feedback and comments during the development of the material:

Reporters: Brazil: Stephen Greene, Damian Williams; Hungary: Eszter Timar; Italy: Elizabeth Gregson; Japan: James Short; Poland: Lech Krzeminski; United Kingdom: Kirsten Colquhoun, Stephanie Dimond-Bayir, John Evans, Eileen Flannigan, Pip Langley, Robert Turland

We are grateful to the following for permission to reproduce copyright material:

Figures:
Figure 6.2 from "Top Ten Languages in the Internet 2010", www.internetworldstats.com, Internet World Stats. Copyright © 2000-2010, Miniwatts Marketing Group.

Tables:
Table 6.2 from "Growth in Internet (2000 - 2010)", www.internetworldstats.com, Internet World Stats. Copyright © 2000-2010, Miniwatts Marketing Group.

Text:
Extract 1.1 adapted from "First Name Terms", The Guardian, 24/09/2007 (Giles Morris), copyright © Guardian News & Media Ltd 2007; Extract 1.2 from "How Myers-Briggs Conquered the Office" BBC Radio 4, copyright © The BBC; Quote 1.3 from Alan Bennett, 'National Portrait Gallery, Interviews with artists and sitters', www.npg.org.uk, copyright © Forelake Ltd. Used by permission of United Agents, www.unitedagents.co.uk on behalf of Forelake Ltd; Quote 1.3 from Germaine Greer 'National Portrait Gallery, Interviews with artists and sitters', www.npg.org.uk. Reproduced with permission from Aitken Alexander Associates, agents for Germaine Greer; Quote 1.3 from Kazuo Ishiguro 'National Portrait Gallery, Interviews with artists and sitters', www.npg.org.uk , copyright © Kazuo Ishiguro. Reproduced by permission of the author c/o Rogers, Coleridge & White Ltd, 20 Powis Mews, London, W11 1JN; Quotes 2.3 from "'Trusted' professions asked about faith in politicians", The BBC, 28/03/2010 by Dr David Bailey, GP, Bedwas, Caerphilly, Mary Davis, Assistant Headteacher, Bryn Hafren Comprehensive School, Barry, and Professor Justin Lewis, Head of the School of Journalism, Media & Cultural Studies, Cardiff University, http://news.bbc.co.uk. Reproduced with kind permission of Dr David Bailey, Mary Davis and Professor Justin Lewis; Extracts 3.1 from "Postcards: Where You've Been and What You've Seen", Lonely Planet, Issue 15, March 2010, pp.11-18 (Alistair McDonald, Anthony McEvoy, Greg Jackson), reproduced with permission from the authors; Extract 3.1 adapted from "Introducing Lisbon", Lonely Planet, Reproduced with permission from the Lonely Planet website www.lonelyplanet.com copyright © 2011 Lonely Planet; Quote and photo in 3.2 from "My space: James Caan", The Observer, 26/07/2009 (Mostyn, E.), copyright © Guardian News & Media Ltd 2009; Quote and photo in 3.2 from "My space: Zandra Rhodes, designer", The Observer, 25/10/2009 (Lutyens, D.), copyright © Guardian News & Media Ltd 2009; Quote and photo in 3.2 from "My space: Jack Vettriano, artist", The Observer, 17/05/2009 (Mostyn, E.), copyright © Guardian News & Media Ltd 2009; Extract 3.3 adapted from "Welcome to The Perfect City", BBC Focus, Issue 210, Dec 2009, pp.70-75 (Frank Swain), copyright © Frank Swain; Extract 4.1 from "Turning Point: I trained as a lawyer to free my innocent brother", Psychologies Magazine, February 2011, p.107 (Betty Anne Waters) copyright © Hachette Filipacchi UK; Extract 5.1 adapted from "Woman's Hour: When and how should you reveal a secret?", BBC Radio 4, copyright © The BBC; Extract 5.2 adapted from "Myths Buster", BBC Focus, March 2010, pp.34-39 (Jo Minihane (Technology Myths), Jo Carlowe (Health Myths) and Caroline Green (Animal Myths and Transport Myths), reproduced with permission of BBC Focus; Extract 6.1 from Longman Dictionary of Contemporary English Pearson Education (2009) copyright © Pearson Education Limited; Extract 6.2 from "Fry's English Delight" BBC Radio 4, copyright © AudioGO Ltd; Extract 7.1 from "I'm an Ig Nobel Winner Get Me Out of Here!", BBC Focus, Issue 211, p.54 (Dr. Elena Bodnar, Charles Spence et al), reproduced with permission of BBC Focus; Extract 8.2 from "Leading Edge: Memory and Smell", BBC Radio 4, copyright © The BBC; Extract 9.2 from "How to Find the Next Big Idea", Psychologies Magazine, December 2010, p.104 (Steven Johnson), copyright © Hachette Filipacchi UK; Extract in Language Bank 9 adapted from "The £40 Art Collection" 2010, www.ed.ac.uk, reproduced with the kind permission of The University of Edinburgh and Mr K. Alexander; Extract 10.1 adapted from "Long Way Round", Radio Times (Jackson, A.), copyright © The BBC Radio Times; Extract 10.2 from Teacher Man: A Memoir (Frank McCourt 2005) pp.3-4, copyright © 2005 Frank McCourt and Green Peril Corp. Reprinted by permission of HarperCollins Publishers Ltd, The Friedrich Agency, and Scribner, a Division of Simon & Schuster, Inc. All rights reserved.

In some instances we have been unable to trace the owners of copyright material, and we would appreciate any information that would enable us to do so.

Illustration acknowledgements: Coburn (Meiklejohn Illustration Agency) pgs 70, 89; Dan Hilliard pgs 67, 71; Fred Blunt (Meiklejohn Illustration Agency) pgs 21, 22, 50, 148, 149, 151, 152, 154, 157; Lyndon Hayes (Dutch Uncle Illustration Agency) p 36; Matt Herring (Début Art Illustration Agency) pgs 11, 67, 74–75, 92–93.

Photo acknowledgements: The publisher would like to thank the following for their kind permission to reproduce their photographs:

(Key: b-bottom; c-centre; l-left; r-right; t-top)

4Corners Images: Andrej Kuzin 117tl, Antonino Bartuccio 38tr, Massimo Borchi 39t, Sophia Simeone 7br; Alamy Images: 53b, 88b, 94tl, 94c, foodfolio 115bc; Alistair McDonald: 32tr; Allstar Picture Library: BBC 43br, 52bc, Warner Bros 46cr; Alpha Press: 16c; Anthony McEvoy: 33tl; BBC Motion Gallery: 55br, 64cl, 79br, 88cl, 124cl; (c) National Portrait Gallery, London: 7bc, 14tr, 15tl, 15tr; Capital Pictures: 115b, 116tr; Corbis: Ada Summer 94tr, Andy Aitchison / In Pictures 62t, Bettmann 91b, Brooks Kraft 8t, Destinations 162cl, Heide Benser 19bl, Image Source 115bl, Keren Su 111c, Lawrence Manning 89br, Michael Haegele 23tr, Mike Kemp / In Pictures 104cr, moodboard 55bc, 63tl, Noel Hendrickson / Blend Images 122tr, Paul Hardy 43bc, Rune Hellestad 19br, Sean Justice 108tl, Walter McBride 28b; DK Images: 74c, 91bc, 92t, 98tr, 117t; Fotolia.com: 19bc, 34tl, 55bl, 59br, 68t, 74tl, 74tc, 74tr, 74cr, 76b, 83cr, 86t, 86tc, 87tl, 92tl, 92c, 93t, 93tl, 93tc, 94t, 94l, 94cl, 94cr, 94r, 94b, 94bl, 94bc, 98t, 99tl, 100b, 108tc, 108c, 108cl, 112b, 117cl, 150tl, 150tr, 150cl, 150cr, 160tr; Getty Images: AFP 47tc, 72bc, Dirk Anschutz 81br, Ariel Skelley 160cl, Bloomberg 86tr, Brad James 117bc, Brian Doben 162bl, Chris Mellor 162cr, De Agostini 158bc, Don Farrall 7bl, Foodcollection 95tr, Fuse 59bl, Ghislain & Marie David de Lossy 91bl, hemis.fr 31bc, 39tl, Ian Cumming 31br, 41br, James Lauritz 62tl, Jeremy Woodhouse 16b, Keiji Iwai 79bl, 83tr, Kevin Schafer 80tr, Larry Goode 103bc, Darryl Leniuk 82br, LWA / Dann Tardif 20cr, Marco Di Lauro 43bl, 48br, Mel Yates 67br, 76bl, Paul Burley 160tl, Pete Turner 117cr, Peter Dazeley 62tc, Peter Macdiarmid 103bl, Randi Shepard 97tr, Robert Gray 19b, 20c, Ron Levine 7b, 8tr, Serdar S. Unal 59cl, SuperStock 158bl, Tanya Constantine 56tr, Tetra Images 115br, The Bridgeman Art Library 64b, Tyler Stableford 84br, Ulf Andersen 120cr, UpperCut Images 123cl, WireImage 12bl, 47cr, Oscar Wong 86tl, ZenShui / Frederic Cirou 55b; Greg Jackson: 31b, 33t; Guardian News and Media Ltd: Lutyens, D 31bl, 35c, Mostyn, E 35t, 35b; Robert Harding World Imagery: 79b, 80tl, 124b; Harper Collins Publishers Ltd © 1996, Frank McCourt: 120cl; Headline Review: 56tl; Kobal Collection Ltd: Dreamworks / Aardman Animations 109tr, Pantheon Entertainment Corporation 43b, 45tl, Paramount / Universal 120tr, Universal 119cl, Warner Bros 46cr; Pearson Education Ltd: 26tc, 27tr, 59cr, 67t, 67tl, 67c, 67cr, 67bc, 71t, 71tl, 71tc, 71tr, 71b, 71bl, 71bc, 71br, 75tl, 98tl, 158br, 160cr; Photolibrary.com: 159br, Andrea Jones 162br, Frank Bean 92tr, H & D Zielske 103br, 112cl, Jason Ingram 106tr, Jorgen Schytte 40bl, Ma Wenxiao 60t, Peter Dazeley 27tc, Radius Images 79bc, Rafael Macia 107tl, Richard B Levine 99tc, Romy Ragan 108tr, Trevor Dixon 108t, Yadid Levy 123tl; Press Association Images: 80cl, 104tc, 119tl; Reuters: Kim Kyung Hoon 67b; Rex Features: 67r, 75tc, 80cr, 91br, 100cl, Action Press 28bl, Andrew Olney / Mood Board 26tl, Dan Callister 37bl, Jeff Blackler 92tc, Nils Jorgensen 104tr, Brian Rasic 47br, Sipa Press 21tc, Steve Black 25tr, Steve Meddle 110cr, Steve Nicholson 51tl; SuperStock: Ambient Images Inc. 111tl, imagebroker.net 8tl, Pixtal 10tl, Radius 26tr, Somos 8tc; www.imagesource.com: 40b, 103bc, 110tr

All other images © Pearson Education

Every effort has been made to trace the copyright holders and we apologise in advance for any unintentional omissions. We would be pleased to insert the appropriate acknowledgement in any subsequent edition of this publication.